PENSION REFORM IN LATIN AMERICA

For Armando and Isabel

Pension Reform in Latin America

ARMANDO BARRIENTOS
Department of Economics, Statistics and Decision Sciences
University of Hertfordshire Business School

LONDON AND NEW YORK

First published 1998 by Ashgate Publishing

Reissued 2018 by Routledge
2 Park Square, Milton Park, Abingdon, Oxon OX14 4RN
711 Third Avenue, New York, NY 10017, USA

Routledge is an imprint of the Taylor & Francis Group, an informa business

Copyright © A. Barrientos 1998

All rights reserved. No part of this book may be reprinted or reproduced or utilised in any form or by any electronic, mechanical, or other means, now known or hereafter invented, including photocopying and recording, or in any information storage or retrieval system, without permission in writing from the publishers.

Notice:
Product or corporate names may be trademarks or registered trademarks, and are used only for identification and explanation without intent to infringe.

Publisher's Note
The publisher has gone to great lengths to ensure the quality of this reprint but points out that some imperfections in the original copies may be apparent.

Disclaimer
The publisher has made every effort to trace copyright holders and welcomes correspondence from those they have been unable to contact.

A Library of Congress record exists under LC control number : 98072852

ISBN 13: 978-1-138-33124-2 (hbk)
ISBN 13: 978-1-138-33129-7 (pbk)
ISBN 13: 978-0-429-44738-9 (ebk)

Contents

Figures and tables	*vii*
Acknowledgements	*xii*
Preface	*xiii*

Introduction	1
Evaluating pension reform	3
The structure of the book	5
1 Background to pension reform in Latin America	9
The origins and evolution of pension schemes	10
Explaining pension scheme deficits	12
Why structural pension reform?	25
Conclusion	32
Appendix One	34
Appendix Two	35
2 The reformed pension schemes	39
The main functions of pension schemes	40
Evaluating pension scheme design	45
The individual capitalization pension scheme in Chile	50
Comparison of pension reform in Latin America	56
Conclusion	66
3 The new pension fund management market	71
Main features of the private pension market in Chile	73
The performance of pension fund managers	88
Competition and regulation in the pension fund management market	96
Issues of efficiency and redistribution	102

The new pension fund management market in Latin America	107
The evolution of the pension fund management market in Chile, Argentina and Peru	114
Conclusion	120

4 Pension reform, saving and capital markets — 125
   Pension reform and saving — 126
   Pension reform and capital markets — 137
   Pension reform and financial markets in Latin America — 151
   Conclusion — 154

5 Pension scheme coverage — 159
   Pension reform and labour market efficiency — 160
   Pension scheme coverage: definitions and policy issues — 165
   Pension scheme coverage in Chile — 168
   Pension scheme coverage in Latin America — 191
   Conclusion — 198

6 Retirement income — 203
   The elderly, retirement income and poverty — 204
   Pension benefits in the new pension scheme in Chile — 208
   The new pension schemes and retirement income — 222
   Conclusion — 236

Conclusion — 241
   An assessment of pension reform in Latin America — 241
   Lessons for other countries — 246
   Future trends and research agenda — 251

Bibliography — 253

Figures and tables

Table 1.1	Population support ratio for selected Latin American countries	15
Table 1.2	Labour market indicators for selected Latin American countries 1980-1992	21
Table 1.3	Pay as you go pension scheme payroll tax under alternative demographic and labour market conditions (% of earnings)	25
Table 1.4	Sequence of structural adjustment and pension reform in Latin America	30
Table 1.A1	Demographic factors relevant to pension schemes in the 1980s	37
Table 2.1	Main features of reformed pension systems in Latin America: structure, contributions and entitlements	58
Table 3.1	Chile: Number of accounts by type	76
Table 3.2	Chile: Commission structure of the AFPs, regulations and practice	78
Figure 3.1	Chile: Operational costs per active contributor 1982-1996	80
Figure 3.2	Chile: Real rates of return of pension funds	82

Table 3.3	Chile: Restrictions on pension fund investment by asset	85
Figure 3.3	Chile: Pension funds investment by asset 1981-1997	86
Chart 3.1	Chile: Pension funds marketing strategy and market segmentation	90
Figure 3.4	Chile: Profitability of pension fund managers 1981-1997	94
Table 3.4	Chile: Mean real rates of return and standard deviation	95
Table 3.5	Chile: Individual retirement account transfers and sales personnel	98
Figure 3.5	Chile: Pension fund management market concentration	100
Table 3.6	Impact of sales costs on pension plan costs	104
Table 3.7	Redistributive impact of alternative allocations of operational costs	106
Table 3.8	Main features of pension fund management in individual capitalization pension schemes in Latin America	108
Table 3.9	Indicators of pension funds growth, and of pension providers costs, returns and efficiency	116
Table 3.10	Indicators of market concentration for Chile, Peru and Argentina	118
Table 3.11	Real annual rates of return in Chile, Peru and Argentina (December of each year)	120
Figure 4.1	Chile: Gross domestic saving as a proportion of GDP	130
Figure 4.2	Chile: Alternative measures of private saving as a proportion of GDP	132

Figure 4.3	Chile: Private saving and components as a proportion of GDP	134
Figure 4.4	Chile: Pension saving under the old and new pension schemes	136
Figure 4.5	Chile: Growth of stock market, pension funds and insurance reserves	140
Figure 4.6	Chile: Pension fund equity investment and stock market capitalization	142
Figure 4.7	Chile: Capital market liquidity and pension fund investment	147
Table 4.1	Chile: Main sources of firm finance	148
Table 4.2	Indicators of capital market development in selected Latin American countries	153
Table 4.3	Life insurance market indicators for selected Latin American countries	154
Figure 5.1	Social insurance and pension scheme coverage for selected Latin American countries	167
Figure 5.2	Chile: Labour force and pension scheme membership 1980-1997	170
Figure 5.3	Chile: Alternative measures of active contributors to the new pension scheme	173
Figure 5.4	Chile: New pension scheme coverage rates 1982-1997	174
Figure 5.5	Chile: Cumulative number of affiliates without contributions to their retirement accounts by length of time	176
Figure 5.6	Chile: New pension scheme coverage rates by sex	177
Figure 5.7	Chile: New pension scheme coverage rates for independent workers	179

Table 5.1	Chile: Pension scheme coverage rates from CASEN94 data	181
Table 5.2	Results from probit models of affiliation and contribution to individual capitalization pension plans	182
Table 5.3	Results from probit models of non-affiliation and non-contribution to pension schemes among employed workers	187
Table 5.4	Number of affiliates and contributors to individual capitalization pension schemes in Chile, Peru, Argentina and Mexico	192
Table 5.5	Pension scheme coverage rates for selected Latin American countries	194
Table 6.1	Income distribution and the elderly in selected Latin American countries	205
Table 6.2	Pension benefits available in the Chilean individual capitalization pension scheme	210
Figure 6.1	Chile: Number of pensions in payment awarded by the new pension scheme, by type	213
Figure 6.2	Chile: Share of different pension types in total number of pensions awarded	214
Figure 6.3	Chile: Share of different pension types in total benefit amount	216
Table 6.3	Comparison of key features of annuity and phased withdrawal pensions	218
Figure 6.4	Chile: Old age and retirement pensions, number and average amount, and minimum pension level	221
Table 6.4	Simulations of pension replacement rates under different assumptions	228

Figure 6.5   Chile: Comparison of replacement rates from phased
              withdrawal and annuity pensions   230

Figure 6.6   Annual age earnings profiles for female workers in
              selected Latin American countries (domestic currency)   232

Figure 6.7   Annual age earnings profiles for male workers in
              selected Latin American countries (domestic currency)   233

Table 6.5   Simulation of pension benefit replacement rates for
              selected Latin American countries   234

Acknowledgements

A number of people made this book possible. My debt to Luis Firinguetti, with whom I have co-authored a number of papers on Chile's pension reform, is evident throughout the book. Eli Balocchi supplied me with published materials from Chile over a considerable period of time. Peter Lloyd-Sherlock helped with materials and suggestions on the elderly in Argentina. Cathy Bennett provided unstinting librarian support. John Adams, Stephanie Barrientos, Claire Morgan, Al Rainnie, and Gareth Thomas read parts of the manuscript. Stephanie Barrientos provided support, encouragement, and criticism throughout the writing of this book. I am grateful to the *Ministerio de Planificación y Cooperación* (MIDEPLAN) in Chile for allowing access to the CASEN data. I am solely responsible for all the errors and inadequacies that remain.

Preface

This book is based on research I have conducted since 1990, initially on the Chilean pension reform, but later extended to other countries in Latin America. In the course of publishing the results of the research, I realized there was a great deal of interest in this topic, but that constraints of space usually meant that the details of the reformed pension schemes in Latin America were inevitably left out. Yet, some familiarity with the detailed regulations, and practices, of pension schemes is vital to the process of understanding, and evaluating, them. The book was conceived to provide a more in depth examination of pension reform in Latin America. The book grew in scope as more countries embarked upon pension reform in the region. The coverage extends to the Mexican pension reform in 1997, and the reform in Costa Rica. I have focused on the new individual capitalization pension plans, which are the main innovation introduced by the reforms. The study of these demand a wide range of expertise, covering the areas of economics, social policy, finance, demography, ageing, and, of course, knowledge of economic and social trends in the region. I have tried to cover the different aspects of pension reform, but the reader will find the limits of my expertise. The wider range provided by the book allowed me to indulge in some of my hobby-horses: that pension schemes make little sense if their insurance properties are ignored, that pension schemes are attached to the labour market by an umbilical chord, and that in the evaluation of public policy, its impact on the least advantaged should be paramount.

Introduction

There has been a rapid spread of pension reform in Latin America in the 1990s. Far reaching pension reform has been implemented in Peru in 1993, Argentina and Colombia in 1994, Uruguay in 1996, Mexico in 1997, and is imminent in Costa Rica. These countries have followed the example of Chile's 1981 pension reform, which replaced its social insurance pension schemes with individual capitalization pension plans. In addition, other countries in Latin America are currently considering pension reform proposals along similar lines, and proposals for reform are very advanced in Bolivia and Paraguay.

The Latin American pension reform is not only important in its own right, but has also provided a model for countries in other regions, both developing and developed, to study and follow. In particular, the Chilean experience of pension reform has attracted attention and praise from multilateral lending institutions such as the World Bank and the IMF (Holzmann, 1997; World Bank, 1994). It would not be an exaggeration to say that the recent pension reform in Latin America, and especially the Chilean reform, provides a paradigm for pension reform.

The basic elements of pension reform are common to all seven Latin American countries that have implemented it. The main aim of the reform is to replace ailing pay as you go social insurance pension schemes, with individual capitalization pension plans. Under the latter workers contribute to individual retirement accounts, enjoying tax privileged status and government guarantees. The contributions are accumulated into a fund managed by private pension fund managers. These invest the pension fund in a set of financial assets yielding returns. The accumulated contributions and returns are used at retirement to make pension arrangements, which include phased withdrawal programs and life annuities.

The new pension schemes have some innovative features. In contrast to the pre-existing social insurance pension schemes, they rely on private pension provision by the newly established pension fund managers, and allow greater scope for individual choice in pension arrangements. A new pension fund management market is created in which competition by fund managers, and extensive regulation, are expected to secure effective pension outcomes. Responsibility for pension arrangements under the new pension schemes is transferred to individual workers. The government's role in pension provision is reduced to that of providing supervision and regulation. The new pension schemes explicitly avoid redistributive objectives.

In the Latin American countries that have embarked upon pension reform, the original proposals involved the straightforward replacement of social insurance pay as you go pension schemes with privately provided individual capitalization pension plans. These proposals were adopted with little change in Chile and Mexico. In all other countries, pension reform resulted in the retention of a reformed social insurance pension scheme in competition with a capitalization scheme. This was a consequence of the influence of political scrutiny and debate, which were severely restricted in Chile, but also resulted from the strong commitment in these countries to social insurance, solidarity, and redistributive values. In Argentina and Uruguay, radical pension reform proposals were also checked by the large liabilities of the pre-existing pension schemes, resulting in large part from their more advanced demographic transition. While pension reform in Latin America shares key common elements, there will be significant diversity in the reformed pension systems.

Proponents of the new individual capitalization pension plans have claimed these will have large positive effects upon the Latin American economies. Firstly, because they will remove many of the distortionary effects of pay as you go pension schemes, particularly as regards saving and labour supply incentives. Secondly, because the new pension schemes will improve the functioning of capital and labour markets. It is claimed that the new pension schemes will increase savings, and will redirect pension saving through the capital markets, contributing to their development and modernization. The new pension schemes are expected to result in lower contribution levels. Individual accumulation for retirement is also expected to create a more effective and direct link between contributions and benefits. These features will, it is claimed, improve the operation of labour markets, and facilitate employment, mobility, and flexibility. To the extent that these expectations are fulfilled, pension reform will contribute to economic growth in the region.

The emphasis being placed on the implications of pension reform for the operation of the economy spring from the fact that the reform is firmly embedded within the wider structural reforms implemented in Latin America following the 1980s crises. Pension reform is expected to facilitate and reinforce these reforms, and to contribute to economic liberalization.

The primary objective of pension schemes is, however, to provide adequate pension benefits for their affiliates. Proponents of pension reform also claim that it will result in improved pension benefits for future groups of pensioners.

Evaluating pension reform

It is important to assess the extent to which these claims are likely to materialize. There is a growing literature aiming to provide this evaluation.[1] The approach of this book will be distinctive in a number of respects, which are as follows.

Pension reform has progressed at a furious pace in Latin America, with more countries adopting and implementing pension reform proposals. This book attempts to provide an up to date study of the different experiences of pension reform in Latin America. In addition to a close examination of pension reform in Chile, Peru, Argentina, Colombia and Uruguay, the book covers the latest two countries embarking upon pension reform, Mexico in 1997, and Costa Rica. It also includes the more important recent changes to pension scheme regulations in Peru, Argentina and Chile. The study of pension reform in these last three countries is based on the most recent available data.

The analysis of pension reform in this book places a strong emphasis on cross-country comparisons. Chile has the longest experience with pension reform, going back to 1981, and as such it merits special attention. In particular, where the analysis requires time series trends, only Chile's pension reform can provide reliable evidence. At the same time, the diversity in the reformed pension systems in Latin America requires that trends in other countries, and especially Argentina and Peru, be considered. Argentina's pension reform, because of its mix of public pay as you go pension schemes, and private capitalization schemes provides an important source of evidence.

Studies of pension reform in Latin America have inevitably glossed over much of the detailed features of the reformed pension systems. This is because the literature, especially the studies done outside Latin America, has naturally focused on the broader, and the more striking, features of pension reform.[2] An important lesson gained from the study of pension schemes and pension design is that familiarity with their detailed features is crucial to an assessment of their worth. An interesting example of this is the debate over the comparative advantages of defined contribution and defined benefit pension schemes. Focusing on stylized versions of pension design emphasizes their distinctive features. It is possible, however, to design the detailed features of these pension schemes in such a way that their properties turn out to be almost indistinguishable (Disney, 1995). An important contribution of this book is provided by the close attention paid both to the broad features of pension schemes in Latin America, and to the details of their design where these have significant effects.

The literature on pension reform in Latin America has downplayed the insurance properties of pension schemes.[3] This is in part because of the structural design of individual capitalization pension plans, in which the basic building bloc consists of individual retirement saving accounts. In part this is due to the short life span of reformed pension schemes in Latin America. Pension schemes have important insurance properties, providing cover for a range of risks affecting consumption in retirement. Pension reform has changed these in important ways. Evaluating pension schemes purely as a mechanism for transferring income from work to retirement, and ignoring the range of consumption insurance provided, is like playing tennis with the net down. The analysis of pension reform in this book pays appropriate attention to the insurance properties of the reformed pension schemes in Latin America.

A further feature of this book is that it makes full use of primary data from the Latin American countries under examination. A positive feature of the introduction of reformed pension schemes in Latin America is that regulators have been required to collect and make available a range of relevant data, including pension fund managers performance indicators, and membership data. The analysis in this book makes full use of these data. Where possible, the analysis of pension scheme coverage, and the simulation of the likely future pension benefits, is supported by available household data.

The evaluation of pension reform in Latin America presented in this book aims to provide a balanced assessment. Pension schemes are long term institutions taking several decades to develop and mature. It is commonplace that new pension schemes invariably appear to be successful at first, when there are large number of contributors and few pensioners. Their introduction is usually accompanied by strong claims concerning their advantages and benefits. It is therefore appropriate that pension reform is considered in a long term perspective, and that its potential advantages and effects are carefully assessed against existing evidence. A further point is that in the evaluation of public policy, the likely outcomes of policy for the least advantaged should be of primary importance. It follows from this that special attention should be paid to the impact of pension reform on the least advantaged. This book approaches its subject matter in precisely these terms.

The structure of the book

The structure of the book is as follows. The next chapter considers the background to recent pension reform in Latin America. It outlines the origins and development of social insurance pension schemes in the area, and identifies the key factors leading to pension reform. Social insurance pension schemes have a long tradition in Latin America. Pension schemes date back to turn of the century in Argentina, and to the 1920s in Chile. They were initially set up for public servants and the armed forces, but from the 1950s onwards expanded very rapidly to cover other workers and contingencies.

In line with social insurance models, pension schemes in Latin America were set up as partially funded defined benefit pension schemes for separate groups of workers. Their accelerated implementation meant that their partial funding element soon fell away, and the government assumed a higher profile in their regulation and funding. The high inflation of the 1970s resulted in rising financial deficits for the pension schemes, and at the same time in a decline in the value of pension benefits. The economic crisis of the early 1980s brought the financial deficits of these pension schemes to a crisis point, and the need for pension reform became urgent. The structural adjustment programs implemented in the wake of the economic crisis identified an important role for pension reform in securing their success. Pension reform became part of a wider strategy of facilitating and reinforcing economic liberalization.

The second chapter focuses on describing and assessing the changes in pension design brought about by the reform. To this end, the main functions of pension schemes are examined. Pension schemes perform three main functions. They provide a mechanism for transferring income from work to retirement, they provide insurance against a range of risks that are likely to impact on retirement income, and they provide a mechanism for supporting redistributive and solidarity objectives. Pension reform, which replaces totally or partially a social insurance pension scheme with individual capitalization pension plans, is bound to lead to a change in the priorities for, and the balance of, the functions performed by pension schemes. The new pension schemes introduced in Latin America are designed to explicitly avoid redistributive properties. And the range of insurance provided by them is narrower, but perhaps more focused, than that provided by the old social insurance pension schemes.

Chile and Mexico have moved to fully replace their old social insurance pension schemes with individual capitalization plans. All the other countries have ended up with a system that retains a reformed social insurance pension scheme set in competition with the new private pension plans. The articulation of pension schemes requires a close study of their main design features. This is done in the last sections of this chapter.

Chapter 3 focuses on the new pension fund management market created by the reforms. The new pension fund managers constitute the main innovation brought in by pension reform, and will provide the key to the future success of the capitalization pension schemes. A pension fund management market will need to be established anew in Latin America. If successful, the new pension fund managers will perform an important role in encouraging the growth and modernization of capital markets, in addition to providing access to the financial sector for a large section of workers. The chapter focuses at first on a close examination and assessment of the evolution of the new pension fund management market in Chile, as this is the country with the oldest, and most developed, market. A comparison with Argentina and Peru serves to identify common trends.

A key theme of this chapter is the role of competition and regulation in establishing and developing this market. In common with financial markets, the effectiveness of the pension fund management market is likely to be undermined by market failure. Supervision and regulation are needed to ensure the orderly functioning of these markets. The experience of Latin American pension reform yields mixed results. The new pension fund managers have been able to become established in a short period of time, and have secured high rates of return for pension savers. At the same time, they have high operational, and especially marketing, costs. The rising marketing costs do not appear to add value to pension provision. Analysis of affiliates' market behaviour confirms that they appear to be relatively insensitive to the parameters affecting their pension fund accumulation. In these circumstances, supervision and regulation are important in securing efficient outcomes. The regulatory choices in the context of the new pension schemes in Latin America appear to be finely balanced.

Chapter 4 discusses the claim that pension reform will have a significant impact on economic growth through raising savings and improving the operation of capital markets. The potential effect of pension reform on saving has received much attention in the literature. It is argued that pension reform replacing pay as you pension schemes with individual retirement pension plans will contribute to raising saving rates by providing a more efficient saving instrument. Economic theory is ambiguous about the potential effects of pension reform on household saving. The empirical evidence is also mixed, but the experience of Chile and other Latin American countries is that the saving effects of pension reform are of marginal significance.

A more promising link between pension reform and economic growth is that existing between the development and modernization of capital markets and improvements in productivity. Pension reform will divert pension saving through the financial and capital markets, and it will help establish an important group of institutional investors. These changes may generate a potential improvement in productivity arising from a more efficient allocation of funds for investment, and a more effective market for corporate control. The late 1980s and 1990s have witnessed a deepening and modernization of the Latin American capital markets. These trends are more pronounced in Chile, where pension reform took place earlier. This chapter examines whether pension reform is responsible for this capital market growth, and evaluates what impact it is likely to have on economic growth.

Chapter 5 focuses on the impact of pension reform on labour markets in Latin America. Proponents of pension reform have claimed it is likely to improve the operation of labour markets by removing the distortions introduced by social insurance pension schemes on labour supply and sectoral employment choice, and by facilitating the employment changes generated by structural adjustment. The core of the chapter concentrates on the analysis of pension coverage trends in Chile, and in other Latin American countries. The main findings are that while the coverage rates of the new pension schemes have been bolstered by workers switching from the old pension schemes, and by the growth in employment which followed the recovery from the 1980s crisis, overall pension system coverage rates have stagnated. The chapter considers what policy changes are needed to raise pension scheme coverage rates in Latin America.

Chapter 6 focuses on the impact of pension reform on retirement income. It begins by noting that current pensioners have a lower poverty incidence than other groups in Latin America, and postulates that this is a factor of the accelerated introduction of pay as you go pension schemes in the region. It describes and evaluates the alternative arrangements for retirement benefits available in the new pension schemes, and the likely future trends. As the pension schemes in Latin America are a long way from achieving maturity, simulations of future pension benefits are constructed. These help to identify which factors will be crucial in determining future retirement income, and the extent to which current pension design will secure adequate pension benefits for pensioners. The main findings are that very favourable conditions will be needed to secure adequate pension benefits in the future, and that inequality among retired groups is likely to grow.

The overall assessment of pension reform in Latin America is by necessity provisional al this stage, but important lessons can be learned. The Conclusion provides some indication of the likely future course of pension reform in Latin America. It also discusses what lessons can be drawn from the spread of pension reform in the region, that should be considered by other countries wishing to embark upon pension reform.

Notes

1. There is a rapidly expanding literature on pension reform in Latin America (Baeza and Margozzini, 1995; Bertín and Perrotto, 1997; CEPAL/PNUD, 1995; Cheyre, 1991; CIEDESS, 1994; Diamond, 1993; Gillion and Bonilla, 1992; Holzmann, 1997; Iglesias and Acuña, 1991; Lo Vuolo, 1996; Mesa-Lago, 1996; Myers, 1992; Queisser, 1995; Shah, 1997; Superintendencia de Administradoras de Fondos de Jubilaciones y Pensiones, 1996; Uthoff, 1994; Vittas, 1997; World Bank, 1994).
2. Two important exceptions are Vittas (1992), and Diamond (1994).
3. An important exception is Diamond (1993).

1 Background to pension reform in Latin America

A number of Latin American countries have embarked upon a radical reshaping of pension provision in the 1990s, following the example of Chile's 1981 pension reform. The rapid spread of pension reform in Latin America helps to underline the fact that common factors are responsible. The key factors explaining recent pension reform in Latin America are the financial deterioration experienced by social insurance funds, the economic crisis in the 1980s, changes in labour market conditions, and the implementation of structural reforms.

The social insurance pension schemes previously in place in most Latin American countries developed large financial imbalances in the 1980s. These were due to a combination of factors. In part, they were the result of long term problems associated with pension scheme design and implementation, and with adverse demographic trends. The acute economic crisis the Latin American economies experienced in the 1980s magnified these longer term trends. The contraction in economic activity, fiscal deficits, and large scale changes in the labour market arising from the 1980s recession, brought about a crisis in social insurance and pension financing and provision.

In response to the economic crisis, a process of structural reform of the Latin American economies was initiated. Structural adjustment programs embedded social insurance and pension reform within the overall objective of economic and market liberalization. The requirements of structural adjustment programs defined the direction and extent of the reform. In all Latin American countries attempting pension reform in the 1990s, individual capitalization pension schemes have fully or partially replaced pay as you go social insurance pension schemes.

This chapter examines the background to pension reform in Latin America. The next section reviews briefly the origins and evolution of social insurance pension schemes. The section that follows identifies, and discusses, the main factors responsible for the large financial imbalances experienced by the Latin American pension schemes. The following section explains the rationale for structural reform of social insurance pension schemes. In particular, it discusses the view that pay as you go pension schemes suffer from structural problems that make them vulnerable to changing demographic and economic conditions. It also inserts pension reform within the wider context of structural adjustment programs. This is important in explaining the orientation of the reforms. A conclusion summarizes the main findings.

The origins and evolution of pension schemes

Pension schemes have a long history in Latin America (Mesa-Lago, 1991). The *Caja Nacional de Jubilaciones y Pensiones Civiles* was set up in 1904 in Argentina to provide old age and service pensions for public administration workers. In Chile, the *Servicio de Seguro Social* was set up in 1924 to provide pensions for blue collar private sector workers, and this was followed in 1925 with similar institutions for white collar private and public sector workers. In Mexico the 1925 *Ley General de Pensiones Civiles de Retiro* set up a pension scheme covering federal, state and municipal workers. The early pension schemes in Latin America shared a number of characteristics. They were organised around a social insurance principle, in that the benefits provided were financed entirely out of contributions, the contributions were fixed and the promised pension benefits aimed to replace a fraction of final salary. They included a partial funding element through the accumulation and investment of initial surpluses, covering clearly defined groups of workers.

The period up to 1980 was characterised by the extension of the social insurance principle to cover other contingencies, such as health, unemployment, sickness, family benefits, and industrial injuries.[1] The schemes also expanded to provide workers with financial support to purchase housing and other merit goods. As the range of benefits expanded, the social insurance schemes developed into small scale welfare states protecting and supporting groups of workers and their dependants from key economic and social risks.

This period was also characterised by an extension of social insurance to other groups of workers. Coverage rates increased steadily during the 1960s and 1970s. By the early 1970s, some countries, such as Chile, Argentina, and Uruguay, had in place social insurance schemes covering over three-quarters of the labour force. In most cases the extension of social insurance coverage led to the creation of a large number of small social insurance funds, or to the proliferation of separate programs within a large social insurance fund.[2] The piecemeal development of social insurance resulted in an enormous diversity of contribution, funding, and entitlement arrangements. It was also responsible in large measure for the complexity, opaqueness, and inequality characterising the operation of social insurance programs.

Atkinson (1989) argues that industrialisation was responsible for the spread of social insurance in developed countries, and in Britain in particular. The shift in employment from rural agriculture to urban manufacture meant, for the workers involved, a change to less secure forms of employment with potentially larger variations in consumption levels. In agriculture, the impact on consumption of unemployment could be ameliorated by subsistence production. In manufacturing, by contrast, industrial unemployment resulted in a more or less total loss of earnings and a therefore a sharp drop in consumption. In addition, higher earnings in manufacturing also had the effect of concentrating employment on a few breadwinners (Goldin, 1994), thus increasing the exposure of workers, and their dependants, to work, sickness, and social risks. Social insurance facilitated the changes required by industrialisation by providing some protection against catastrophic falls in consumption.

The establishment and expansion of social insurance in Latin America is also closely connected with the process of industrialisation, and with the dominant import substitution model of industrialisation (Huber, 1996). Industrialisation created a large urban labour force, and sizeable public sector employment. The state had a key role in implementing these policies, as they required a significant diversion of resources from agriculture to industry. At a political level, manufacturing and public sector workers played an important role in the political alliances that sustained import substitution policies. The expansion of welfare provision for urban workers was a product of these, and helped sustained these political alliances. It enabled these groups to share in the benefits arising from the redistribution of resources imposed by such a model. [3]

In the pioneer countries, social insurance funds began life as quasi-public bodies. The government provided the initial impetus and the legal framework for social insurance funds, but these were operationally autonomous. It helped that public servants were, in most cases, the first group of workers covered by social insurance. Over time, the role played by government in social insurance expanded. Initially in the 1950s and 1960s this was a consequence of government attempts to harmonise and consolidate provision. Later in the 1970s it was a consequence of rising funding subsidies needed to shore up the funds' booming financial deficits.

The rising government profile in social insurance provision facilitated the expansion of social insurance benefits, but also led to a departure from the partial funding principle. The extension of the scope and value of the benefits provided by social insurance, together with rising inflation, spelt the end of partial funding in the 1970s. Most social insurance funds became strictly pay as you go, and increasingly dependent on government support.

Argentina provides a good example of the typical evolution of social insurance pension schemes in the region. In Argentina the unification of the plethora of pension schemes began in 1954 (Schulthess and Demarco, 1993). The existing social insurance funds were consolidated into thirteen in 1954, which became three in 1967, and later two in 1969. In managing and underwriting this consolidation the government inevitably raised its involvement in pension schemes, leading to a shift in the status of the funds from partial funding to pay as you go. In Argentina, the social insurance funds had, by the 1950s, accumulated significant surpluses totalling around 28 percent of GDP. The government took over these surpluses providing the social insurance funds with government fixed interest debt instruments in their place. Interest rates paid on these instruments were fixed in nominal terms at between 4 and 8 percent. The value of these debt instruments declined dramatically with the onset of high inflation in the late 1960s and 1970s (Durán, 1993). The partial funding of the social insurance funds in Argentina soon disappeared. As the social insurance system plunged into deficit in mid 1970s, government funding support increased. By 1975, government subsidies came to account for 20 percent of total social insurance revenue.

In the 1980s, the great majority of social insurance funds in Latin America were experiencing acute financial imbalances, and relied to an increasing extent on government funding. Public concern over the sustainability of social insurance rose. This focused on the declining value of pension benefits, sharp inequalities in the benefits provided, and the administrative and financial shortcomings which became increasingly apparent from the operation of the funds. The stage was thus set for the reform of social insurance.

Explaining pension scheme deficits

The mounting financial deficits experienced by the social insurance funds were already apparent before the 1980s economic crisis. They were a consequence of some key design features of pension schemes and problems associated with their accelerated implementation. These design and implementation problems made them particularly vulnerable to adverse demographic and economic trends. The financial deficits of social insurance pension schemes mounted in the wake of the early 1980s economic crisis, which had a strong impact on government finances and the labour market.

This section reviews the key factors leading to the mounting financial deficits of pension schemes in Latin America.

Financial equilibrium in a pay as you go pension scheme

In pay as you go pension schemes financial balance requires that for a given period, contributions are sufficient to finance benefits plus administration costs.[4] For a mature pay as you go pension scheme, and assuming constant population, financial balance requires that the revenue collected covers expenditures.

If pension scheme income is

$$Y = C\,t\,W^x + GS \tag{1.1}$$

where Y is pension scheme revenue, C is the number of contributors, t is the contribution rate, W^x represents contributory earnings, and GS is government subsidy.

And pension scheme expenditure is

$$E = P\,b\,W^z + AC \tag{1.2}$$

where E is pension expenditure, P is the number of pensioners, b is the target replacement rate, W^z represents the final salary base on which the pension benefit is calculated, and AC represents administrative costs. Financial equilibrium for a mature pay as you go pension scheme must satisfy the condition

$$Y = C\,t\,W^x + GS = P\,b\,W^z + AC = E \tag{1.3}$$

For a given target replacement rate (1.3) can be reorganised as

$$b = (C/P)\,t\,(W^x/W^z) + GS/PW^z - AC/PW^z \tag{1.4}$$

This equation identifies the factors that may be responsible for a deterioration of the financial balance of a pay as you go pension scheme. For a given target pension benefit replacement rate a deterioration of pension scheme finances will result from: (i) a deterioration in the pension scheme support ratio, the ratio of contributors to pensioners; (ii) a fall in contribution rates; (iii) a decline in the real earnings of workers relative to the earnings of retirees; (iv) a fall in government support; and (v) an increase in the administrative costs (Iglesias and Acuña, 1991). These factors are discussed below in the context of the Latin American countries that have embarked upon pension reform.

The fall in the pension scheme support ratio

A key factor in the financial deterioration of social insurance pension schemes in Latin America has been a sharp fall in the ratio of active contributors to passive beneficiaries. Most countries in Latin America have experienced a rapid increase in the number of pensioners while at the same time the number of contributors has stagnated or even declined. The ratio of active to passive members of pension schemes in Chile fell from 10.8 in 1960 to 2.2 in 1980. In Argentina the same ratio for dependent workers was 2.1 in 1990 and is expected to fall below 1.9 in the year 2000. In Peru the ratio declined from 13.6 in 1980 to 7.8 in 1990. In Mexico the ratio was 16 for the affiliates to the *Instituto Mexicano de Seguro Social* (IMSS) in 1970 and fell to 9.1 in 1990. And in Colombia the pension scheme dependency ratio is predicted to decline from 13 in 1990 to 8.8 in the year 2000. These figures show that the pension scheme support ratio has deteriorated fast for all the countries in Latin America. The reasons behind this deterioration are complex and will need to be examined closely.

Demographic trends: population ageing in Latin America

A contributory factor in the deterioration of pension scheme support ratio for Latin American countries is the demographic transition these countries are experiencing. Population ageing is the result of a combined rise in life expectancy and fall in fertility. Both these processes are underway in Latin America. Moreover, the indications are that the population ageing will happen faster in Latin America than it did in the developed nations (World Bank, 1994). Population ageing is already quite advanced in a handful of Latin American countries that include Uruguay and Argentina. Population projections for Latin America show that the ratio of the population of working age to the population over 65 will fall steadily during the first half of the twenty-first century to just under three potential workers per pensioner. Table 1.1 below shows the population support ratio for the countries under examination. As the retired population rises relative to those of working age, the ratio of contributors to pensioners must necessarily fall.

Although population ageing has played a part in the recent financial deterioration of pension funds in Latin America, it has not been an important one. Population ageing is a gradual process that will take some time to uncoil. It alone cannot explain the large deficits in pension schemes that emerged in the 1980s. And the financial imbalances experienced by countries like Argentina and Uruguay that are well ahead in their demographic transition are also much in evidence in those countries like Peru and Colombia that are yet to experience serious demographic pressures. At the same time, given the population projections in the table below, pension reform will need to take account of the demographic changes ahead (Barrientos, 1996a). [5]

Table 1.1
Population support ratio for selected Latin American countries

population 20-64 years of age / 65 and over

Country	1990	2020	2050
Argentina	5.9	4.8	2.7
Chile	9.0	5.5	2.7
Colombia	12.5	7.7	2.8
Costa Rica	12.5	6.6	2.7
Mexico	12.5	8.3	3.0
Peru	14.3	10.0	3.7
Uruguay	4.8	3.8	2.4

Population projections from The World Bank(1994).

Social insurance pension scheme design and implementation

There are other long term trends explaining the fall in the support ratio of social insurance pensions schemes. These schemes have pension benefits aiming to replace a given proportion of final salary. They also aim to generate significant redistribution. These features of social insurance pension schemes weaken, for individual contributors, the link existing between contributions and entitlements. The favourable demographic conditions in Latin America facilitated an accelerated implementation of these pension schemes. As a result, pension entitlements pre-requisites were significantly relaxed for older workers. One important implication from this is that the incentives for regular contributors were weakened, with adverse implications for the support ratio. Moreover, labour market conditions in Latin America, with a large informal sector, reinforced these trends.

In common with the experience of many other countries with pay as you go pension schemes, initial entitlement regulations in Latin America allowed for an accelerated implementation of the schemes. Benefit entitlement regulations were relaxed to provide pensions for those close to retirement. This usually took the form of short qualifying contribution periods, and even shorter periods used in the calculation of pension benefits. This meant that the number of pensioners increased very rapidly following the extension of pension scheme coverage in the 1950s and 1960s.

Whilst enabling workers to build up entitlements in a short period of time, these relaxed entitlement requirements enhanced incentives for workers to make contributions for only a fraction of their working lives. Contribution incentives were strong only in the years leading to retirement, and the incentives for younger members of the labour force to make regular contributions were considerably weakened. These generous entitlement requirements had adverse consequences for the number of active contributors to pension schemes.

For example, in the main Chilean social insurance funds, the pension benefit was fixed as a fraction of final salary calculated from the last 3 to 5 years of employment. The required contribution record was 15 years for blue collar workers and 10 years for public sector white collar workers. In Colombia, private sector worker's pension benefit is calculated on a fraction of the average of the last two years of employment. As regards the required period of contribution, the first 10 years of contributions buy 45 percent of this final salary, with extra years adding additional 3 percentage points up to a maximum of 90 percent. Ayala (1992) reports, not surprisingly, a bunching of current pensioners with 10 years contribution records. The design of entitlement requisites aimed at facilitating the accelerated implementation of the pension schemes also created disincentives for regular contributions.

The conditions of Latin American labour markets, with a sizeable informal sector and generally inadequate mechanisms for enforcing labour market regulations, greatly facilitated avoidance and evasion of pension scheme contributions. Adverse labour market conditions arising from the 1980s economic crisis, especially the rise in unemployment and the growing informalisation of employment, reinforced these trends. These factors are primarily responsible for the fall in the pension scheme support ratio in the Latin American schemes, and consequently for their rising financial deficits.

Non-contributory pensions and underreporting of contributory earnings

As was noted, the accelerated implementation of pension schemes in Latin America meant that the number of pensioners rose rapidly soon after the extension of pension scheme coverage in the 1950s and 1960s. In Chile, for example, the proportion of the population over retirement age receiving a retirement pension increased from 39 percent in 1961, to 54 percent in 1965, and further to 63 percent in 1975 (Arellano, 1990). In addition, the extension of pension benefits to workers without the necessary contribution requisites, and to non-contributors, placed further pressure upon the support ratio.

The rapid rise in the number of non-contributory pensions was a factor of the growth in the volume and value of disability pensions. In many of the countries under study, requirements for disability pension were easier to satisfy than those applying to old age, or service, pensions. This created incentives for disability pension applications. In Argentina, for example, disability pension benefits trebled in value during the 1980s, and non-contributory pensions came to account for 5 percent of all pensions (Schulthess and Demarco, 1993). The growth of non-contributory pensions had the effect of increasing the number of pensioners relative to contributors.

In addition to workers not contributing regularly through their working lives, the short period used in the pension benefit calculation created incentives for the under reporting of contributory earnings. This is because the level of contributory earnings is only important for the pension benefit within the period used for the final salary calculation.

These are the main factors responsible for the decline in the support ratio of pension schemes in Latin America.[6] In addition to demographic factors, the accelerated implementation of social insurance pension schemes, together with the specific labour market conditions in Latin America, combined to produce a fall in the pension schemes support ratio.

Responses to the mounting financial deficits

In order to maintain financial balance in a pay as you go pension scheme which is experiencing a fall in the support ratio, compensating changes are needed. A number of options are possible responses to the problem. One possibility is to allow a decline in the target replacement ratio, effectively lowering pension commitments. Alternatively, the target replacement ratio can be sustained if the fall in the support ratio is compensated for by changes in the other variables. This can be done by raising contribution rates, increasing government subsidies, or by reducing administration costs. It is also possible to combine these with a tightening up of entitlement pre-requisites.

In the Latin American pension schemes, attempts have been made to restore financial balances by scaling down entitlements, raising contribution rates, increasing government financial support, and by reducing administrative costs.

Of these, scaling down entitlements by reducing pension benefit levels is the most difficult to implement, especially as the majority of pensioners receive pension benefits that are very close to the minimum. In the early 1990s in Argentina, the average pension benefit was around a quarter of the minimum wage (Schulthess and Demarco, 1993). In the same period in Chile, two thirds of pensioners received the minimum pension benefit (Cheyre, 1991). A different avenue for scaling down entitlements is that of restricting pension benefit awards. Argentina attempted to clamp down on especial pension programs without much success, and in Chile the 1980 pension reform eliminated service pensions in the pay as you go scheme.

The improvements in pension scheme finances arising from these measures are initially very small, as pension entitlements can only be amended for new pensioners.

A different response is to increase contribution levels. There has been a strong upward trend in the pension and social insurance contribution rates in the Latin American pension schemes. In Chile, the combined employer and employee social insurance scheme contribution rate for blue collar workers rose from 47.9 percent of earnings in 1968, to just over 60 percent in 1974. The rate then declined in the latter part of the 1970s, the period leading to the pension reform in 1980. Contribution rates for white collar workers peaked in the mid 1970s at 68.5 percent for those in the private sector, and 58.75 percent for those in the public sector. The pension scheme contribution rate alone stayed at around 25 percent of earnings for private sector white collar workers. Chile is in some ways an unusual case as the hike in contribution rates in the 1970s took place in the context of very limited political and organised labour opposition. The rise in contribution rates in other countries in the region has been much more gradual, but the trend if clearly observable.

The problem with this method of financial adjustment is that it impacts back on labour market incentives, by further encouraging evasion and avoidance of contributions. High, or rising, contribution rates reinforce incentives for the underreporting of earnings for contribution purposes, the evasion of contribution payments, and the shift of employment to the non-covered sector.

The level of government support funding for social insurance schemes, and the pension schemes within them, had been rising in real terms through the 1970s and 1980s. The rise in government subsidies to social insurance programs acquired a high profile in the context of the drive to reduce government expenditure. There are therefore clear limits to using government funding as a means of rebalancing financially the pension schemes.

The administrative costs of the social insurance schemes have not been particularly large, although they are much higher than those for similar programs in developed countries (Mesa-Lago, 1991). More importantly, administrative costs have shown a gradual upward trend. Pension scheme administrative costs as a proportion of total expenditure were 2.3 percent in Argentina in 1974, rising to 2,7 percent in 1990. In Mexico's IMSS they were reported as 13.7 percent in 1980 rising to 14.5 percent in 1989. And in Colombia they were 5 percent in the early 1990s. In addition, pension scheme administration in many countries in Latin America has some reputation for bureaucracy and inefficiency.[7] On the whole, savings in the administrative costs of pension schemes can provide at best a marginal solution to the financial imbalances.

Pension scheme redistribution and inequality

The aim of restoring financial balance in the social insurance pension schemes has been complicated by the perverse redistribution and the inequalities in pension provision some pension schemes have produced.

The governance of pension schemes in Latin America has been criticised for a marked generosity towards favoured groups. Pay as you go pension schemes have the advantage that they facilitate redistribution, both across and within cohorts, through the manipulation of contribution and entitlement formulas. The redistribution of income towards the poor was a central objective of social insurance pension schemes. The redistribution generated by pension schemes has tended, in practice, to benefit favoured client groups instead. This has taken many forms in Latin America, including lower retirement age, shorter service pension requirements, higher replacement rates, and indexed pension benefits. This perverse redistribution became more accentuated in the 1970s and 1980s with the attempts by these groups to ameliorate the effects of rising inflation on their pension entitlements. Their privileged pensions made rising demand upon resources, further contributing to pension scheme financial imbalances.

There are large inequalities in pension scheme entitlements, and returns, with significant demonstration effects for non-favoured workers. By inequality in pension entitlement, it is meant that workers with the same working lives and earnings paths could end up receiving different entitlements from the pension scheme. Inequalities in pension entitlements have the effect of further undermining confidence in the pension scheme. Through the demonstration effect, these also encourage rent seeking. There were substantial inequalities in entitlement present in the Latin American pay as you go pension schemes. Thus, for example, white collar workers in Chile with similar working experiences would have received different pension entitlements simply because they belonged to different schemes with different rules concerning entitlements. Whereas public sector workers accumulated pension entitlements at a rate of 1/30th of final salary per year of services, private sector workers did so at 1/35th. As indicated above, inequalities increased as a result of the inflationary conditions of the 1970s and early 1980s.

The 1980s economic crisis in Latin America

The rising deficits of social insurance pension schemes and the failure of piecemeal efforts at pension reform were exacerbated by the acute economic crises experienced by Latin American economies in the early 1980s.

Labour market and macroeconomic conditions in the 1980s were particularly adverse for the Latin American economies. The 1970s debt crisis and its aftermath plunged these economies into a deep recession in the early 1980s. The balance of payment imbalances that followed the abrupt ending of capital inflows necessitated the implementation of stabilization programs to reduce inflation, domestic demand, and public expenditure. These initially reinforced recessionary trends. Chile's gross domestic product, for example, contracted by as much as 14 percent in 1982. This contraction generated high rates of unemployment and a consequent rise in poverty. For most countries in the region, the balance sheet for the entire decade was depressing, leading commentators to pen the term 'the lost decade' to describe the 1980s.

The crisis and the macroeconomic stabilization programs that followed produced significant upheaval and change in the Latin American economies, and created the conditions for more fundamental structural reforms. The core of structural reform consisted of far reaching economic liberalization prioritising market resource allocation and openness to international competition. One after the other, Latin American economies abandoned import substitution strategies, and embraced export-led growth, and embarked upon financial and labour market liberalization.

The impact on labour markets was acute. Table 1.2 below presents data on key labour market indicators for the Latin American countries under examination. A sharp contraction in real wages in the 1980s can be observed in all the countries under examination. The contraction in real earnings was large and prolonged. As earnings related contributions financed most social insurance pension schemes, the decline in real earnings directly reduced pension scheme revenues. By contrast, pension benefits, which are commonly indexed to prices, did not show a corresponding decline. This has the implication that financial deficits are inevitable.

The decline in real earnings accelerated the rise in female participation rates in the region, with all the countries under examination showing this trend. In part this is a factor of a long term rise in female activity rates, but the acceleration of this trend in the 1980s reflects the 'added worker' effect of unemployment and falling real wages (Arriagada, 1994). This impacts upon the support ratio as women usually have lower rates of pension scheme coverage.

Public sector employment was particularly hard hit by the crisis and stabilization programs. Cutting down the size of the public sector was perceived as an important objective, as it contributed to the reduction in the balance of payments and fiscal deficits. Traditionally, membership of pension schemes had been high among public sector workers. The decline in public sector employment had a large effect upon pension scheme coverage rates. In addition to the contraction in public sector employment, public sector workers suffered large cuts in pay, in both absolute and relative terms, as austerity packages were implemented. These trends contributed to the fall in the support ratio.

Table 1.2
Labour market indicators for selected Latin American countries
1980-1992

	Annual rate of labour force growth (%)[a]		Female Activity Rate (%)[a]		Male Activity Rate (%)[a]		Public Sector (% of PEA)	
	1981/ 1990	1991/ 2000	1980	1991	1980	1991	1980	1993
Argentina	1.2	1.7	34	[d]34	83	86	18.9	16.8
Chile	2.5	1.8	29	35	75	80	11.9	7.9
Colombia	2.8	2.3	24	54	81	84	13.8	9.9
Costa Rica	3.1	2.6	29	36	86	86	26.7	21.0
Mexico	3.1	2.6	31	36	84	86	21.8	23.0
Peru	2.7	2.6	32	46	81	75		
Uruguay	0.6	0.9	[e]53	58	90	91		

	Unemployment Rate (%)			Real Wage in Manufacturing 1985=100[a]		Real Minimum Wage 1980=100[h]		Informal Sector (% of PEA)	
	1980[a]	1984[b]	1993[b]	1980	1991	1981	1989	1980[c]	1993
Argentina	2.0	4.6	9.6	97	93	98	42	39.4	50.8
Chile	10.0	18.5	4.0	111	124	99	64	50.4	49.9
Colombia	9.0	13.4	8.7	88	101	98	110	52.5	60.3
Costa Rica	6.0	6.6	4.0	95	97	90	119	36.4	52.5
Mexico	5.0	5.7	3.4	139	88	100	47	49.1	57.0
Peru		8.9	9.9	177	59	94	25	[g]40.5	[g]48.8
Uruguay	7.0	14.0	8.4	102	120	103	79	35.2	37.9

a. From ILO (1995).
b. From World Bank (1995).
c. From CEPAL/PNUD (1995). Informal sector comprises the self-employed minus professionals, unwaged relatives, and workers in microenterprises.
d. 1990.
e. 1984.
f. 1983.
g. From Webb (1995),1984 instead of 1980.
h. From Morley (1995).

Trade liberalization added to the changes forced upon the labour market, as it encouraged production of tradeables, and opened up protected manufacturing sectors to the rigours of international competition (Horton, Kanbur and Mazumdar, 1994b). Chile and Uruguay began to dismantle trade barriers in the mid-1970s by eliminating trade quotas and reducing tariffs, and most other countries undertook this process during the 1980s. Trade liberalization brought about large shifts in employment, with a stagnation of employment in manufacturing. It encouraged employment growth in non-traditional exports, which are predominantly natural resource based. Agricultural employment in agribusiness expanded in Costa Rica and Chile (Glinding and Berry, 1994; Riveros, 1994).[8] These shifts in employment also had a significant impact upon pension scheme support ratios. Manufacturing workers traditionally have a higher pension scheme membership density than agriculture or services, and therefore these shifts in employment further reduced the contributor base of these schemes.

Finally, labour market liberalization, which becomes the linchpin of both stabilization and trade liberalization, increased the informalisation of employment relations. Labour market regulation in Latin America emerged from the rise in industrialisation of the 1940s and 1950s and was based on the principle that workers are the weaker part in the employment relationship and need to be protected (Marquez, 1995). Labour market liberalization aims to deregulate employment contracts and to facilitate non-standard employment. It also aims to make employment contracts more flexible and to encourage worker mobility by scaling down hiring and termination restrictions (Marshall, 1996). The dismantling of government intervention in the labour market, the reduction of social security contributions and other payroll taxes, and the decentralisation of collective bargaining are key objectives of labour market liberalization. Labour market liberalization is itself a precondition to the successful implementation of stabilization programs, trade liberalization, and structural adjustment.

The key role of labour market liberalization in sustaining and facilitating economic reform in Latin America has not been given the attention it deserves. In part this is because it has been implemented in a piecemeal fashion, and therefore it does not have the 'big-bang' feel of trade liberalization. In part the lower profile of labour market liberalization has been due to the difficulty in distinguishing between de facto changes from more formal legal changes. This is particularly the case in labour markets with a large informal sector component in which labour market regulation never did apply. Labour market liberalization could simply take the subtle form of an extension of the informal or non-covered sector of the labour market.

In Chile, for example, de facto liberalization of the labour market followed the military coup of 1973 as a result of the repression of political and labour organisations. Employers had, to a large extent, carte blanche as far as the management of their labour force was concerned. Legal changes did not take place until the introduction of the *Plan Laboral* in 1979. Furthermore, key changes in the legal framework of the employment relationship were introduced in the wake of the 1982 economic crisis, and only crystallised in a 1987 revision to the Labour Code (Barrientos and Barrientos, 1996).

Taking the size of the measured informal sector as an indicator of labour market liberalization provides an indication of the scope and significance of this change in Latin America in the period under examination. Labour market liberalization translates directly into lower rates of pension and social insurance coverage. As the margins between the covered and non-covered sectors widened, these facilitated avoidance of payroll contributions by workers and employers. For many workers with low pay and insecure employment, the probability of collecting pension benefits looked increasingly unlikely. In any case, acute present need made future benefits less desirable. Studies of the incidence of evasion in Argentina indicate this is a large-scale problem. Durán (1993) estimates evasion from a comparison of a measure of earnings in the economy, and a measure of declared contributory earnings. She concludes that evasion, as a proportion of actual contributions collected, was 54 percent in 1992, or 3.6 percent of GDP. Lo Vuolo (1993) uses employment and pension scheme affiliation data, and concludes that around 48 percent of potential contributors in fact fail to do so.

The rising unemployment and falling real wages that followed the crisis and the stabilization programs were responsible for a significant increase in poverty and inequality. Morley (1995) estimates poverty incidence in Latin America as a whole to have increased from 26.5 percent in 1980 to 31 percent in 1989. Unemployment and poverty have exerted considerable pressure on the capacity of social insurance schemes to deal with dramatic rises in benefit claims (Mesa-Lago, 1997). In the more advanced countries in the region, pension schemes were used to cushion unemployment via a relaxation in disability and early retirement entitlement requirements. These further aggravated the financial imbalances in the pay as you go pension schemes.

The rise in poverty and inequality also placed a spotlight on the administrative inefficiency and inequality of provision, in social insurance. As the economic crisis affected the poorest sectors of the population most, the large gaps in the safety net provided by social insurance became more clearly observable.

The overall impact of these changes was to engineer a sharp fall in the support ratio of social insurance pension schemes. They also accentuated the distortions in the pattern of contribution and affiliation incentives produced by the design and governance of social insurance pension schemes, by further encouraging rent seeking among participants. The deterioration in labour market conditions has been largely responsible for the rising financial disequilibrium in pay as you go social insurance schemes, by reducing revenues and coverage, and encouraging evasion. These labour market changes have added considerable weight and urgency to the need for pension reform.

Assessing the relative significance of the factors explaining pension scheme financial deficits

The deterioration in labour market conditions in the 1980s as a result of the economic crisis, the stabilization programs that followed, and labour market liberalization in the 1990s had a dominant role in the rising financial deficits of pay as you go pension schemes in the region.

A simulation of the potential impact of changes in labour market conditions on the financial balance of the pension schemes underlines this point. A simple model of pension scheme financial balance that takes account of changes in demographic and labour market conditions is developed in Appendix Two. This model shows that the pension payroll tax required for financial balance is dependent upon the rate of growth of real wages, the rate of change in the activity rate, the rate of change in the proportion of active contributors, and the rate of growth of the labour force. The pension payroll tax required to balance pension schemes is then predicted based on the changes observed for these variables in the Latin American countries under examination in the 1980s (as reported in Table 1.2 above).[9] Alternative assumptions regarding the behaviour of these variables are then simulated. The results provide some indication of the impact of different variables on the predicted pension payroll tax. The results are reported in Table 1.3 below.

The simulations suggest that the deterioration in labour market conditions in Latin America have a stronger impact upon the financial balances of social insurance pension schemes than demographic factors. In particular, the largest increase in notional pension payroll tax would result from extrapolating Mexico's real wage decline to the other countries. Only Peru would show lower payroll tax rates in this case, as real wages in Peru declined in 1990 to one third of their 1980 level. The rise in payroll tax resulting from labour market informality is not very marked because most of the countries under examination, Chile and Colombia are the exception, have experienced significant increases in the relative size of their informal sector. A rise in activity rates, particularly of women, would work to reduce the predicted pension payroll tax. The impact of demographic variables can be observed in the predicted payroll contribution arising from imposing Uruguay's survival ratio across the other countries. This raises pension payroll tax significantly, but the impact is felt more strongly in those countries that are less advanced in their population ageing.[10]

Table 1.3
Pay as you go pension scheme payroll tax under alternative demographic and labour market conditions (% of earnings)

Country	(1) Benchmark based on own country conditions	(2) Same as (1) but assumed survival rate of 0.33	(3) Same as (1) but with survival ratio as in Uruguay	(4) Same as (1) but with female activity rate as in Colombia	(5) Same as (1) but with informal sector as in Argentina	(6) Same as (1) but with real wage changes as in Mexico
Argentina	35	23	37	22	35	53
Chile	17	16	25	12	19	30
Colombia	17	18	19	17	18	31
Costa Rica	37	22	34	25	35	61
Mexico	31	32	51	20	32	31
Peru	79	69	96	53	82	42
Uruguay	27	17	27	17	30	51

The model used in the simulations is described in Appendix Two. Labour market data used are from Table 1.2. Demographic data used are in Table 1.A1 below.

The conclusion from this simulation exercise is that labour market, and macroeconomic, conditions constitute the key factors explaining the financial deterioration in the social insurance pension schemes in Latin America.

Why structural pension reform?

When the factors explaining the financial imbalances of the pay as you go pension schemes in Latin America are brought together, these appear to suggest that nothing short of a fundamental restructuring of pension provision would succeed in bringing the pension schemes back to health. This has been the conclusion of the majority of studies on the subject (Ayala, 1992; Cheyre, 1991; Durán, 1993; Iglesias and Acuña, 1991; Schulthess and Demarco, 1993; World Bank, 1994). They find that structural reform of social insurance pension schemes is needed to create the conditions for sustainable pension schemes in Latin America. A distinction is made between structural and operational problems in the unreformed pension schemes. Whereas operational problems could in principle be solved through partial reform, structural problems point to a major overhaul of the pension scheme. This section briefly reviews the main structural problems identified in pay as you go pension schemes in Latin America.

The impact of external factors on pay as you go pension schemes

To what extent can the financial imbalances experienced by Latin American pension schemes be attributed to fundamental flaws in their design? Some commentators have argued that the financial disequilibrium suffered by pension schemes in Latin America flows from a fundamental lack of symmetry in the way that exogenous variables impact upon the income and expenditure sides of a pay as you go pension scheme (Iglesias and Acuña, 1991).

Noting the requirements for financial equilibrium specified in equation (1.3) above, it is apparent that changes in the exogenous (non-policy) variables, essentially the demographic and economic variables, have asymmetric effects upon the revenues and expenditures of pay as you go pension schemes. Population ageing, for example, reduces the support ratio and therefore revenue, without generating a compensating change in expenditures. In fact, expenditures will exhibit a rising trend in the face of population ageing. Along similar lines, an economic downturn reduces both the support ratio and the level of contributory earnings, without inducing a compensating effect upon the expenditure side. In fact, in the context of social insurance as a whole, expenditure demand rises with an economic downturn.

The argument is that the asymmetric effects of key exogenous factors upon the balance sheet of pay as you go pension schemes imply that these are not self-sustaining. Pay as you go pension schemes will work well in favourable demographic and labour market conditions, such as those that existed in the 1950s and 1960s. However, in the harsh environment of the late 1970s and 1980s, pay as you go pension schemes would find it hard to operate without building up large deficits. In so far as this claim is justified, it would point to the need for fundamental pension reform which replaces pay as you go pension schemes with a pension scheme design that incorporates more appropriate (or better still, automatic) mechanisms for adjusting expenditures to revenues.

In the original design of social insurance pension schemes in Latin America, there existed a mechanism for generating this adjustment. Partial funding was intended to ensure the accumulation of surpluses. A gradual build up of entitlements would have created significant surpluses in the early years of the pension schemes which, wisely invested, could have provided a reserve to cushion external shocks. Even with this pension scheme reserve fund, discretionary adjustments of expenditures to revenues may have been required with large changes in the external variables influencing the funding of pension schemes.

Pension scheme governance and political processes

The need for periodic adjustment to the key parameters of a pay as you go pension scheme highlights the importance of pension scheme governance, and, in the context of public schemes, that of political processes. Adjustments required by population ageing can be anticipated and implemented by a forward looking pension scheme administration. This in most cases necessitates a political input, in initiating a review, collecting the relevant information, and taking a decision to alter pension scheme regulations.

From the experience of pension schemes in Latin America it can be concluded that pension scheme governance may have contributed to the financial imbalances. It is a commonplace that while the extension of pension scheme coverage and benefits does not prove particularly difficult, there exist large political costs associated with bringing social insurance pension schemes back into financial balance. This is confirmed by the extension of pension scheme benefit coverage without corresponding increases in revenue sources, and by the elimination of partial funding. The discretionary relaxation of entitlement pre-requisites for favoured groups provides another example. All these measures have operated to deepen the financial imbalances of pension schemes. On the other hand, pension schemes in Latin America have been largely unsuccessful in their attempts at implementing the reforms needed to bring the pension schemes back into financial balance.

The financial balance of pay as you go pension schemes necessitates regular adjustments to the scheme rules. Given the experience with public governance of pension schemes in Latin America, there must be some significant level of uncertainty attached to the ability of political processes to ensure the financial balance of pay as you go pension schemes. In this context, insulating pension schemes from political processes emerges as a desirable design property of reformed pension schemes (Diamond, 1997).

Lack of correlation between contribution and benefits at the individual level

A different structural problem with pay as you go pension scheme design is associated with the lack of direct correlation between pension contributions and benefits for individual affiliates, and the incentives effects that result from this. The absence of a direct correlation between contributions and benefits in the context of a pay as you go pension scheme reduces incentives for individual workers to maximize contribution density and levels. This has been an important argument deployed against pay as you go pension schemes and in favour of individual capitalization pension schemes.

There are a number of reasons why contributions may not be directly correlated with benefits in a pay as you go pension scheme. The first reason has to do with the redistributive properties of pay as you go pension schemes, which operate within and across cohorts. These schemes can redistribute from cohorts currently in work to those cohorts in retirement through, for example, a discretionary increase of pension benefits. They can also redistribute within a cohort by, for example, reducing the entitlement requisites as regards retirement age for women. The associated redistribution would introduce a wedge between contributions paid and benefits received by different individuals.

A second reason why there could be a lack of correlation between contributions and benefits for individual affiliates relates to the insurance properties of social insurance schemes. The realization of insurance will necessarily imply redistribution of retirement income from those who did not suffer the insured contingencies, to those who did. Finally, a further reason has to do with discretionary redistribution towards favoured groups. The first two reasons are of a structural nature, in so far as they emerge from the nature of pension schemes as such. The last one really belongs to the specifics of the governance and administration of pension schemes.

The redistribution and insurance elements of pay as you go pension schemes[11] necessarily introduce a wedge between contribution and benefits for individual affiliates. This is an intrinsic feature of the institution itself, and, specific design issues aside, one that is eminently desirable as far as the participants are concerned.

In sum, there are structural reasons why pay as you go pension schemes may be particularly vulnerable to adverse external conditions, such as demographic change and economic crisis. The central issues here have to do with the discretionary changes required by pay as you go pension schemes, the associated political inputs, and the pattern of incentives generated by the absence of a direct link between contribution and benefits. Whether pay as you pension schemes can be designed in ways that could minimize the impact of these factors has been a subject of longstanding debate. This issue will be considered more fully in the next chapter. In the case of Latin America, however, the views presented in this section found an echo in the structural reforms which followed the 1980s economic crisis.

Structural adjustment and pension reform

Whilst the financial deficits of social insurance pension schemes and the recent labour market changes have added urgency to pension reform in Latin America, the catalyst was provided by the spread of structural adjustment and reform in the region in the late 1980s and 1990s. Chile is a special case since it pioneered these reforms from mid 1970s. In the other countries under study, structural reform gathered momentum after the severe crisis in the early 1980s, but it shows considerable diversity in both depth and timing. Pension reform followed the wider structural reforms.

Most Latin American economies began implementing structural adjustment programs in the second half of the 1980s and at the beginning of the 1990s, but the process is still underway (Morley, 1995).[12] The change in economic policy orientation evolved in two phases. The first phase consisted of a macroeconomic stabilization program. It aimed to correct balance of payments deficits by engineering a devaluation of the exchange rate buttressed by a contraction in government expenditure and monetary policy, and by downward pressure on real wages. Most countries in Latin America implemented stabilization programs in the early 1980s. Chile and Uruguay did so in mid 1970s, after military takeovers (Cassoni, Labadie and Allen, 1995). The stabilization programs generated high inflation and unemployment.

The second phase consisted of structural adjustment aimed at reorienting the economies in the region to the new export led growth strategy. The foundation blocks of the structural adjustment programs included further trade liberalization, the downsizing of the public sector, privatization of public sector enterprises, and capital and labour market liberalization (Edwards, 1995). Chile was, again, a pioneer country in this process as the first wholesale privatization had already began in mid 1970s.

Pension reform plays an important role in structural adjustment in so far as it supports and facilitates a number of other reforms. Pension reform that replaces public pay as you go pension schemes with individual capitalization retirement accounts is expected to make a significant contribution to the success of structural adjustment. It is expected to reduce disincentives to work and save, which are seen as key drawbacks in pay as you go pension schemes. It is also expected to facilitate the liberalization of the labour market by reducing payroll taxes, which constrain employment creation, and by lowering barriers to labour mobility. Pension reform is also expected to improve incentives for pension saving by providing workers with a more efficient and secure saving instrument. Similarly, by channelling pension saving through the financial markets, pension reform facilitates the modernization of these markets (Edwards, 1995). The accumulation and investment of pension contributions, and the emergence of large institutional pension fund investors are expected to contribute significantly to the deepening and development of financial markets. Pension reform comes to play a key role in structural adjustment programs (Piñera, 1991).

Chile's experience with pension reform provides a seemingly compelling paradigm for the inclusion of pension reform in structural adjustment packages, and of the contribution that it can make to the overall success of the economic reforms.

The politics of pension reform

In all cases, pension reform has been embedded in structural adjustment programs. Pension reform in Latin America was mainly motivated, as far as the designers and proponents were concerned, by the expectation that it had an important role to play in the success of structural adjustment programs. Table 1.4 below shows key dates in both structural adjustment and pension reform. The sharp recession in the early 1980s was crucial in hastening the implementation of pension reform in Chile. In all the other Latin American countries, the recession of the early 1990s had the same effect of concentrating the mind of pension reformers and legislators.

Table 1.4
Sequence of structural adjustment and pension reform in Latin America

Structural Reforms Start date [a]	Country	Pension Reform Proposal date (legislation date) [b]	Implementation date [b]
1975	Chile	1980 (1980)	1981
1991	Peru	1991 (1992)	1993
1990/1	Argentina	1991 (1993)	1994
1990/1	Colombia	1992 (1993)	1994
1987/8	Uruguay	1994 (1995)	1996
1985/6	Mexico		
	SAR[c]	1991 (1992)	1992
	RAI[c]	1994 (1995)	1997
1988	Costa Rica	? (1995)	-

a. from Edwards (1995)
b. from Barrientos (1997a)
c. SAR is *Sistema de Ahorro para el Retiro*, RAI is *Regimen de Ahorro Individual*.

It is inevitable that pension reform will generate strong opposition. In voting models of policy reform, it is assumed that groups will decide whether to support or oppose reforms based on a calculation of the benefits, and the losses, each is expected to experience. Pension reform that reduces the generosity and scope of benefits is likely to be opposed by workers who are closer to retirement, or have retired. Political, labour, and business organisations will also adopt positions in line with the perceived interests of their supporters. The expectation is that the political passage of pension reform legislation, and its implementation, will be problematic. The initial pension scheme design proposals may also have to be altered to secure the support of voters.

Disney (1996a) shows that, in the context of an ageing population, both discounted benefits and the rates of return attaching to contributions will decline in pay as you go pension schemes. Even in this situation middle aged generations and those close to retirement may continue to support pension schemes with declining expected benefits simply because the alternatives could be worse. Exogenous factors, such as economic, or pension scheme, crises may be important in generating a switch in allegiance by these groups of workers.

In Chile these constraints on pension reform were not important as normal political processes were suspended, and the executive did not have to satisfy parliamentary scrutiny. The original proposal for pension reform involved transferring all workers from the social insurance funds to the new individual capitalization pension plans. Consultations were carried out with the military, some sectors of the right, and some trade union representatives, but these resulted in few alterations to the proposal (Piñera, 1991). The key amendments made on the initial proposals were the exemption of the military from the pension reform, and the continuation of social insurance pension scheme for those workers who wished to remain in it. The political conditions in Chile also account for the speed with which the proposals were approved and implemented. The whole process of design, consultation and implementation took a matter of months.[13]

In all other countries, parliamentary scrutiny of the pension reform proposals was fully exercised. As a result, the process of discussion, approval and implementation of pension reform was longer than Chile's, and the resulting pension reforms differed in important respects from the original proposals. In Peru, Argentina and Colombia, the original proposals for pension reform involved a purely private pillar of pension provision, but the pension system which came out of the reforms included the continuation of the public final salary pension scheme in competition with the new private individual capitalization scheme. The compromise ensured that the legislators who supported the continuation of the old pension scheme could then persuaded to support pension reform. These countries have as a result a pension pillar in which there is competition between the public and private pension schemes. The political compromise also accounts for the complexity and sensitivity of the rules governing the public and private components, which will prove to be crucial for the future development of pension systems in these countries.

The experiences of Latin American countries that have embarked upon pension reform confirm that exogenous shocks are important in securing political support for the reforms. In Latin America, the acute economic crises of the early 1980s and early 1990s provided the conditions for structural reform in which pension reform was embedded. Lack of confidence in the financial health of pay as you go pension schemes, and compromises with those groups who supported the existing schemes, ensured the political support necessary for the approval of pension reform.

Conclusion

This chapter has examined the origins and evolution of social insurance pension schemes in Latin America, and the factors that led to mounting financial deficits in the 1980s and 1990s, and to the recent spread of pension reform.

The pension schemes introduced in Latin America in the early part of the century had common features. They included an element of partial funding, covered homogeneous groups of workers, and operated as autonomous bodies. Social insurance pension schemes developed in a piecemeal fashion. Industrialisation and growing government sponsorship of social insurance led to the expansion of social insurance to cover a wider range of benefits and workers. The implementation of pension schemes was accelerated enabling a rapid build up of entitlements. The larger role of government in pension provision resulted in the elimination of partial funding, and an increasing dependence of pension schemes on government finance.

The economic crisis of the 1980s imposed mounting deficits on the social insurance pension schemes. There were many factors leading to the financial imbalances of social insurance pension schemes in Latin America. Some of these are longer term, such as those associated with adverse demographic trends and those resulting from the accelerated implementation of pension schemes. The economic crisis of the 1980s, and the rapid deterioration in labour market conditions and government finances brought the social insurance pension schemes to a crisis point. The need for pension reform acquired urgency.

It has proved difficult for countries in Latin America to restore pension schemes, and social insurance programs, to financial health.[14] A major factor in the financial deterioration of social insurance pension schemes has been a steep fall in the support ratio, the ratio of active to passive members of a pension scheme. This is principally a consequence of labour market trends characterised by rising unemployment, and a growing informalisation of employment. Reducing the commitments to passive members of pension schemes is an almost impossible task, given the pension benefits currently received by the majority of pensioners are very low. In the end, for most Latin American countries the catalyst for pension reform was the structural adjustment program that followed the 1980s crisis.

Proponents of pension reform in Latin America have pointed to the existence of structural problems with pay as you go pension schemes which appear to provide a strong justification for their reform. The priorities for economic policy imposed by structural adjustment have dictated the extent and orientation of pension reform. A common feature of pension reform in Latin America has been the replacement of pay as you go final salary pension schemes with individual capitalization pension plans. Pension reform is embedded in structural adjustment programs and is expected to make a significant contribution to the success of these programs.

Appendix One

The impact of pension design and implementation problems and of labour market changes on the financial balance of social insurance pension scheme can be represented more formally in the following equations.

The impact of labour market trends upon the number of active contributors, and therefore the support ratio, can be represented as

$$C = L(1-u)(h)(1-e) \qquad (A1.1)$$

where L is the labour force, u is the unemployment rate, h is the fraction of workers in the covered sector, and e is the fraction of workers who evade paying pension contributions.

The ratio of pensioners receiving non-contributory pensions to those receiving contributory pensions P^c can be denoted as n. Therefore the total number of passive members of the pension scheme P become

$$P = P^c(1+n) \qquad (A1.2)$$

With W^d representing declared contributory earnings, and m representing the fraction of under-declared earnings or evasion coefficient, W^x now becomes

$$W^x = W^d(1-m), \qquad 0<m<1 \qquad (A1.3)$$

Gathering these factors together by inserting (A1.1) through (A1.3) into (1.4) above results in

$$b = \{[L(1-u)(h)(1-e)] / P^c(1+n)\}t\,[W^x(1-m) / W^z] \\ +(GS / PW^z) - (AC / PW^z) \qquad (A1.4)$$

This formulation describes in more detail the main factors responsible for the mounting financial deficits experienced pension schemes in Latin America.

Appendix Two

The relative significance of the different factors leading to the financial imbalances of the social insurance pension schemes can be clarified with the aid of some simulations.

The first stage is to develop a model of the contribution rate required to ensure the financial balance of a pay as you go pension scheme, which takes account of changes in the key variables. The basic requirement for financial balance in pay as you go pension schemes identified in (1.3) above provides a starting point. It may be useful to ignore government subsidies and administrative costs for the time being. The condition for financial equilibrium can be written as

$$P\, b\, W^z = t\, W^x\, C \tag{A2.1}$$

and solving for the pension payroll tax *t* yields

$$t = (P/C)(b\, W^z / W^x) \tag{A2.2}$$

The payroll contribution required for financial equilibrium depends on the dependency ratio and the replacement ratio. This implies that under most plausible scenarios the contribution rate must rise to accommodate the rise in the dependency ratio.

This assumes that all other relevant variables remain constant. However, most variables influencing the financial parameters of pension schemes are non-stationary. Extending the analysis to include non-stationary conditions becomes enormously complicated, but the essentials of the problem can be handled by making the simplifying assumption that there are two generations or cohorts, one of which is in work while the other is in retirement (Disney, 1996a; Rosen, 1984). Indexing the last period as -1, and assuming that pension benefits are calculated in lifetime salary (A2.1) becomes

$$b\, W^z_{-1}\, P = t\, W^x\, C \tag{A2.3}$$

Some linkages can be established between current pensioners and past contributors through a survival parameter *s* denoting expected retirement years as a fraction of years worked (this assumes that retirement is exogenous and age dependent, and that retirees do not work), so that

$$P = s\, C_{-1} \tag{A2.4}$$

Similarly, the ratio of active workers to the population of working age is denoted by the activity rate a; and the ratio of active contributors to the pension scheme as a proportion of the labour force is denoted by the contributor rate r. The current labour force relates to the labour force in the previous period through a rate of growth g as in $L = L_{-1}(1+g)$, so that,

$$C = r\, a\, g\, L_{-1} \qquad (A2.5)$$

with contributors in the last period being $C_{-1} = r_{-1}\, a_{-1}\, L_{-1}$, and therefore

$$L_{-1} = C_{-1} / (r_{-1}\, a_{-1}) \qquad (A2.6)$$

Writing v for the change in activity rate (a / a_{-1}); and h for the change in the proportion of the labour who actively contribute (r / r_{-1}). And after replacing (A2.6) in (A2.5), it can be shown that

$$C = (1+v)(1+h)(1+g)\, C_{-1} \qquad (A2.7)$$

Defining W^x as $(1+w)\, W_{-1}$, and substituting into (A2.3) gives

$$b\, W_{-1}\, s\, C_{-1} = t\, [(1+w)\, W_{-1}]\, (1+v)(1+h)(1+g)\, C_{-1} \qquad (A2.8)$$

Finally, solving for t yields

$$t = b\, s / (1+w)(1+v)(1+h)(1+g) \qquad (A2.9)$$

and the implicit rate of return is

$$b\, s / t = (1+w)(1+v)(1+h)(1+g) \qquad (A2.10)$$

The implicit rate of return is dependent upon the rate of growth of real wages, the rate of change in the activity rate, the rate of change in the proportion of active contributors, and the rate of growth of the labour force.

The simulations for the Latin American countries reported in the text are based on computing (A2.9) using the data shown in Table 1.2 in the text, and Table 1.A1 below.

Table 1.A1
Demographic factors relevant to pension schemes in the 1980s

Countries	legal retirement age[a]		life expectancy at retirement[a]		survival ratio[b]	female share of labour force[c]
	male	female	male	female	All	
Argentina	60	55	16.2	24.2	0.51	0.37
Chile	65	60	13.2	19.4	0.36	0.35
Colombia	60	55	15.6	21.4	0.49	0.48
Costa Rica	57	50	19.1	24.2	0.59	0.28
Mexico	65	65	14.4	15.7	0.33	0.38
Peru	60	55	15.2	20.7	0.45	0.33
Uruguay	60	55	16.2	24.1	0.54	0.49

a. Data from McGreevey (1990).
b. Survival ratio is calculated as life expectancy at retirement over legal retirement age minus 20. Males and females survival ratios are weighted by proportion of each sex in labour force.
c. from Psacharopoulos (1992b).

Notes

1 Soto (1992) lists twelve additional benefits provided by the Mexican pension scheme between 1943 and 1990 including disability pensions, indexed pensions, bonuses, marriage benefit, etc.; and ten large increases in the value of existing pension benefits. He also notes that these changes were introduced without any adjustment to the contribution rates, which remained at 6 percent of contributory earnings for the entire 47 year period.

2 Ayala (1992) notes that the 1.3 million workers in the public sector in Colombia are affiliated to just under 1000 insurance funds, although 16 of these provide cover for around 70 percent of these workers.

3 As Huber notes, "ISI created urban constituencies for social insurance, that is, employed middle and working classes with an interest in protection from loss of earnings due to accidents, illness and old age... Politically, passage of social insurance schemes with relatively generous benefits for those covered was facilitated by the fact that employers did not really have to absorb the costs of their contributions but rather could pass them on to consumers because they were operating in protected markets"(1996, p.144)

4 In the initial stages of such a scheme, contributions will be greater than benefits and a surplus will build up. This surplus could be used to supplement contributions, and/or smooth over short term variations, in a second stage.

5   Population projections are, of course, subject to considerable uncertainty and change. Expected length of life of old age pensioners in Mexico was estimated at 6.16 in 1942, and at 13.13 in 1990 (Soto-Perez, 1992).
6   A more formal presentation of these factors is discussed in Appendix One.
7   Ayala (1992) notes evidence of corruption and considerable delay in the processing of pension claims in Colombia. Godoy (1997) reports that discretionary indexation of pensions played a part in the political cycle in Chile.
8   Reviewing the impact of structural adjustment programs in developing countries, Horton et al. conclude that "in response to structural adjustment, labor has moved in the direction opposite to that usually associated with economic development. Labor has shifted back into agriculture, out of manufacturing, and out of the public sector... Recession plus adjustment has also resulted in an increased informalisation, increased used of casual labor, decreased worker benefits and declines in skill and possibly education differentials. These trends are observed even in the most successful adjustment cases in Asia"(Horton, Kanbur and Mazumdar, 1994a, p.57)
9   The survival rate assumptions are in Table 1.A1 in Appendix Two.
10 These last two points are connected in that the rise in women's activity rates has everywhere been accompanied by a fall in fertility rates.
11 The redistributive and insurance properties of pension schemes are discussed in more detail in chapter 2.
12 The World Bank and the IMF played an important role in orchestrating this change on economic orientation. The World Bank in particular began structural adjustment program lending in the early 1980s (Mosley, Harrigan and Toye, 1991).
13 Piñera notes that the first study meeting with government officials and advisors took place in August 1979, the first briefing to the Military Junta was done in April 1980, and was followed by a public announcement of the initiative in May 1980. The Decree-Law approving the pension reform was signed on 4 November 1980 (Piñera, 1991).
14 In Chile, for example, all three administrations preceding the 1973 military coup attempted to reform the social insurance scheme without success.

2 The reformed pension schemes

Pension reform in Argentina, Chile, Colombia, Costa Rica, Mexico, Peru and Uruguay has been aimed at replacing, totally or partially, the existing social insurance pension schemes with individual capitalization pension plans. This is the dominant common factor in the recent spread of pension reform in Latin America. Chile's pension reform supplied the paradigm by introducing compulsory individual capitalization pension plans as the sole pension scheme available for workers entering the labour market. Over time, therefore, the old social insurance pension scheme will be phased out. Of the other countries that have embarked upon pension reform in Latin America, only Mexico will follow Chile in fully replacing its social insurance pension schemes. The remaining countries will reform and retain the social insurance pension schemes alongside the new capitalization pension schemes.

Pension reform involves a fundamental shift in pension provision. This is characterised by an emphasis on individual responsibility and choice in retirement saving, a larger private sector role in pension provision, and a curtailment of the redistributive properties of pension schemes. These characteristics are shared by all examples of recent pension reform in Latin America. The retention of social insurance pension schemes in most countries, and their articulation within overall pension provision, will result in diversity of provision, and especially in the resulting mix of individual capitalization and social insurance pension schemes. These issues are explored in this chapter. The main objective of this chapter is to evaluate the broad implications of alternative forms of pension design by comparing the main features of the reformed pension schemes in Latin America.

In order to do this it is necessary to sketch out first the main functions performed by pension schemes. The next section identifies and examines these pension scheme functions. There are mainly three: income transfer, insurance, and redistribution. Pension schemes have a set of design features that perform, with greater or lesser effectiveness, a range of these functions. Different pension scheme design will support a different range of functions. The discussion in this section emphasises the importance of the insurance functions fulfilled by pension schemes.

A further section compares the key design features of final salary or defined benefit pension schemes as against defined contribution pension schemes, a distinction that is crucial in the analysis of recent pension reform in Latin America. The two sections that follow concentrate on providing a more detailed examination of the key features of the reformed pension systems, first in Chile, and then in Latin America. The final section provides conclusions.

The main functions of pension schemes

Pension schemes perform three main functions. Firstly, they provide a mechanism for transferring income between work and retirement, and therefore smooth out consumption over the life cycle. Secondly, they provide insurance against a number of contingencies, such as disability or death, resulting in severe income shortfalls for the beneficiaries and their dependants. As such, pension schemes help secure greater certainty in the provision of retirement income. Thirdly, they provide an instrument for solidarity and redistribution across and within generations. This Section discusses each one in turn.

The life-cycle model, pension schemes and income transfers

Pension schemes consist of long term contracts which best make sense in the context of life cycle models of consumption. A central finding of life cycle models of consumption is that, under certain assumptions, individuals will maximise their welfare by securing constant levels of consumption throughout their lives.[1] For an individual or household, the timing and size of income receipts and consumption expenditures are unlikely to coincide precisely, with the consequence that matching strategies are required. As the vast majority of households depend mainly on labour income, and to a lesser extent on income from other sources, securing income in retirement involves saving while in work to finance consumption while in retirement.

There is a range of alternative instruments that can be used to transfer income to retirement. Pension schemes are dedicated sets of contracts providing a means by which a fraction of income received while in work is set aside and saved. The contributions secure pension benefit entitlements after retirement, thus smoothing out consumption over the life cycle.

Investment in financial, monetary, and real estate assets can also facilitate the accumulation of entitlements while in work which can be redeemed to support consumption in retirement. Retirement income entitlements can also be secured via income transfers within a household, or group, leading to reciprocal transfers to support consumption of its retired members. Individuals and households will seek to use a combination of these in order to acquire retirement income entitlements.

Pension schemes have a number of advantages over alternative vehicles for transferring income from work to retirement. They are set up specifically for this purpose, they normally enjoy privileged tax treatment, and are usually backed by government guarantees. Pension schemes also have other advantages in that they have properties providing insurance against certain contingencies, and supporting solidarity and redistributive objectives.

Insurance properties of pension schemes

Pension schemes also provide insurance against certain contingencies that may affect consumption in retirement. Pension schemes can provide insurance against consumption shortfalls suffered by the beneficiary or his or her dependants due to unexpected length of life and/or working life. If life is longer than expected, a longevity risk arises that individuals may outlive their resources. If, on the other hand, life is shorter than expected, there is a risk that dependants' consumption will be subject to shortfalls. There is also a risk that an individual's working life is cut short by disability, or by the need to care for others. Pension schemes provide insurance against these contingencies affecting the length of life and working life.

The great majority of pension schemes provide cover for longevity risks.[2] Disability and survivor insurance are commonly integrated within pension schemes and provide pension benefits in the event a beneficiary is permanently incapacitated, and to his or her dependants in the event of death. What distinguishes the insurance cover provided by pension schemes from other insurance providing contracts is that the former concentrate on providing cover for beneficiaries who are unlikely to be in a position to return to the labour market to make good their consumption shortfall. This applies to the contingencies affecting those who have retired from the labour market due to old age or disability.

There are also contingencies that may affect the accumulation of retirement saving while in work. As the accumulation of retirement saving in most cases depends upon labour market participation and earnings, the contingencies affecting these will also impact upon retirement income. Some pension schemes provide some insurance against earnings variability associated with employment gaps (due to unemployment or inactivity) or with earnings variability over the working life. The Mexican public pension scheme, for example, provides a pension benefit if older workers who have not yet reached the age of retirement are made unemployed and are unable to find another job. Pension schemes that calculate a pension benefit on the basis of earnings during a fraction of a person's working life effectively insure against years of low earnings. Under the British basic state pension scheme, individuals caring for children or others can include these spells as contributory years for the purposes of claiming pension entitlements. What is common to all the contingencies listed above is that they impact directly upon the earnings capacity of the insured. Pension schemes normally provide insurance against a range of contingencies which may affect a worker's ability to accumulate retirement saving.

Finally, pension schemes also provide some insurance against risks affecting retirement income itself, such as inflation and macroeconomic performance. This is the case where pension benefits are linked to a price index, or an earnings index. In the former the pension scheme covers the risk that inflation may reduce retirement income and consumption. Indexing pension benefits to earnings links the level of pension benefits to general improvements in productivity. This provides some insurance against the risk that workers may retire in periods of poor macroeconomic performance lowering pension benefits permanently.

The insurance properties of different pension schemes depend crucially on the, sometimes subtle, details of pension and entitlement design. As a result, identifying and evaluating the insurance properties of different pension scheme requires intensive knowledge of their design and does not generalise easily. There are very few studies focusing on the insurance properties of pension schemes, and most concentrate on comparing generic types of pension schemes (Bodie, Marcus and Merton, 1988; Brugiavini, Disney and Whitehouse, 1993; Disney, 1996b).

The failure to pay sufficient attention to the insurance aspects of pension schemes has important implications for the understanding of pension scheme design and evaluation (Bodie, 1990). It would be difficult to justify the very existence of pension schemes without an understanding of their insurance properties. It would not be difficult to find, for any retiring worker who has contributed to a pension scheme, a portfolio of assets that could have generated a larger fund at retirement, and consequently a higher pension benefit. Looked at in this way pension schemes appear to be less effective than alternatives in providing retirement income. This is only because *ex post* the risks covered by pension schemes disappear from view. Ignoring the important insurance properties of pension funds effectively biases selection of optimal pension design towards basic retirement saving pension schemes. These appear as simpler, and more transparent, and as a more effective means of transferring income to retirement.

Solidarity and redistribution in pension schemes

Pension schemes also have properties, which can effect redistribution of income both across and within generations. The redistributive effects of pension schemes follow directly from the specific regulations concerning contributions and benefit entitlement. Pension schemes that collect earnings related contributions and pay fixed level benefits would typically redistribute from high to low earners. Similarly, pension schemes that offer an annuity type benefit will redistribute from short-lived individuals to longer-lived ones. As noted in the previous chapter, pension schemes have very powerful redistributive properties, which are not always sufficiently understood. The redistributive effects of pension schemes are likely to be very sensitive to the details of pension scheme regulations.

In the standard pay as you go public pension schemes, generations in work pay contributions to cover pension benefits to the generations in retirement. These pension schemes can support redistribution of income across generations, which is one of their key advantages. As noted in the previous chapter, the introduction of pay as you go pension schemes in most countries generated redistribution towards generations close to retirement (Disney and Whitehouse, 1993; Schwarz, 1993). In large part this emerged from their accelerated accrual and generosity in setting benefit levels, which allowed older workers to draw pensions without having made lifetime contributions. As pay as you go pension schemes mature, the constraints operating on this cross-cohort redistribution become stronger, and actuarially fair pensions become the norm. An advantage of pay as you go pension schemes involving several generations is that they make possible redistribution towards generations that have been particularly affected by macroeconomic factors.[3]

Pension schemes can also redistribute within generations. The extent of this redistribution is also dependent on the specific regulations governing contribution requirements and benefit entitlements. Pension schemes including a minimum pension level redistribute from high earners to low earners. On the other hand, systematic differential mortality across income and occupational groups generates redistribution from low earners to high earners (Creedy, Disney and Whitehouse, 1992). Unisex benefits usually involve redistribution from men to women, as the latter have, on average, longer lives and shorter contribution records. Where pension benefits include entitlements for dependants, pension schemes redistribute towards members with dependants.

Funded pension schemes also have redistributive properties, which again depend on the regulations covering contributions and entitlements. Even basic defined contribution pension schemes explicitly eschewing redistributive properties, as Chile's, involve some redistribution arising from the allocation of pension scheme costs, or the design of pension benefits. Where pension scheme costs are constant per contributor, but are financed from charges related in a proportional way to contributions or earnings, redistribution takes place from high to low earners. If on the other hand, pension costs rise with the size of contributions, but are charged as a fixed amount, these produce redistribution from low to high earners. The combination of fixed and variable costs and charges can generate a complex pattern of redistribution.

Employer provided defined benefit pension schemes usually involve earnings related contributions and final salary, and tenure related, pension benefits. These pension schemes intentionally redistribute from short tenured to long tenured workers and from workers with flat age earnings profiles to those with rising age earnings profiles (Ippolito, 1991; Lazear, 1985). Employer provided pension schemes have some limited redistributive properties across generations, depending on the longevity of the pension scheme, but enjoy powerful within generation redistributive properties.

As can be seen from this brief review, pension scheme have powerful, and rich, redistributive effects. These effects spring mainly from the regulations covering contribution requirements and benefit entitlements, but demographic and tax regimes are also important. Evaluating the net redistributive effects of pension schemes can be, as a result, quite complex. It is difficult to draw some general conclusions regarding the redistributive effects of pension schemes, except that pay as you go public pension schemes have cross-cohort redistributive properties which are much less likely to be present in funded defined benefit or defined contribution pension schemes. Another general point is that pension schemes with individual pension plans have much fewer redistributive properties compared to group pension schemes with wider membership.

When examining the redistributive effects of pension schemes it is important to keep in mind the following important points for the discussion that follows. Firstly, the redistributive effects of pension schemes may be exaggerated if their insurance properties are not fully considered. As Diamond aptly notes, ex ante insurance is likely to result in ex post redistribution (1996a). It is therefore important to measure redistributive effects net of insurance outcomes. Secondly, when considering the redistributive effects of pension schemes it is important to distinguish between intentional from unintentional redistribution. In complex pension schemes with intricate contribution incidence and rates, and with complex entitlement regulations, the extent of unintentional redistribution is likely to be greater. Thirdly, it should be acknowledged that individuals are likely to respond to the incentives created by redistribution. The discussion in this section provides a powerful argument in favour of the application of

Occam's razor to pension design, and therefore in favour of selecting simpler and more transparent pension schemes.

Functional separation and multipillar pension systems: The World Bank's view

In their report *Averting the Old Age Crisis* the World Bank examined different country experiences with pension scheme design, and recommended pension reform aimed at creating a multipillar pension system (World Bank, 1994). A key justification for this multipillar pension system is that it can best facilitate a separation of the income transfer function from the redistributive function of pension schemes.[4]

According to the World Bank, the private sector has a comparative advantage in securing income transfers from work to retirement. The report begins by noting the "economic and political advantages of having a large, funded, privately managed component of the old age security system" (James, 1996, p.111). At the same time, it is acknowledged that the public sector has a comparative advantage in implementing redistribution. It argues that if redistribution is needed, the government can manage it more effectively. The comparative effectiveness of the private and public sectors in performing these two different functions of pension schemes would justify having separate pillars each focused on one of these two functions. The redistributive function could be best handled by a public minimum pension scheme, means tested, and funded out of general taxation. The income transfer function could best be handled by private pension schemes, preferably of a defined contribution type. The different management and funding mechanisms justify having separate pension pillars.[5]

A third pillar consisting of either defined contribution or defined benefit voluntary pension plans could be added. In the World Bank's framework, the insurance function is distributed across the three pillars.

Evaluating pension scheme design

The extent to which different pension schemes support income transfers, insurance and redistribution functions will depend ultimately upon the details of pension scheme regulations, can be evaluated in broad terms for generic types of pension schemes. For our purposes, it will be useful to focus on the design properties of two broadly defined pension schemes: unfunded defined benefit (DB thereafter) pension schemes on the one hand; and fully funded defined contribution (DC thereafter) pension schemes with mandatory life annuity purchase on the other.[6] These are the broad alternatives common to most Latin American countries involved in pension reform. To simplify matters the analysis that follows concentrates on old age and retirement pensions only.

Unfunded DB pension schemes promise participants a pension benefit calculated as a fraction of final salary. The formula used in the determination of the pension benefit is defined in advance. From the discussion in the last chapter it is clear that the social insurance pension schemes existing in Latin America prior to the reforms belonged to this category. They all shared the basic features of pay as you go final salary pension schemes. There existed important differences in terms of contribution rates and incidence, the measure of final salary used, and the accrual parameters, across different pension schemes within a country, as well as across countries.[7] These differences are, however, of second order in the context of the current discussion of pension design properties.

In fully funded DC pension plans, on the other hand, there is no defined target replacement rate, but the pension benefit depends on the pension fund accumulated at retirement. The pension scheme sets the contribution rates and incidence in advance. In the variant adopted in Latin America, individual workers contribute to a pension fund. This fund is used at retirement to purchase a life annuity, or agree a phased withdrawal program. Dedicated private pension fund managers manage the individuals' retirement accounts.[8]

Income transfer properties

It is difficult to compare the income transfer properties of DB and DC plans, in so far as these are likely to depend upon a large number of exogenous factors. In addition, the set of factors likely to influence income transfers under DC pension schemes may prove to be different than that influencing them under DB pension schemes.

Perhaps it would be useful to focus on the rate of return to contributions paid as an indicator of the extent to which contributions on labour earnings are preserved as income in retirement. In DB plans, what the pension scheme promises is a pension benefit replacing income while in work. The rate of return on contributions will depend on a large number of factors, mainly demographic and labour market conditions. Given changes in these, rates of return could be positive or negative. Empirical studies have shown that in the initial stages of unfunded DB pension schemes rates of return are positive for workers closer to retirement, they are also positive where population growth rates are high, and when labour market conditions are improving. By contrast, slower population growth, poor labour market conditions, and the maturity of pension schemes are associated with declining, or even negative, rates of return on contributions. Under unfunded DB pension schemes, there is scope for government intervention on the rates of return applying to contributions. In sum, the income transfer properties of unfunded, pay as you go pension schemes are dependent on a number of exogenous factors and can be negative or positive.

The income transfer properties of DC pension plans also depend on a number of exogenous factors, but these are on the whole a different set. The capacity of DC pension funds to preserve and expand contributions paid depends on the effectiveness of pension fund managers in investing the accumulated contributions, and on macroeconomic and financial market conditions which raise the rates of return of pension funds. Rates of return applying to individuals' pension contributions under DC pension plans can also be negative or positive. It has been argued that DC plans have better income transfer properties in so far as redistributive features affect them to a lesser extent. In contrast to DB pension schemes, government intervention aimed at reducing rates of return on contributions is less likely as it can only arise from changes in the tax regime, or the permitted structure of charges, applying to contributions.

In conclusion, while some differences in the range of factors affecting income transfer properties of DB and DC plans can be established, it remains difficult to conclude that one pension design type dominates over the other in respect of income transfer. DC plans may have advantages over public DB pension schemes in reducing the scope for government intervention in reducing rates of return. Rates of return can be either positive or negative in both DB and DC pension schemes.

Redistributive properties

As regards redistribution, it is necessary to distinguish between intergenerational, and intragenerational redistribution. Taking intergenerational redistribution first, a further distinction needs to be made between the redistributive effects arising from the initial introduction of a pension scheme, and the distributional effects present when the pension scheme has reached maturity.

In the initial period DB and DC pension schemes will have redistributive effects which operate in different directions. The introduction of a DC pension scheme where a DB was already in place will impose on generations in work a double burden of saving for their own retirement and providing for the retired generations. Overall this implies redistribution from generations currently in work to those who have retired. The introduction of a DB plan, on the other hand, usually involves redistribution from young and future generations to those generations currently in work. The redistributive effects arising in the transitional period disappear when the pension scheme reaches maturity. At a later stage, DC pension schemes have no intergenerational redistributive properties, but DB pension schemes continue to support intergenerational redistribution dependent on the legislated contribution and benefit formulas.

As regards intragenerational redistribution, DC pension schemes have no redistribution properties providing that commissions and charges accurately reflect participant costs and that pension annuities reflect only systematic differences in survival probabilities.

DB pension schemes on the other hand do have significant intragenerational redistributive properties though these may differ in practice from the intention and rhetoric of the legislators (James, 1997b). Most DB pension schemes combine a minimum safety level pension with an earnings related supplement. The first element redistributes towards low earners by securing a basic income in retirement. The second element, on the other hand, redistributes to high earners since this group are more likely to have longer life expectancy and therefore retirement, are also likely to benefit from rising age earnings profiles, and are more likely to be in a position to take early retirement. The annuity nature of most DB plan benefits usually enforces redistribution from low to high earners in so far as these groups have systematic differences in longevity. Higher income groups have, on average, longer lives than lower income groups. The net redistributive impact of DB plans is therefore an empirical matter.[9] Studies for the USA and the UK have found a large net redistribution to high earners (Creedy, Disney and Whitehouse, 1992; Hurd and Shoven, 1985).

With regards to gender redistribution, DB plans with a unisex benefit formula usually redistribute from males to females insofar as females have on average longer lives, can retire early, and normally have a shorter contribution record (James, 1997b).

Insurance properties

Both DC and DB pension schemes insure against longevity risk. The extent of risk coverage varies according to the type of pension benefit provided. Where real annuities, or annuity like benefits, are provided these can provide insurance for inflation risk, productivity risk, and investment risk. This depends on whether the pension benefits are indexed to consumer prices, wages, equity prices, or a mixture of these. To the extent that pension schemes do not have provision for early retirement, they therefore involve some retirement date risk. In practice, DC pension schemes are more flexible in this respect.

As the DB plan is assumed to be unfunded, it insures against investment and capital market risk. In our stereotypical DC pension schemes, on the other hand, the investment risk is in large measure borne by the pension scheme participant. The extent of this risk depends, however, on the diversification of the pension fund asset portfolio.

Conditions in the labour market involve a separate range of risks. With regards to risks associated with short careers or labour market interruptions, DC pension schemes provide very little insurance, except that associated with the pattern of accumulation of the retirement fund. Employment or contribution gaps that occur late in someone's working life matter less to the pension benefit under DC plans. DB pension schemes, on the other hand, provide some insurance against short career risk to the extent that the pension benefit formula is calculated on a fraction of lifetime earnings. In these pension schemes, interruptions that take place earlier in a person's career matter less to the pension benefit. The extent of the insurance depends largely on the period used for pension benefit calculation, and on whether individuals have flexibility in selecting portions of their working life for this purpose.

In terms of wage path risk, DC pension schemes provide better risk coverage, as the benefit depends on some average of lifetime earnings. DB plans may provide some cover against this risk if there is flexibility in the fraction of a person's lifetime earnings that can be used in the benefit calculation. More commonly, DB pension schemes are vulnerable to wage path risks in the later stages of worker's careers.

Neither DC nor DB pension schemes can provide effective insurance against macroeconomic or social risks, although DB pension schemes are more flexible in this respect. In DB pension schemes legislated changes can alter intergenerational distribution, thus allowing the possibility of insuring against the risk that adverse macroeconomic conditions seriously affect particular cohorts. Of course, this insurance would depend to an important extent on whether legislation is timely, accurate and effective, and could be neutralised by the risk that government may make wrong decisions.

Governance risk is important in both types of pension schemes. Governance risk in private DC pension schemes is dependent upon the extent and effectiveness of the regulatory framework. Governance risk in public DB pension schemes is also important, and has provided a powerful argument for pension reform in Latin America. Proponents of private provision of DC pension plans effectively assume that government risk is not diversifiable, and therefore cannot be insured against. On the other hand, supporters of public DB pension schemes assume that governance risk for private pension provider is large and equally difficult to diversify.[10]

In conclusion, the two stylised pension schemes show some differences in their income transfer, insurance, and redistributive properties. These arise from their basic design features. A closer examination of the detailed features of pension schemes would be needed to establish with greater accuracy the properties of specific pension schemes. This discussion shows that it is difficult to evaluate the risk coverage and redistribution packages provided by the two stylised DB and DC pension schemes. A basic comparison of their properties reveals that no pension scheme design dominates (Disney, 1996b).

The detailed features of the reformed pension schemes in Latin America will be discussed in more detail below. The key element of pension reform in Latin America is the introduction of privately provided, defined contribution pension schemes. The outline of insurance and redistributive properties of pension schemes provided in this section suggests that reform will produce an important rebalancing of the capacity of the pension system and pension schemes to perform their functions. A closer examination of the main features of the reformed pension systems in these countries could indicate to what extent these changes are likely to lead to an improvement in welfare for the pension scheme participants. The next sections concentrate on describing and assessing the key features of pension scheme design in Chile and other Latin American countries, and suggest the likely rebalancing of pension scheme functions they will produce.

The individual capitalization pension scheme in Chile

As the Chilean pension reform has provided the model for pension reform elsewhere in Latin America, this section will briefly outline Chile's social insurance system, and the characteristics of the reform process, before focusing on the key design features of the new pension scheme.

The social insurance system in Chile

The Chilean social insurance system dates back to 1924 when a compulsory social insurance system covering old age, sickness, disability and industrial injury was set up for blue-collar workers. The system operated through Insurance Funds (*Cajas de Previsión*) which collected contributions and paid benefits. The creation of the first Insurance Fund, the *Servicio de Seguro Social*, in 1924 was followed by similar institutions for white-collar workers in the public and private sectors (*Caja Nacional de Empleados Públicos* and *Caja Nacional de Empleados Particulares* respectively) in 1925. Chile was one of the first countries to set up social insurance in Latin America.[11]

The social insurance system expanded over time to cover a wider range of contingencies, and workers. The coverage of insurance funds expanded to include preventive private medicine in 1938, and child and unemployment benefits in 1953. By 1973 the system comprised 35 separate Insurance Funds covering 76 percent of the labour force (Cheyre, 1991). The first three insurance funds established in the mid 1920s remained the largest, covering over one half of the labour force, with the minor insurance funds covering a further 12 percent.

Within the social insurance funds, pension schemes were a key component. The early pension schemes included an element of partial funding, but this fell away later on. While there were significant differences in the contribution rates, and entitlements across pension schemes, they shared a basic defined benefit design (Cheyre, 1991). Pension schemes provided old age, service, disability, and survivor pensions, in addition to funeral expenses. The requisites for entitlement and the generosity of the benefits provided varied across insurance funds.

It may be useful to describe some of the pension schemes' features.[12] The main blue collar worker pension scheme, the *Servicio de Seguro Social*, did not provide a service pensions, while entitlements to old age pension benefits began at 65 years of age for men, and 55 for women and required 15 years of contribution. The old age pension benefit was calculated as a fraction of final salary averaged over the last three years, times the number of years of service up to a maximum of 70 percent of final salary.

The pension scheme covering public sector white collar workers, the *Caja Nacional de Empleados Públicos*, on the other hand, provided more comprehensive and generous benefits. Old age pension entitlements began at 65 years of age, but service pensions could be obtained after 30 years of contributions, whatever the age of the worker. Only ten years of contribution were required for entitlement to old age and disability pensions. The pension benefit was calculated as one thirtieth of final salary per year of service. The final salary was the average of the last three years of monthly earnings, with the pension benefit having a maximum of 100 percent of this.

Some of the pension schemes of the smaller insurance funds provided even more generous benefits. The great majority of pension benefits were set in nominal terms with ad hoc inflation adjustments. Some high status workers were entitled to pension benefits adjusted in line with the earnings of like workers in employment.

Although successful, the Chilean social insurance system was not free from problems arising from its design and implementation, and from its piecemeal development. The evolution of the Chilean Social insurance system, and its rising financial deficits fit in well with the broad picture described in the previous chapter. By the 1970s, the insurance funds in Chile showed a considerable lack of uniformity in the level of contributions, entitlements and coverage. These reflected the status, earnings, and influence of the workers they covered, and contributed greatly to the preservation of social and economic inequalities in old age. In common with the experience of other Latin American countries, successive governments dispensed patronage by raising entitlements for client groups.

The social insurance system became complex and increasingly reliant on government support. By 1980 social security expenditure was 11 percent of GDP. Evasion of social insurance contributions by employers and employees rose significantly. And the administrative costs of running the scheme reached 7 percent of contributions. At the same time, the level of benefits paid declined sharply during the 1970s owing to the severe contraction of the economy, and to inflationary pressures. In 1980, 70 percent of those retired received only the minimum pension entitlement.

Social insurance and pension reform

Successive governments had attempted to reform the Social insurance system but faced considerable opposition and failed (Godoy and Valdés-Prieto, 1997). The military government that came to power in Chile in 1973 became committed to the reform of the social insurance system in line with the requirements of structural adjustment and the neoliberal economic program that underpinned it. At first, the government introduced a number of changes to the social insurance system aimed at improving their finances by cutting entitlements and increasing contribution rates. These changes were also aimed at harmonising contribution and entitlement rules across the insurance funds. Then in 1980, the government took the decision to radically reform social insurance.

The reforms split social insurance programs into three groups: pension, health, and the residual. A new individual capitalization pension scheme was introduced to replace the social insurance pension schemes. The new pension scheme was based on mandatory contributions to individual retirement accounts managed by private pension fund managers. The health programs of the social insurance system were replaced with health insurance schemes, offered competitively by private providers (*Institutos de Salud Previsional*, ISAPRES) and a public, but autonomous, provider (*Fondo Nacional de Salud*, FONASA). The other programs were restructured or eliminated and became the responsibility of government agencies.[13]

Decree Law 3500 approved the pension reform in November 1980, and the new pension scheme became fully operational in May 1981. The decision making process was *sui generis*, as normal political processes were suspended at the time. The architect of the pension reform, the then Minister for Labour and Social Security Mr. José Piñera, has written a personal and colourful account of discussions and events surrounding the passage of the legislation (Piñera, 1991). The first meeting with officials and advisors took place in August 1979, and the first briefing to the members of the Military Junta was done in May 1980. Opposition to the proposal was stronger from trade union and opposition political leaders, from academics and political figures of the traditional (more paternalistic) right. There was also opposition from within the military. Objections from this last group were met by exempting the military from the pension reform. The objections from the other groups were largely ignored. The promulgation of the pension reform Decree Law came in November 1980 less than six months from the first briefing to the Junta.

A key element of pension reform was the transfer of pension provision to the private sector. The wider structural reforms were founded on a strong belief in the greater efficiency of private sector provision. Thus private pension provision was expected to have far a reaching impact on reducing the government's financial commitments, strengthening and improving the workings of capital and labour markets, and widening the scope for individual choice and responsibility for pension arrangements. The new pension scheme was also expected to raise saving, and therefore investment, thus contributing to economic growth. A further objective associated with pension reform was the reduction in employer costs and the elimination of social insurance payroll tax distortions, leading to higher levels of employment and to greater worker mobility. [14]

The new individual capitalization pension scheme

Pension reform introduced a new individual capitalization pension scheme. Under this new scheme workers contribute 10 percent of their monthly earnings to an individual retirement account kept with a pension fund manager (*Administradora de Fondos de Pensiones*, or AFP). In addition to this basic contribution, an additional contribution is paid to cover a disability and dependent survival insurance, and the management of the accounts by the AFPs.[15] This additional contribution is competitively set and at present amounts to a further 3 percent of earnings. The funds accumulated in the retirement accounts are invested by the AFPs in a range of permitted assets, and the returns are added to the account.

On reaching retirement age (65 for men and 60 for women) workers can use their accumulated funds to make pension arrangements. The funds can only be used for this purpose. There are three possible pension arrangements. Individuals can use their accumulated fund to purchase a life annuity from an insurance company. Alternatively, they can agree a phased withdrawal program with an AFP. The regulations prescribe a maximum monthly withdrawal according to a formula that takes account of the life expectancy of the beneficiary and his/her dependants. The maximum monthly withdrawals are reviewed once a year. The pension fund of the individuals who choose this pension arrangement can continue to accumulate returns, and is transferred to his/her estate in the event of the death of the pensioner. Finally, it is also possible to agree a phased withdrawal pension with a life annuity to begin at a later date.

Other entitlements provided for in the new pension scheme include a lump sum withdrawal at the time of retirement, and early retirement, providing the accumulated pension fund can support a minimum level of pension benefit.[16] There is also provision for disability and survivor pension benefits in the event these contingencies materialise. And for workers with at least 20 years of contributions, the government provides a minimum pension guarantee, securing a minimum pension level if the accumulated funds prove insufficient.

The new pension scheme is compulsory for dependent workers who entered employment after December 1983, and voluntary for independent workers, and for those who contributed to the old pension scheme. It is therefore possible for workers who participated in the social insurance pension scheme to switch to the new pension scheme, but it is not possible to transfer from the new pension scheme to the old one. Workers who switch from the old pension scheme are provided with a Recognition Bond (*Bono de Reconocimiento*) reflecting the value of their entitlements under the old pension scheme. This Bond is calculated at the time of the switch, is inflation proof, and earns a real rate of return of 4 percent annually until the beneficiary reaches retirement age when it is redeemed.

The pension fund managers compete for retirement accounts by offering lower charges and commissions, higher returns, or better service. Workers are free to transfer their retirement accounts from one fund manager to another. In practice, the length of the administrative procedures involved in the transfer allows a maximum of three transfers a year. Pension fund managers can only operate a single pension fund for all their affiliates, and this must be kept separate from the fund managers' own capital. Entry to the pension fund management market requires a minimum initial capital. It also requires approval by the regulator, the *Superintendencia de Administradoras de Fondos de Pensiones* or SAFP.

The pension fund is invested in a range of permitted assets. The regulations set maximum levels of investment by instrument, issuer, and sector. These regulations are in place for prudential reasons, to ensure the pension fund managers do not take unreasonable risks, and remain solvent. The pension funds are expressed in units which are valued daily. Pension fund managers are required to provide affiliates with standard information at regular intervals, and to report daily on their financial transaction to the SAFP. The incidence, but not the level, of commissions of the AFPs is subject to regulation.

In addition to ensuring the proper functioning of the regulatory framework, the government provides a number of guarantees. It guarantees the value of retirement accounts and a minimum level of returns. It guarantees pension annuities in full up to the minimum pension level, and three quarters of the excess up to an upper level.

Pension reform and pension scheme functions

The insurance and redistributive properties of pension schemes depend crucially on the detailed features of pension design. The individual capitalization pension scheme introduced in Chile in 1980 has design features that differ in some important respects from the insurance properties identified for the stylised DC pension schemes discussed in the previous section. I shall examine these briefly here.

Membership of the new Chilean pension scheme is restricted to workers drawing earnings. This means that workers who suffer some interruption in their employment or self-employment cannot make contributions to individual retirement accounts. This has some implications for the extent of the labour market risk cover provided by the new pension plans. As regards old age and retirement pensions, the gap in contributions paid to the retirement fund will directly affect workers pension benefits. These effects can be ameliorated through voluntary extra contributions when the worker is active again. Where gaps occur earlier on in a person's employment or are frequent and/or prolonged, these will seriously affect pension entitlements. The effect of labour market risks on pension benefits is reduced through the minimum pension guarantee to which workers with over twenty years of contribution are entitled. Yet this minimum pension benefit is not indexed, so that considerable uncertainty over variations in retirement income remains. A disability and survivor insurance also cover contributors to the pension scheme in Chile who are below retirement age, but this is dependent upon workers making regular contributions. Unemployed workers have had, since 1990, the benefit of an extension in insurance cover for these risks for up to twelve months after the start of an unemployment spell.

The legislators have attempted to reduce investment risk for participants by placing restrictions upon the investment portfolio of pension funds, and by requiring that rates of return achieved by individual pension funds do not deviate too much from the average of the funds. The government guarantees the pension funds in the event of a pension fund failure, and also guarantees pension annuities in the event of an insurance company failure. The legislators have also attempted to reduce governance risk by restricting pension providers to those that satisfy minimum solvency and governance standards.

Other features of the Chilean pension scheme increase risk exposure for participants. On reaching retirement pension scheme contributors can choose whether to take up a pension annuity or a phased withdrawal program. Under this latter pension mode, the individual bears both longevity and investment risk in full.[17]

Comparison of pension reform in Latin America

Having studied the main design features of the Chilean new pension scheme, this section extends the examination to cover the key design features of pension reform in the other six Latin American countries. Cross-country comparisons are very helpful in showing how far pension reform has gone in these countries, and in highlighting the different ways in which Latin American countries have attempted to combine a restructured social insurance pension scheme with the new individual capitalization pension plans. The section will outline the existing differences and similarities in the pattern of contributions and entitlements in these different pension schemes.

The extent of pension reform: a broad characterization of reformed pension systems

After Chile's pension reform in 1981, a further six countries in Latin America have introduced individual capitalization pension plans in the 1990s. The design of the new pension plans has in the main followed the basic features of the Chilean model. In terms of the reform of the pension system, however, most countries have not gone as far as Chile in phasing out the old social insurance pension scheme. Mexico is the only other country apart from Chile where the new individual capitalization pension plans are intended to fully replace social insurance pensions. In all other countries the social insurance pension schemes have been restructured and retained.

There are many reasons why the majority of countries that embarked upon pension reform have decided to retain some of the social insurance pension programs. A key factor, especially in contrast to the Chilean experience, has been the influence of democratic processes, which have allowed opposition to pension reform to enforce compromises in the design of the reformed pension systems. Opposition to pension reform has been naturally stronger in countries with a longer tradition in social insurance, and a deeper commitment to the solidarity and redistributive principles entrenched in social insurance. These countries also have a large retired population. Another factor has been the existence of large pension liabilities in the countries with older social insurance schemes and populations. Pension reform makes explicit the pre-existing pension scheme debt, and focuses attention on the issue of how to meet future pension scheme liabilities. In addition the setting up of a new pension scheme generates significant costs for the government associated with accounting, administration, regulation and supervision functions. These liabilities and costs can be very high and force government to opt for more gradual reforms.

Most countries therefore decided to revamp and retain elements of the old public pension schemes as part of their pension reform. Table 2.1 below shows the main pension design features across the countries under study.[18] The discussion that follows highlights the differences and similarities in pension design. In order to develop a broad characterization of the extent of pension reform across the Latin American countries it may be useful to classify the reformed pension systems into three groups: unitary, dual, and mixed. *Unitary* pension systems are those, like the Chilean one, which consist of a single pillar.[19] The Mexican pension reform will also put in place a unitary pension system as members of the existing social insurance systems will be transferred *en masse* to the newly introduced individual capitalization pension scheme.

Dual pension systems also consist of a single pillar, but one including two alternative pension schemes. One of these is a reformed public pension scheme designed along social insurance lines, with contributions entitling participants to a pension benefit defined under a formula including years of contribution, or service, and final salary. The other is the new individual capitalization pension scheme.

In *dual* pension systems, workers select one of the alternatives. Peru and Colombia are examples of a dual pension system. In both these countries the initial pension reform proposals included a unitary system, with the dissolution of the old social insurance system and its replacement by individual capitalization pension plans. Changes forced by the legislatures resulted in the retention of a revamped social insurance system. Workers are allowed to select one or the other pension schemes, and to transfer across them.

There is a question mark over whether this proves to be a stable model. The initial Peruvian pension reform in 1993 made the public sector scheme more attractive by, for example, setting differential contribution rates across the two pension schemes.[20] Changes since then in the regulations affecting pension schemes in Peru have aimed to equalize contribution and entitlement rules across the pension schemes. Marginal changes in the regulations affecting transfers across the private and public pension schemes could gradually transform the dual pension system into a unitary one.

Finally, *Mixed* pension systems are those combining a first pillar, containing a government provided basic pension benefit, and a second pillar consisting mainly of individual capitalization pension plans, but, transitionally, a defined benefit public pension scheme as well. *Mixed* pension systems have been adopted in Argentina, Uruguay and Costa Rica. These countries, and especially Argentina and Uruguay, have longstanding social insurance systems, older populations, higher income per capita levels, and a stronger commitment to solidarity and redistributive principles entrenched in social insurance.

Table 2.1
Main features of reformed pension systems in Latin America: structure, contributions and entitlements

	Chile	Peru	Argentina	Colombia	Mexico	Uruguay	Costa Rica
Title	Sistema de Pensiones de Capitalización Individual	Sistema Nacional de Pensiones (SNP) and Sistema Privado de Administración de Fondos de Pensiones (SPAFP)	Sistema Integrado de Jubilaciones y Pensiones	Régimen Solidario con Prima Media de Prestación Definida (RSPMPD) and Régimen de Ahorro Individual con Solidaridad (RAIS)	Sistema Previsional de Mexico, including Sistema de Ahorro para el Retiro (SAR) 1992; superseded by Régimen de Ahorro Individual 1995	Régimen de Jubilación por Solidaridad Inter-generacional (RJSI) and Régimen de Jubilación por Ahorro Individual Obligatorio (RJAIO)	Sistema Previsional Costarricense including Régimen Privado de Pensiones Complementarias (RPPC)
date law	DL 3500 11/1980	DL 25897 12/1992	Ley 24241 09/1993	Ley 1000 12/1993	Ley Seguro Social 12/1995	Ley 16713 9/1995	Ley 7523 8/1995
date start	01/05/81	06/93 relaunched 7/95	15/07/94	01/04/94	01/07/97	01/04/96	
pension system structure	UNITARY, only capitalization scheme for new workers; but residual public scheme	DUAL, choice between SNP and SPAFP	MIXED, first pillar government provided; second pillar either public payg DB scheme or private capitalization sch.	DUAL, , choice between RSPMPD and RAIS	UNITARY; compulsory transfer to individual capitalization accounts	MIXED; first pillar public payg DB scheme, second pillar capitalization scheme	MIXED, first pillar public DB scheme; second pillar contractual individual capitalization sch.
retirement age (Men, Women)	65M ; 60W	private: 65M/60W ; public: 65, or M55 & 30 years contrib. W50 & 25	current 60M/55W rising to 65 for all	55W/60M rising to 57W/62M by 2014	65 & 1250 weeks of contributions	RJSI: 60 & 35 years of service or 70 & 15 years; RJAIO: 60 & 35	62M/60W in public scheme; contractual in RPPC

58

Table 2.1 Continued

	Chile	Peru	Argentina	Colombia	Mexico	Uruguay	Costa Rica
legal coverage (civilian workers)	compulsory for dependent workers; voluntary for independents	compulsory for dependent workers; voluntary for independents	compulsory for all dependent and independent workers over 18; except provincial government and foreign workers	compulsory for dependent workers, voluntary for independents	compulsory for dependent workers, voluntary for independent, domestic service, and public sector workers	capitalization compulsory for all workers below 40 years of age or entering the labour market	public scheme is compulsory for dependent workers and voluntary for independents; capitalization scheme is voluntary
contribution rates (as % of earnings)	employees: 10% plus additional contribution covering charges and invalidity and survivor insurance	employees: 10% plus survivor and disability insurance premiums plus charges plus solidarity tax; since 1997 public scheme contributions can be no less than 13%	employees: 11%, charges, disability and survivor insurance premiums are deducted; remainder to retirement account; employers: 16% to public schemes; independents 27%	13.5 % from 1997: 10% to retirement account and 3.5% disability and survivor insurance, also solidarity contrib. Split 75/25% employer/employee independents pay 13.5%	9% in all: 6.5% for retirement and 2.5% invalidity and survivor insurance; contributions split between employer (70%), employee (20%) and government (10%).	employees: 15% on $0-15000 ($May 1995) of earnings; contributions up to $5000 earnings go to public scheme. Employers: on $1-15000 earnings at 12.5% in private sector	public scheme are 4.75% from employers, 2.5% from employees, and 0.25% from government; contributions are voluntary and contractual in RPPC
minimum pension or first pillar	minimum pension if 20 years contributions and retirement age; currently is 80% of minimum wage	minimum pension introduced by legislation in 1995 but has not been implemented	basic pension (Pension Basica Universal or PBU) is 2.5 times mean contributions (Aporte Medio Previsional Obligatorio)	minimum pension is one minimum wage if 62M/57W and 1150 weeks of contributions	if 65, minimum pension is one minimum wage, if required contribution record is satisfied	minimum pension is UR$ 550, price indexed, rising if retirement is postponed; capitalization minimum pension is 75% of this	public scheme: if retirement age and 39 years of contributions; level is 60% of base salary plus 0.0835 per 3 months over 240 months contrib

Table 2.1 Continued

old age main pension benefit	from balance of capitalization account at retirement	public scheme pension benefit is 50% of reference salary (average of last 12 months); capitalization scheme from balance of retirement account	capitaliz. benefit from balance of retirement fund ; public scheme (*Prestación Adicional por Permanencia*) of 0.85% of mean salary times contrib.years; old pension scheme (*Prestación Compensatoria*)	public scheme benefit is 65% of average of last 10 years earnings if 1000 weeks contributions; rising with longer contribution record up to a maximum of 85%. Capitalization scheme benefit from fund balance	pension benefit from retirement account balance	basic pension benefit is 50% of base salary plus 0.5% per year of service over 35 up to 2.5%; or 100% if aged 70; RJAIO pension benefit from balance of retirement account	public scheme benefit is 60% of average of best 48 salaries in last 60 months, rising by 0.0835% for every month contributed over 240, and by postponing retirement; capitaliz. benefit from balance of retirement account
capitalization scheme pension options	pension annuity, phased withdrawal, or deferred annuity	pension annuity, phased withdrawal, or deferred annuity	pension annuity, phased withdrawal, or fractional withdrawal if annuity<50% PBU	pension annuity, phased withdrawal, or deferred annuity	choice to receive pension under old scheme; or new scheme: pension annuity or phased withdrawal	annuity only	partial or total withdrawal; and partial or total annuity
early retirement	whenever pension benefit greater than 110% of minimum pension or 50% of average of last 10 years earnings	whenever potential pension benefit greater than 50% of average of last 120 months earnings	whenever potential pension benefit greater than 50% of average of last 5 years salary or greater 2 PBUs	whenever potential pension benefit of at least 110% of the minimum wage	whenever potential pension benefit greater than 130% of minimum guaranteed pension	capitalization scheme: if 35 years of contributions	capitalization scheme: if 5 years of contributions
disability/ survivor insurance cover	disability: total (2/3 loss of capacity) or partial (1/2 loss of capacity). Survivor: wife and children below 18 or 24 if in full time education	public: disability if 1/3 loss of capacity. Capitaliz.: partial disability if 1/2 loss or total if 2/3 loss. Survivor: same for both schemes, spouse, children<18	disability if 2/3 loss of incapacity	disability if 1/2 loss of capacity; benefits and entitlements are the same for public and capitalization schemes:	disability if 1/2 loss of capacity. Survivor: widows and children below 16 or 25 if in full-time education. Insurance cover is managed by IMSS	disability and dependant survivor cover	public: disability if 2/3 loss of capacity; survivor covers widow and children <18 or 25 if in education, single daughters < 55. capitaliz: voluntary

Table 2.1 Continued

	Chile	Peru	Argentina	Colombia	Mexico	Uruguay	Costa Rica
disability/ survivor insurance qualification	if contributing; if unemployed and contributed six months in last 12, cover is extended for 12 months after beginning of unemployment spell	public: contributing or contributed for 15 years; or less if contribution record; capitalization : if 3 contributions before disability/ death, or 4 in last 6 months	if regular contributor (contributions in 30 of last 36 months) ; or irregular contributor if contributed for 18 months out of last 36	entitled to disability if contributed 26 weeks before disability, or at least 26 weeks contributions in year prior to disability	entitled if minimum 150 weeks contributions	AFAP disability and survivor benefits if 2 years contributions and 6 months immediately before disability	disability requires 36 monthly contributions and having affiliated before age 55; survivor requires 24 monthly contributions
disability/ survivor pension benefit (as % of reference salary)	survivor and total disability is 70% and partial disability is 50% of average of last 120 earnings; if unemployed then 50% and 35% respectively	public scheme: disability is 50%, plus 1% per year if contributed over 3; survivor is 50% for widow plus 20% children; capitalization: disability is 70% for total, and 50% for partial disability; survivor is 35% spouse, 14% children.	capitalization: disability benefit is 70%; survivor is 50%	disability benefit depends on level of disability; survivor is 45% for first 500 weeks of contributions, rising by 2% for each 50 weeks above that with a maximum of 75%; if death of pensioner then 100% of the pension benefit	invalidity pension is 35% of basic wage if 250 weeks contribution or 150 weeks if more than 3/4 loss of capacity; survivor is 90% if 150 weeks contribution or if in receipt of a pension benefit	RJSI total invalidity is 65%; survivors receive accumulated entitlements; RJAIO disability is 45% of average last 10 years pay; survivor benefit is accumulated entitlements with a minimum of 45% of reference salary	disability is 60% of reference salary plus 0.0835 for every month contributed above 240; survivor calculated as a proportion of the potential old age pension

Compiled from several sources (Asociación Internacional de Organismos de Supervisión de Fondos de Pensiones, 1997; Asociación Gremial de AFPs, 1996; Baeza and Margozzini, 1995; Bertin and Perrotto, 1997; CEPAL/PNUD, 1995; CIEDESS, 1995; Sales, Solís and Villagómez, 1996; Superintendencia de Administradoras de Fondos de Jubilaciones y Pensiones, 1996; Vittas, 1994).

As noted, in all countries except Chile and Mexico, the social insurance pension schemes have been restructured and retained. These will compete with, and/or complement, the individual capitalization pension plans. It is interesting to examine the existing structure and regulations applying to the reformed pension systems, in order to asses what is the likely future status of the public scheme components. In countries with a mixed pension system, the public basic state pension is likely to be a permanent feature. In dual pension systems, and in the second pillar of mixed pension systems, the situation is somewhat different. It is apparent that in these cases the public pension scheme components are not intended to survive beyond the transitional phase. This is because transfers from the private to the public pension scheme are restricted, while transfers from the public to the private pension scheme are encouraged. The situation is not yet settled. In Argentina, for example, the original legislation did not allow the possibility of transfers from the private to the public pension schemes in the second pillar. Later changes have allowed a single move back to the public pension scheme from the private scheme for a restricted period. In Peru, on the other hand, the original legislation included no restrictions in the transfers across the public and private components, but later changes have placed increasing restrictions on such transfers.

In Argentina, the first pillar is financed by a combination of employer contributions and taxation. It is intended that when the liabilities of the old pension scheme are met as older workers retire, the employer contributions will gradually be eliminated (Vittas, 1997). After the transition period is completed, it is foreseen by pension designers in Argentina that the pension system will have a first pillar financed from general taxation, and a second pillar consisting exclusively of the individual capitalization pension scheme.

Legal coverage of pension schemes

Membership of pension schemes is compulsory for dependent civilian workers in all countries. Mandatory participation in pension schemes can be justified in terms of paternalistic concerns based on the belief that, if left to themselves, individuals will fail to plan their retirement income adequately. In the context of individual capitalization pension plans that place greater choice and responsibility in pension arrangements on the workers themselves, this justification does not appear to have great force. A stronger justification for the compulsory nature of pension schemes derives from the government's role of provider of last resort, and consequently, the need to reduce future retirement income liabilities to a minimum. As Latin American countries have a sizeable informal sector, which has grown in the 1980s and early 1990s, mandatory participation in pension schemes does not apply universally.[21]

Except for Argentina, participation in pension schemes by independent workers is voluntary. Argentina is the only country where independent workers are mandated to join a pension scheme. Argentina has, exceptionally among Latin American countries, attempted to include independent workers in pension schemes. Prior to the pension reform in Argentina there was a social insurance pension fund aimed specifically at independent workers (Schulthess and LoVuolo, 1991).

In all cases, members of the armed forces and foreign workers are exempted from participating in the reformed pension schemes.[22] In most countries, workers joining the labour force anew are mandated to affiliate to the private pension schemes.

Contributions and benefits in the new pension schemes

Comparison of contribution rates and entitlements for the new pension schemes across the Latin American countries under examination is greatly facilitated by their broad similarities. An important feature of the new individual capitalization pension schemes is that only employees are required to make contributions. The exceptions are Mexico and Costa Rica, where the contributions to the pension scheme are split between the employer, the employee and government. In Uruguay employees contribute to the first pillar, while employers pay the contributions to the second pillar. In Argentina, employers contribute 16 percent of earnings to finance the public schemes, and employees contribute 11 percent of earnings to finance the second tier private scheme. The employee contribution includes the charges and commissions of the pension fund managers, and the disability and survivor insurance

In Chile, Peru and Colombia, a basic contribution rate of 10 percent of earnings is required, with an additional contribution covering charges and commissions and disability and survivor insurance.

Contributions entitle workers to old age, disability and survivor pension benefits. The individual capitalization pension schemes do not include service pensions, but allow for the possibility or early retirement where workers have a more than sufficient accumulation of retirement funds. While old age pension benefits under the individual capitalization pension scheme depend on the pension fund accumulated at retirement, disability and survivor pension benefits are of a defined benefit type.

At retirement, workers can select pension benefit arrangements from a menu including life annuity, phased withdrawal, or phased withdrawal with a life annuity at a later date. This is in line with the options available in the Chilean new pension scheme. Uruguay is the exception in restricting choice of pension arrangements to life annuities only.

All countries have roughly the same pattern of provision for disability and survivor pension insurance. This is secured, in most cases, by an extra earnings related contribution ranging from 2.5 to 3.5 percent of earnings. The pension fund managers assume the disability and survivor liabilities, but can arrange reinsurance with private insurance companies. Most countries grant entitlement to disability pensions if two thirds of an individual's capacity to work is lost. Colombia and Mexico have a lower threshold for disability pension entitlement of one half. This latter threshold generates entitlement to partial disability in Chile and Peru.

Normal retirement age

Pension reform has pushed retirement age upward towards 65. This upward drift of normal retirement age, together with the elimination of service pensions, represents an important reduction in future pension liabilities. These changes are justified by predicted demographic trends, which they aim to accommodate. The new pension scheme in Mexico has equalized retirement ages for men and women at 65, and Argentina intends to move gradually towards this target. Uruguay has unisex retirement age at 60. All the other countries allow for an earlier retirement age for women. In view of the fact that women live on average longer than men, and of the rise in women's labour force participation, the trend towards unisex retirement ages for men and women should be welcomed (Barrientos and Firinguetti, 1996).

Retirement income security: short working life and minimum pensions

All countries have included provision for a minimum pension securing a basic level of retirement income. This minimum pension is provided by the government and normally funded out of general revenues (in Argentina, minimum pensions are also funded by employer contributions and earmarked taxes). In Peru a minimum pension is included in the legislation but it is yet to be implemented. Entitlement to a minimum pension benefit requires reaching retirement age and having contributed for an extended period (20 years for Chile, 22 years for Colombia, and 30 years for Argentina). The level of minimum pension benefits vary in their degree of generosity from 50 percent of the minimum wage in Colombia, through 80 percent of the minimum wage in Chile, and 100 percent in Mexico.

Given the extent of low pay and irregular employment in Latin American countries, minimum pensions are likely to be an important source of income in old age, and will become in practice a first tier of pension provision in the future. The extended qualification period poses a difficult problem. These regulations are in place to encourage regular contributions to the pension scheme. At the same time these discourage workers with low pay or irregular employment from affiliating, particularly if they are unlikely to fulfil the qualification period.

Entitlement rules for disability and survivor pension benefits restrict coverage in most cases only to active and regular contributors. This restriction is in place to prevent workers who become disabled from joining a pension scheme to obtain benefits. At the same time, labour market conditions in Latin America are such that, for a large proportion of the labour force, regular contributions to pension schemes present considerable difficulties. Employment gaps will make workers vulnerable to this contingency.[23] Survivor pension beneficiaries are restricted to the immediate family, widows, children under 18, and dependent parents. Most countries also cover children up to 21 or 25 years of age as beneficiaries if they are in full-time education. Colombia and Chile provide disability and survivor pension benefits for unmarried long term partners.

Solidarity and redistribution

Individual capitalization pension schemes have very limited redistributive features. The minimum pension guarantee provides a safety net measure of redistribution, but governments usually provide these as a separate entity. Some countries have attempted to integrate a solidarity element into their individual capitalization pension schemes. In Peru, the contribution rate to the private pension scheme includes a solidarity tax used to finance redistributive public programs. In Colombia, workers with earnings greater than four times the minimum wage are required to make an extra one percent contribution to subsidize pension contributions for vulnerable workers.

Those countries with a mixed pension system are in a better position to effect redistribution within and across cohorts. In Argentina, for example, the first pillar basic pension benefit is calculated as 2.5 times the average pension amount contributed to pension schemes, this is called the *Aporte Medio Previsional Obligatorio* or AMPO. As a flat benefit it redistributes from high earners to low earners, and by linking the basic pension benefit to earnings growth it redistributes from cohorts in work to those in retirement. Recent legislative changes, passed in March 1995 and prompted by the 1994 Mexican crisis, have considerably watered down the minimum pension guarantee by withdrawing automatic indexation and by capping payments within budget resources (Vittas, 1997).

In sum, there are striking similarities in the design of the individual capitalization pension schemes recently introduced in Latin America. At the same time, the overall configuration of the reformed pension systems show significant differences, as some countries have chosen to retain and revamp elements of their social insurance pension schemes. These are likely to result in diversity of performance and outcomes.

Conclusion

This chapter began by studying the basic functions performed by pension schemes as a preliminary to the analysis of the reformed pension system in Latin America. Pension schemes perform three main functions. They help transfer income from work to retirement, they provide insurance against a range of contingencies which affect retirement income, and they support redistributive and solidarity objectives. Different types of pension schemes have different sets of income transfer, insurance and redistributive properties. This means that diversity of pension scheme design will result in pension schemes having a different balance of, and priorities for, function performance.

A brief analysis was undertaken of the main properties of two stylised pension schemes, an unfunded defined benefit pension scheme on the one hand, and a fully funded defined contribution pension scheme on the other. These two pension scheme types represent in broad terms the two main pension scheme designs involved in the Latin American pension reform, the old social insurance pension schemes and the new individual capitalization pension plans. The comparative analysis of the stylised pension schemes led to the conclusion that each supported a different range of pension scheme functions. As a result, neither pension scheme design dominated. A further conclusion was that the detailed features of pension scheme design are crucial in identifying the likely function performance of pension schemes.

The next two sections aimed to provide a description and evaluation of the main features of the reformed pension systems in Latin America. The main features of the Chilean pension reform, and its new individual capitalization pension scheme were considered first. Another section provided a comparison of the main features of the reformed pension schemes across the seven countries that have undertaken recent pension reform in Latin America. These sections suggest the broad conclusion that pension reform will produce a rebalancing of the income transfer, insurance and redistributive functions performed by pension schemes in Latin America. The new individual capitalization pension schemes have design properties that restrict solidarity and redistributive functions. And the insurance properties of the new pension schemes are narrower in range, although more precisely focused.

In terms of the details of the new individual capitalization pension schemes in Latin America, they all share a common basic structure. Contributions are earnings related at uniform rates, with disability and survivor insurance financed separately. Dependent workers are required to make contributions to a retirement account with a private pension fund manager. These contributions are invested in a range of assets yielding returns. At retirement, workers have a restricted choice of pension arrangements.

Apart from Chile and Mexico, all other countries in Latin America that have embarked upon pension reform in the 1990s have retained a reformed social insurance pension scheme. In Peru and Colombia, the new individual capitalization pension plans are in direct competition with the reformed public pay as you go pension schemes. In Argentina, Uruguay and Costa Rica, the reformed pension systems include several pillars. A first pillar provides a basic pension benefit, with a second pillar including a private individual capitalization pension scheme.

In so far as public and private pension schemes coexist in direct competition with one another, the configuration of pension systems is not settled yet. The regulations concerning pension scheme affiliation by workers encourage transfer from the public to the private schemes, and restrict them in the opposite direction. This would indicate that public pension schemes, except where they provide a basic pension pillar, are not intended to survive the transitional phase of pension reform. Whether this intention materialises or not, the differences observed in the configuration of pension systems are likely to provide an interesting range of pension scheme outcomes, as regards articulation of the three main pension schemes functions.

Notes

1 Assume for simplicity a single individual who lives in two periods, 0 and 1, and who works only in period 0 earning a wage y_0, and consumes c_0 and c_1. Initial wealth is A_0. The individual in question will need to save some of her income in period 0 to support consumption in period 1. This can be done through a financial asset providing a riskless rate of return r, which is assumed equal to the individual's rate of discount. The individual will maximise indirect utility U, that is

$$\max U = u[c_0, c_1] \qquad (A2.1)$$

subject to the budget constraint

$$Y = A_0 + y_0 = [c_0 + c_1/(1+r)] = C \qquad (A2.2)$$

assuming utility of consumption is separable in the two periods, implying that $U = u(c_0, c_1) = u(c_0) + u(c_1)$, the first order condition is

$$u'[c_0] = u'[c_1](1+r) \qquad (A2.3)$$

2. Pension schemes providing a benefit in the form of a lump sum do not provide longevity risk insurance.
3. Estelle James points out that the redistribution across cohorts generated by pay as you go pension schemes tends to becomes largely automatic, and that as a result the redistribution they effect is not properly discussed or agreed upon (James, 1997b).
4. The report acknowledges the difficulties involved in separating the income transfer and redistributive functions from the insurance function.
5. The World Bank report is particularly critical of the management of public pay as you go pension schemes, and of their vulnerability to political manipulation.
6. It is important to keep in mind that these are stereotypical pension scheme types. In fact the extent to which particular pension schemes support income transfers, insurance and redistribution functions will, as noted, depend upon the specific details of pension design.
7. Outside Latin America, there is a much wider variety of defined benefit pension schemes. Some are employer or government provided, as is the case with occupational pension schemes and SERPS in the UK; or partially funded, as is the case with the public pension scheme in the USA.
8. The exception is Argentina where a public pension fund manager is in competition with private providers. There are also different variants to this basic design in other countries outside Latin America. Employer provided defined contribution pension schemes have the capacity to link contributions, and pension fund accumulation, to the performance of a firm as in the USA. It is also possible to provide group, rather than individual, pension plans.
9. Although these can be broadly identified from simulation studies (Schwarz, 1993).
10. Diamond (1997) notes that repeated legislation provides some form of insurance against macroeconomic shocks or demographic change affecting public pension schemes. The extent to this insurance depends upon the effectiveness of the repeated legislation.
11. Mesa-Lago (1991) notes that the other pioneer countries in terms of social insurance in Latin America were Uruguay, Argentina, Cuba and Brazil.
12. Further details can be found in Cheyre (1991).
13. A description of the changes to these programs can be found in CIEDESS (1994).
14. In the view of Piñera, pension reform also had political objectives. He notes that "by transforming every worker into a proprietor, the reform would

commit him to the responsible management of the economy and to the search for political stability and social peace" (1991, p.171).

15 The disability and survivor insurance is provided by the pension fund managers, and it is their responsibility. It has been the practice of pension fund managers to reinsure their liabilities in this respect with insurance companies. The additional contribution allows pension fund managers to finance the insurance.

16 The government sets the level of the minimum pension. This and the other entitlements are explored in more detail in chapter 6 below.

17 These issues are explored in more detail in chapter 6 below.

18 A cross-country comparison and discussion of the main features of the pension fund management market is included in the next chapter.

19 I am ignoring here the fact that the social insurance pension scheme will continue for those workers who decided to remain in it. The old pension scheme will be phased out gradually, as these workers retire. The social insurance pension scheme is closed to all other workers.

20 Workers who remained in the public pension scheme contributed 3 percent of their earnings (plus a contribution of 6 percent from their employers), while workers who joined the new pension scheme contributed 10 percent of their earnings plus an additional contribution (of up to 5 percent) (Cáceres, 1996). The workers joining the new pension scheme received a one off wage rise to compensate them for the employer contributions. Regulatory changes introduced later on require that from 1997 the public pension scheme has contribution rates at or above 13 percent of earnings.

21 Issues of pension scheme coverage are discussed in more detail in chapter 5 below.

22 The exemptions that apply to the participation of members of the armed forces in the new pension scheme can be justified on several grounds. There are security issues relating to information on military personnel being held by private pension fund managers. And there is a need to design pension benefits differently for armed forces personnel. Usually, pension schemes for military personnel include long vesting periods, and support up-or-out promotion schemes. As regards the exemption applying to foreign workers, this will have to be reviewed later on. An important implication of the homogeneity of pension schemes in Latin America following pension reform will be that worker cross-country mobility and regional integration are likely to be greatly facilitated (Asociación Internacional de Organismos de Supervisión de Fondos de Pensiones, 1997).

23 This will be examined in more detail in chapter 6 below.

3 The new pension fund management market

The most important innovation introduced by pension reform in Latin America is the creation of a pension fund management market. The new pension providers are pension fund managers, in charge of managing and investing workers' pension contributions. These contribute a central element to the new individual capitalization pension schemes in Latin America. The success or failure of the new pension schemes will come to depend on whether the pension fund managers are effective as pension providers. This in turn will depend on whether the market environment in which they operate is adequately regulated, encourages competition, and generates the right set of incentives for both pension fund managers and affiliates.

The pension fund managers have many important functions. These include: to collect workers contributions, to invest these in a range of assets combining high returns and low risk, to arrange disability and survivor insurance for active contributors, to provide a range of supporting services such as voluntary saving accounts and information, and to provide phased withdrawal pensions. The designers of the new pension schemes in Latin America aimed for the pension fund managers to operate in a competitive environment. They also required that market participants are subject to detailed supervision and regulation. The regulation is set by government authorities and implemented by an ad hoc regulator. Competition extends to the quality of the service provided, commissions and charges, and rates of return. In the new pension schemes, contributors are able to transfer easily from one pension fund manager to another in search of a better deal. This particular feature of the new pension schemes is in place to ensure, in theory at least, that competitive pressures spur the pension fund managers.

In Latin America, this is a novel way of organising pension provision. The conditions predating pension reform did not encourage the development of a pension fund management market. The dominance of pay as you go pension schemes, together with the controls upon the financial sector in place before the 1980s, precluded the spontaneous development of this market. In addition, the life insurance sector remained considerably underdeveloped. Pension reform will establish the pension fund management market anew. The success of pension reform in Latin America will depend upon the rapid development of this market, and upon an equally rapid development of the life insurance sector.

The objective of this chapter is to examine these important issues. The chapter begins with a detailed study of the design, evolution, and performance of the pension fund management market in Chile. Chile's introduction of individual retirement pension plans was the earliest, and most radical, in Latin America and as a result its pension fund market is the most developed. The new pension scheme in Chile also appears to be the most successful, and as such it enjoys paradigmatic status. To a large extent, the other Latin American countries studied here have introduced fund management structures and regulations that are very similar to Chile's. This is why a central focus of this chapter is on a detailed analysis of Chile's pension fund management market. In addition the chapter will look at the incipient pension fund management markets in Peru and Argentina. A comparison of their design and development with those experienced in Chile will be useful in identifying common trends as well as design innovations and their outcomes.

The first section provides a description of the main features of the Chilean pension fund management market as a whole. It provides information on providers, products, commissions, revenues, operational costs, and rates of return. It discusses the existing regulatory structure, and identifies the main trends. The next section examines the pension fund managers at a more disaggregated level. It discusses their market share, size, costs, strategy, and performance over time. The next two sections focus on issues of competition and regulation. One section evaluates the effectiveness of the current mix of competition and regulation. The following section traces the implications of this for future pension provision.

The final sections of the chapter extend the study of the pension fund management market to other Latin American countries. One section focuses on a comparison of the main features of the pension fund management market in Chile with those that have emerged, or are likely to emerge, from pension reform in other countries. The similarities and differences in the design framework are interesting in themselves, as each country has tried to avoid design flaws perceived in others, and take account of their own specific conditions and objectives. A further section contrasts the evolution of the pension market in Chile, Argentina and Peru to date, and identifies common trends and problems. A final section provides some conclusions.

Main features of the private pension market in Chile

Pension Fund Managers

Under the Chilean individual capitalization pension scheme, dependent workers are required to contribute a fraction of their earnings to an individual retirement account. Independent workers can make voluntary contributions. The administration, investment and management of individual retirement accounts is provided by *Administradoras de Fondos de Pensiones* or AFPs. The AFPs are corporations set up with the exclusive objective of managing individual retirement accounts. The private pension market is regulated by the *Superintendencia de Administradoras de Fondos de Pensiones* or SAFP. The interactions of private providers, savers, and the regulatory body make up the private pension market.[1]

Market behaviour and outcomes are dominated by the twin principles of competition and regulation. The AFPs are expected to compete for business, by attracting and retaining savers. They can compete on the basis of the rate of returns they can secure on the pension fund; the levels and incidence of commissions; and the quality of the service provided. At the same time they are subject to extensive regulation. This regulation restricts, *inter alia*, their services to standard products, and their ability to charge commissions. The regulatory framework also includes prudential regulation on pension funds' investment portfolios and rates of return, as well as regulations requiring information disclosure to both contributors and the regulator.

The AFPs manage their own assets, and separately a pension fund for their affiliates. AFPs can only administer a single pension fund for all their affiliates, which is insulated from their own assets.[2] The AFP's own assets belong to its investors to whom profits are distributed. The pension fund, on the other hand, is owned by the affiliates. The only flows allowed between the pension fund and the AFP's assets consist of permitted deductions for commissions. The pension fund is divided into equal units, and its value is calculated daily from changes in the value of the instruments it is invested in.

The market entry requirements for AFPs include a minimum capital of UF 5000[3], a reserve of 1 percent of the pension fund[4], and approval from the SAFP. The number of providers remained stable throughout the 1980s, oscillating between 12 and 14. In 1992 and 1993 the number of AFPs in the market rose to 22, but subsequent mergers had reduced these to 13 by August 1997. The rise in the number of providers in the early 1990s was a consequence of a relaxation in the entry regulations allowing trade unions and regional organisations to set up AFPs, and the remarkably high profits secured by them in the early 1990s.[5]

Products

The AFPs are prohibited from offering services other than those specified in the regulations. These are outlined below.

Individual retirement accounts (Cuentas de Capitalización Individual). The main product offered by the AFPs is the management of individual retirement accounts. AFPs receive contributions, invest these in a range of financial assets, credit the accounts with the returns, and keep a record of the accounts. Pension plan contributions are collected and deposited by employers in the case of dependent workers, or deposited directly by independent workers. The AFPs also handle transfers where affiliates move their accounts to a different provider. All affiliates have a book listing the movement in their accounts, and receive information on the balance of their accounts every four months.[6] The frequency and format of the information are strictly regulated.[7]

In addition to the normal contributions, it is possible for affiliates to agree with their employers either single or regular contributions to their individual retirement account with charge to the employer, or to make additional voluntary contributions to reduce contribution gaps.

Retirement pension. Once the affiliate reaches retirement age, s/he has to decide on pension arrangements. If the affiliate selects either a phased withdrawal or a deferred annuity, these will involve an AFP in receiving the recognition bond from the government, assessing the pension benefit, paying the benefit and continuing to manage the individual retirement account.

Survivor and disability insurance and benefits. In addition the AFPs must provide their affiliates who are below the age of retirement with a survivor and disability insurance. The contingencies insured and the benefits to be provided are standard. The AFPs reinsure with insurance companies some of the risk, and must handle these insurance contracts. A medical commission determines the incidence, and level, of disability, but the AFPs are responsible for assessing and paying survivor and disability pensions where these are awarded.

Voluntary saving account (Cuenta de Ahorro Voluntario). These were introduced in August 1987 as a means of encouraging personal saving. Voluntary savings are invested in pension fund units. Any person can open a voluntary saving account, and make deposits at will but there is a maximum of four permitted withdrawals per year. The balance in the voluntary saving accounts can be used to supplement individual retirement accounts. While the deposits are exempted from tax, withdrawals other than those transferring monies to individual retirement accounts are subject to capital gains tax.[8] The voluntary saving account services provided by the AFPs are pretty much the same as in the individual retirement accounts, except that the presence of withdrawals must be more resource intensive to handle.

Severance saving accounts (Cuenta de Ahorro de Indemnización). These accounts were introduced in November 1990 and are aimed at providing severance benefits for workers.[9] These are mandatory for domestic workers, and voluntary for all other dependent workers. Legal responsibility for the payment of severance contributions falls upon the employer. Employers are required to deposit 4.11 percent of a worker's pensionable monthly earnings for up to a maximum of 11 years.[10] These contributions are exempted from tax, and are invested by the AFP in pension fund units with returns being credited accordingly. In the event of the termination of employment, domestic workers can use the balance of the accounts. For all other workers statutory severance benefit rules apply, but these can be replaced from the seventh to the eleventh year of employment by a severance saving account. In addition, workers can agree with their employer to extend the severance saving contributions beyond the eleventh year.

Funeral benefit. In the event of death before retirement, a Funeral Benefit of 15 UF is available to finance funeral expenses.

The evolution in the number of accounts handled by the AFPs is shown in Table 3.1 below. The number of affiliates has increased from 1.4 to 5.6 million in the period 1982 to 1997. The number of active contributors has also risen, but at a slower rate than the number of affiliates. Affiliates are those who have, at any point in time, opened a retirement account with an AFP. Active contributors, on the other hand, are those who contributed in December, for earnings in the previous month. There is a widening gap existing between the numbers of affiliates and contributors. Non-contributing affiliates include those workers below retirement age who have become inactive or the unemployed, and those in work who fail to contribute.

Since their introduction, the number of voluntary saving and severance saving accounts has increased markedly. By November 1996, 17 percent of affiliates had a voluntary saving account. Banks also provide voluntary saving accounts, but the AFPs can reach a much wider set of potential savers. The growth in the proportion of affiliated independent workers with voluntary saving accounts since 1989 is much higher than that of affiliated dependent workers, indicating that independent workers have found these accounts especially attractive. The balances of these accounts earn the same returns as retirement accounts. The advantage of voluntary saving accounts is that they provide an opportunity for withdrawals. Severance saving accounts have also risen in number to 392,344 by December 1995, of which 95 percent belong to domestic workers (Superintendencia de Administradoras de Fondos de Pensiones, 1996a).

Table 3.1
Chile: Number of accounts by type

	Individual retirement accounts		Voluntary saving accounts	Severance saving accounts
	Active affiliates	Active contributors		
1982	1,440,000	1,060,000		
1983	1,620,000	1,230,000		
1984	1,930,353	1,360,000		
1985	2,283,830	1,321,938		
1986	2,591,484	1,493,568		
1987	2,890,680	1,675,615		
1988	3,183,002	1,772,371		
1989	3,470,845	1,917,629	189,948	
1990	3,739,542	1,961,547	256,226	
1991	4,109,184	2,118,373	414,762	176,484
1992	4,434,795	2,297,853	601,960	255,850
1993	4,708,840	2,366,728	692,332	290,821
1994	5,014,444	2,436,266	834,074	343,505
1995	5,320,913	2,489,533	961,636	392,344
1996	5,571,482	2,548,362	930,396	
1997[a]	5,683,223	2,505,013	962,783	

[a] June
Source: (Iglesias and Acuña, 1991; Superintendencia de Administradoras de Fondos de Pensiones, several issues).

As regards pensions, these are not quantitatively significant as yet. To a large extent, the pensions awarded by the AFPs to date have been financed with government transfers, or insurance cover.[11]

Commissions

Pension fund managers charge savers commissions for their services, which are the main source of revenue for the AFPs. The regulatory framework defines what services the AFPs can charge commission for, and the type of commission. The AFPs are free to decide whether to charge these commissions, and their level. Since the start of the new pension scheme there has been considerable change in the commission structure due to changes in the regulatory framework, and to the marketing practices of AFPs. Of all the areas of activity of the AFPs this has proved the most difficult to regulate effectively. Table 3.2 below summarises current commission regulations and practice by pension fund managers.

Initially, the AFPs charged fixed and proportional commissions for fund maintenance. One effect of this was to reduce dramatically the pension fund of workers who, due to unemployment or inactivity, ceased to contribute regularly. Adverse public perception of the new pension scheme arising from this practice led to changes in the regulations. In mid 1983, inactive contributors were exempted from this commission, and in January 1988 this commission was eliminated for all.

Since 1988, the mainstay of commission earnings by the AFPs has been the fixed and earnings related commissions charged on deposits. These have a different impact on the pension fund. The fixed commission on deposits is deducted from the individual affiliates' retirement account, thus reducing directly his/her pension fund. The earnings related commission on deposits, on the other hand, is charged as an additional contribution over the basic 10 percent of earnings. The earnings related commission on deposits does not directly reduce the pension fund. It is also noteworthy that because the additional contribution conflates an element of commission as well as the survivor and disability insurance premiums, the actual level of the proportional commission is not transparent.

There has been concern over the regressive impact of fixed commissions as they have a greater impact upon low earning workers, and their accumulated pension fund. Fixed commissions also generate a distortion in the distribution of the pension fund returns secured by an AFP to the individual retirement accounts. Fixed commissions drive a wedge between the rates of return secured by the pension fund units and the rates of return gained by individual retirement accounts. They also create a wedge in the net rates of return applying to affiliates with different earning levels within a single pension fund. Since fixed commissions are discounted from individual retirement account balances, a given rate of return for the pension fund will translate into lower rates of return for workers with lower earnings, and higher rates of return for workers with higher earnings. In 1987, for example the average wedge existing between the rate of return applying to lower

Table 3.2
Chile: Commission structure of the AFPs, regulations and practice

Service	Fund management	Individual Retirement Accounts				Voluntary Saving Accounts	Severance Saving Accounts
		Affiliates		Retired		Withdrawals or Transfers	Deposits
		Deposits	Transfers	Withdrawals			Proportion of deposits
Type	Fixed and proportion of Fund	Fixed and proportion of pensionable earnings	Fixed or proportion of Fund	Fixed and proportion of Withdrawal		Fixed	Proportion of deposits
Whether charged, and changes in regulations	Initially charged, but in 1983 eliminated for inactives, in 1988 eliminated for all	Both charged, but few AFPs now charge fixed commission		Sporadic, very few instances		Sporadic	Never
November 1997 range	–	Fixed: Ch $100–1,495; Earnings related: 2.55–3.4%		Ch $1,495 (only one AFP charges)		0	0

Source: Superintendencia de Administradoras de Fondos de Pension (several issues).

earnings workers and that applying to higher earnings workers was close to 1.5 percentage points. Over time, fewer AFPs are charging fixed commissions on deposits and the wedge has gradually disappeared.[12]

The earnings related commission on deposits has therefore become the main source of earnings for the AFPs. As will be discussed below, this practice also has undesirable consequences. Since the costs of providing these services are either constant, or decreasing, in the number of affiliates, AFPs have an incentive in capturing high earning workers. This is a key factor responsible for the rising marketing costs of the new pension scheme.

The pension fund managers have been reluctant to use the full range of permitted commissions. Competition and marketing policy by the AFPs has ensured they have charged for transfers to other AFPs only very occasionally. Charging commissions on transfers may reduce the potential market of an AFP and generate retaliatory responses from other pension fund managers (Valdés-Prieto, 1995).

Competitive pressures also explain the AFPs' decision not to charge for the management of retirement accounts of those members who retire and take up the phased withdrawal pension option.[13] This helps the AFPs to compete with pension annuities that are provided by insurance companies.

Similarly, AFPs have never charged commission on voluntary saving and severance saving accounts. This has made these accounts more attractive to potential savers. The absence of charges on voluntary saving accounts in particular has helped the AFPs attract savers away from banks. As noted above, voluntary saving and severance saving accounts have risen in number to around 1.5 million by December 1995.

The changes in regulations and in the practices of the AFPs have produced a situation in which the entire costs of operating the private pension market fall upon the regular contributors to individual retirement accounts. As will be discussed below, this situation has a number of undesirable implications.

Operational costs of the AFPs

The AFPs are required to submit annual financial reports to the regulator on both their own assets and their pension fund.[14] As regards the AFPs' own assets, the reports provide information on their revenues, costs, and profits. From this information it is possible to identify overall trends in their operational costs. Operational costs include costs of personnel (administrative, sales and management), administrative, computing and marketing costs, and amortisation and depreciation. Figure 3.1 below, shows the evolution of annual average operational costs per active contributor. To facilitate comparison across time, the series are reported in constant prices.

Data Source: Superintendencia de Administradoras de Fondos de Pensiones (1996a); Superintendencia de Administradoras de Fondos de Pensiones (several issues); Iglesias (1991).

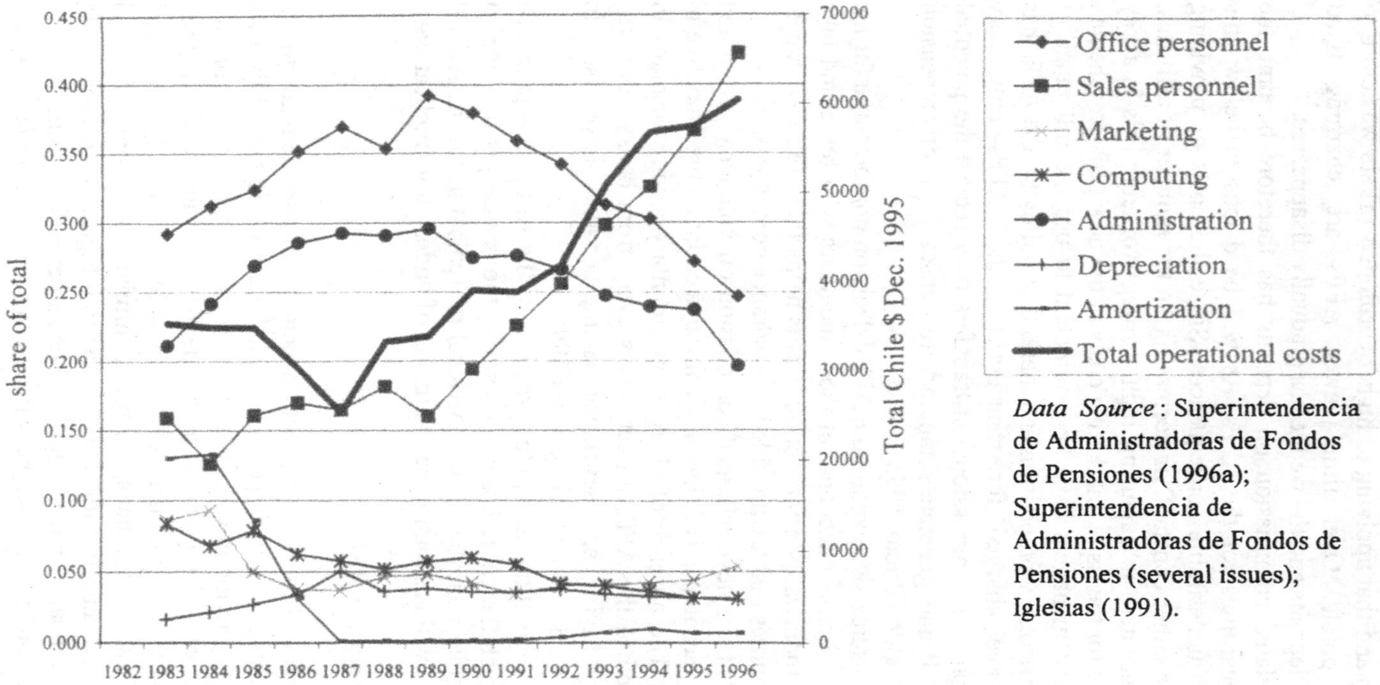

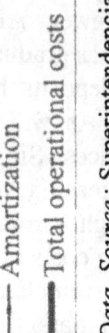

Figure 3.1 Chile: Operational costs per active contributor 1982-1996

Focusing on operational costs per active contributor can be justified on two counts: firstly, as has been noted, the commission charges fall almost exclusively on active contributors; and secondly, the core business of the AFPs is the management of active contributors' accounts. The trend in the total operational costs per contributor exhibits three main phases. The costs of the AFPs were high at the start of their operation due to the large set up costs involved. From 1982 to 1987, operational costs per contributor declined as a result of the rapid increase in the number of affiliates, and the amortisation of the set up costs. From 1987, however, operational costs rose steadily. This reflects the expansion in the services provided by the AFPs, and rising marketing and sales costs. In the last phase, since 1994, operational costs per contributor have stabilised at a high level.

The breakdown of operational costs per contributor shows the main factors behind these two trends. The initial fall in operational costs was mainly due to the rapid fall in amortisation, computing and administration costs. This is to be expected as the growth of the new pension scheme ensures the initial set up costs are spread more widely across time and across contributors. Gains from economies of scale and technical efficiency were exploited in the initial period.

The rise in operational costs after 1987, on the other hand, is a factor of the expansion in the range of services provided and of the rise in sales personnel, and to a lesser extent in marketing costs. While the number of active contributors rises only very slowly from the late 1980s, the services provided expand to include voluntary saving and severance saving accounts, leading to a rise in office personnel and administration costs. The most important factor in the rise in operational costs per contributor is the impact on sales personnel of a large number of new fund managers entering the market in 1992. The strategy of the new entrants was aimed at capturing market share by attracting contributors from existing AFPs, hence the emphasis on sales personnel. At the same time, the existing AFPs reacted by expanding their sales force to protect their market share. From 1994 onwards, the AFPs have employed more personnel in sales than in administration, and the salary costs of sales personnel are greater than the salary costs of administrative and management personnel combined. In addition the number of transfers increased generating extra costs.

Rates of return and investment portfolio regulations

Trends in real rates of return. The rates of return experienced by the AFPs are perhaps the most notable feature of the new pension scheme in Chile. Some summary statistics are presented in Figure 3.2 below. Since their inception in July 1981, to July 1997, the weighted mean annual rate of return of the combined pension funds was 12.4 percent.

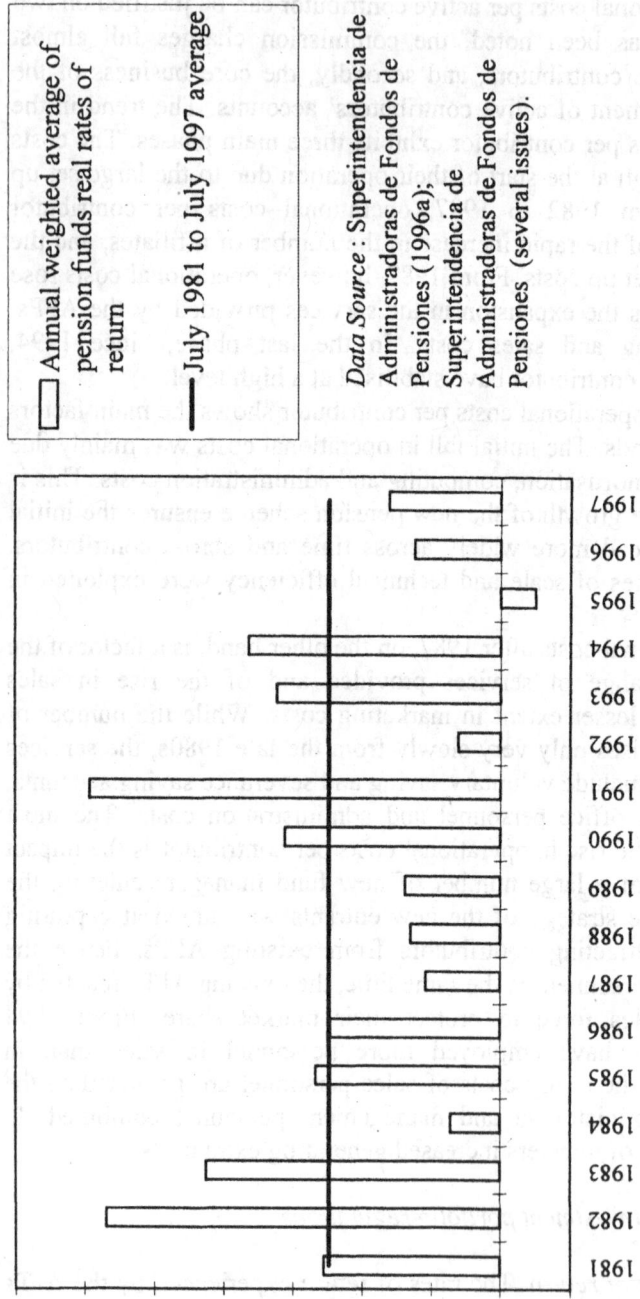

Figure 3.2 Chile: Real rates of return of pension funds

The high rates of return have exceeded all expectations and has contributed hugely to the successful implementation of the new pension scheme in Chile.

There is considerable variation in the mean annual rate of return over the period, ranging from a low of –2.5 in 1995 and a high of 29.7 in 1991, with standard deviation at just over 9. Rates of return rose and then fell with the recessions in the early 1980s and early 1990s. While rates of return show considerable variation over time, there is very little variation in rates of return across pension funds, implying that the variation over time is a factor of general economic and capital market conditions, rather than of active portfolio management. In any case regulations on relative rates of return and on investment portfolios, together with the shallowness of the capital market, provide significant restrictions upon the investment behaviour of pension fund managers.

Rate of return regulations. There are prudential regulations affecting the pension funds rates of return, and their investment portfolios. The regulations on the relative rates of return of the pension funds aim to protect the affiliates, and to minimise the liabilities arising from the government guarantees. The AFPs are required to ensure their monthly real rates of return are above a minimum level. This minimum level is defined as the lowest of the following two:

- The mean real rate of return of all the AFPs in the last twelve months minus 2 percentage points;
- One half of the mean real rate of return of all the AFPs in the last twelve months.

In the event a pension fund has rates of return below this minimum level, it is required to supplement the pension fund up to the minimum level from its rate of return fluctuation fund, and in case this is insufficient, from the AFPs' reserves. The rate of return fluctuations fund is built up where a pension fund's rate of return exceeds the upper level defined as the higher of the following two:

- The mean real rate of return of all the AFPs in the last twelve months plus 2 percentage points;
- One and a half times the mean real rate of return of all the AFPs in the last twelve months.

If these two reserves prove insufficient, the government guarantee applies. Under the terms of this guarantee, the government is required to supplement the fund up to the minimum level and then ensure the orderly transfer of the pension fund to a new pension fund manager.

These regulations ensure that the rates of return of individual pension funds do not stray too far from the mean, and therefore strengthen incentives for the pension funds to imitate each other's market behaviour.[15]

Investment portfolio regulations. The regulations applying to the investment portfolio of the pension funds have as their main objective that of securing an appropriate risk-return trade off, but an important secondary objective is ensuring the development of pension funds investment in line with government objectives, and capital market absorption capacity. Government objectives in connection with pension funds' investment portfolios include: (i) financing of liabilities from the old pension scheme; (ii) facilitating the privatization program; (iii) contributing to the modernization and deconcentration of capital markets; (iv) financing of housing and infrastructure projects; and (v) securing balances in the capital account of the balance of payments.

The regulations affecting the investment portfolio of the pension funds set maximum limits to their investment in specified assets, issuers, issues and sectors. The regulations have evolved considerably over time in line with the growth in the pension funds and the modernization of capital markets. The fast growth of the pension funds has forced the regulators to extend the range of assets the AFPs are permitted to invest in. The 1995 Capital Market Law has extended permitted assets to cover infrastructure and housing projects, venture capital, securitised funds, futures, and foreign instruments. And a new regulatory framework empowers the Central Bank to extend this list further without the need for further legislation.

The current regulations applying to pension funds' investment by assets are noted in Table 3.3 below, together with key changes in the regulatory framework. The regulations applying to pension funds investment portfolios have been gradually relaxed. Initially, the majority of the pension funds were placed in bonds issued by government and financial institutions, and investment in equities was not allowed. This helped the government finance the liabilities of the old scheme, such as the payment of pension benefits to the members of the old pension scheme and the recognition bonds paid to those who retired under the new pension scheme. The initial reluctance to allow pension fund investment in equity was justified by the shallowness and concentration of the Chilean capital market. The ban on equity investment by the pension funds was extremely fortuitous in that the AFPs were spared large losses from the 1984 financial crash.

Table 3.3
Chile: Restrictions on pension fund investment by asset

Asset type	Current limits (limit set by Central Bank if different)	Main changes
Government paper	35 – 50%	Prior to 1995 0-45%
Time deposits in, or Bonds secured by, Financial Institutions	30 – 50%	Prior to 1995 0-50%
Bonds issued by Financial Institutions	35 – 50%	Prior to 1995 40-100%
Corporate Bonds	30 – 50% (45%)	Initially 0-60%, then up to 1995 30-100%
Shares	30 – 40% (37%)	0% up to 1985, then 0-30%; then 20-40% prior to 1995
Venture Capital	2 – 5%	Prior to 1995 0-5%
Mortgage Bonds + Securitised Mortgage Loans	5 – 10%	Prior to 1995 10-20%
Short-term Debt paper (≤ 1 year)	10-20%	Prior to 1995 10-100%
Foreign Instruments	6 – 12% fixed interest (9%); 3- 6 % if variable interest (4.5%); 12% all	Prior to 1991, limit was 1%; then 0 – 10% but fixed interest assets permitted only
Risk coverage Instruments	5 – 15% (9%)	Not permitted before 1995
Securitised Funds	5 - 10 % (5%)	Not permitted before 1995
Shares in other AFPs	Not permitted after 1995	20 – 100% before 1995
Other Instruments authorised by the Central Bank	1-5%	Not permitted before 1995

Source: (Iglesias, Acuña and Chamorro, 1991; Superintendencia de Administradoras de Fondos de Pensiones, 1996b; Superintendencia de Administradoras de Fondos de Pensiones, 1996c).

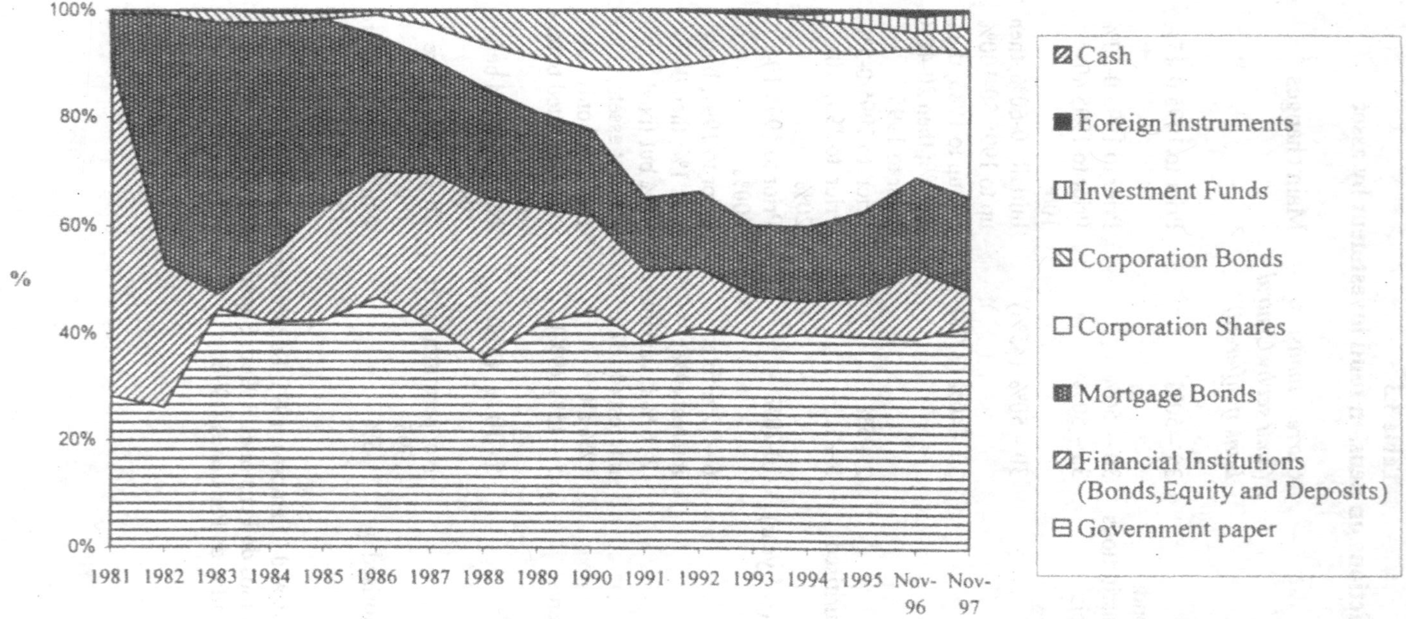

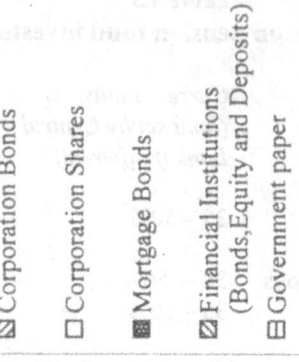

Figure 3.3 Chile: Pension funds investment by asset 1981-1997

Data Source: Superintendencia de Administradoras de Fondos de Pensiones (several issues).

The harsh recession of 1982 forced the government to embark upon a second large privatization program. Placing large public utilities in the private sector was facilitated considerably by allowing the AFPs to invest in equity in 1985. The pension funds were only permitted to invest in deconcentrated corporations, which effectively meant they could only invest in the privatised utilities. The privatization program was extremely important in generating the high rates of return experienced by the pension funds after 1986. The pension funds were able to benefit from the rapid rise in share prices of these companies.[16]

The actual asset distribution in the combined investment portfolios of the pension funds is shown in Figure 3.3 above. The initial investment portfolio of the pension funds relied to a large extent on instruments issued by the financial sector (especially mortgage and time deposits), and government paper. Since 1985, the share of equity has risen very fast towards the prescribed limits.[17] By May 1997, investment in government instruments amounted to 41.3 percent of the combined pension funds; equity holdings made up 26.7 percent of the pension funds; mortgage instruments reached 17.4 percent, and corporate and financial bonds accounted for a further 4.6 percent. Investment in foreign instruments barely reached 0.48 percent.

In addition to restrictions by asset, the regulatory framework for pension fund investment includes restrictions by issuer, by issue, and by sector. These are too detailed to cover in full here, but a brief review of some of the key ones will provide a flavour of the regulations.[18] AFPs cannot exceed upper limits of investment in a single open corporation. These are set as the lowest of the following two: 5 percent of the pension fund, or 7 percent of the share capital of the issuer. Open corporations are those which satisfy minimum governance and price transparency standards. This limit is adjusted by reference to three factors taking account of the liquidity, concentration, and the capital of the corporation. The liquidity factor takes a value of one if the majority shareholder controls 32 percent or less of the corporation's equity, and a value of 0.6 if s/he controls between 50 and 65 percent. As regards the liquidity factor, this takes a value of 1 if a corporation's trading ratio is more than 70 percent, but a factor of 0.3 if the trading ratio is equal to, or less than, 20 percent. The limit is also adjusted downwards if there is any financial association between the AFP and the issuer.

The restrictions applying to bond holdings by the pension funds require that these have a continuous and satisfactory risk classification. The actual limits take account of the type of instrument and the issuer. For example, AFPs are required not to exceed a limit of 20 percent of their fund's holdings of financial and mortgage bonds issued, or backed, by financial institutions, and having a A or BBB risk classification. These restrictions have the objective of protecting the pension funds from mismanagement, but also have had a significant impact upon the development and effectiveness of the capital markets.[19]

As noted, the restrictions applying to the AFPs' rates of return, and the restrictions on their investment portfolio, help explain the absence of variation in rate of return performance across the pension funds. It has been suggested that the prudential regulations on the investment portfolios of the pension funds have a more restrictive impact on the larger pension funds than the small ones, an effect compounded by the shallowness of the capital market in Chile. Smaller pension funds have more freedom to organise their investment strategy, but also they are more flexible in responding to market changes. Walker investigated this issue econometrically and was able to find evidence of an inverse relationship between rates of return and size of the pension funds, but this size effect is very small (1993a; 1993b).

The performance of pension fund managers

This section aims to provide some information and discussion on the differences in market share and performance across pension fund managers. This is important because the individual capitalization pension scheme in Chile relies to an important extent on competition.

Market shares of pension fund managers

The new pension scheme began in 1981 with twelve pension fund managers. The conditions of entry then were tougher than those currently in place and required substantial starting capital.[20] In addition, the military government was not sympathetic to labour organisations and groups connected to the old pension scheme, which prevented their early participation. The initial AFPs were set up in the main by business groups and employer organisations, although a few had links to trade unions.

Between 1981 and 1984 there were no changes in the number of pension fund managers, although some important changes in ownership took place. The acute economic crisis of 1982 affected the financial sector in particular. Some financial and business groups failed and were taken over by the government as financial guarantor of last resort. The AFPs owned by these groups continued to operate successfully under government ownership and were subsequently sold off. The debt-for-equity swap facility allowed international financial groups to acquire a stake in the Chilean pension market. Two AFPs, Alameda and San Cristóbal were merged into AFP Unión in 1984 and sold to a group in which the American International Group held a controlling interest. Other international financial groups also acquired shares in the AFPs. These included Bankers Trust which bought into Provida, AETNA which bought into Santa María, and Mitsomuri Shoji which purchased part of Invierta (Errázuriz, 1987).

The next important change in the market took place in 1986 when the AFP Protección, sponsored by workers in the Banco del Estado was set up. This is the first AFP which implements a selective recruitment strategy aimed at high earning workers. Foreign investment continued in 1991, with a French insurance company buying shares in the AFP Protección.

Despite a relaxation in the entry requirement conditions in 1983 and 1987, which lowered the required starting capital, the entry of new pension fund managers into the market only began to take place in 1992. This was also encouraged by a more sympathetic attitude towards trade union and regional bodies shown by the democratic government which took office in 1990. The high profit levels experienced by the AFPs provided a further incentive for market entry. In 1992 six new pension fund managers entered the market (Banguardia, Bansander, Fomenta, Previpán, Qualitas and Valora), and in 1993 three new AFPs joined them (Aporta, Genera, Norprevision). In 1994 only one AFP enters the market, Armoniza. By 1994 as many as 22 pension fund managers are operating in the pension market.

The rise in the number of pension fund managers increased competition for market share, and generally raised marketing and sales costs. It also proved to be short lived as some of the new entrants did not survive long. Failures and mergers combined to reduce the number of providers to 13 in November 1996.

Despite the entry of new competitors in 1992 and 1993, the pension market remains concentrated, with the largest three AFPs attracting over 65 percent of active contributors, and controlling over 50 percent of pension fund assets throughout the 1990s. The main three largest providers have in fact retained their leading position since 1982 (Provida, Habitat and Santa María). Data on market shares by active contributors and by pension fund for selected years are included in Chart 1 below. Taking market shares by active contributors first, these show some stability through time. This indicates that pension fund managers entering the market and managing to remain in it, can secure some market share stability through time. There is less stability in market shares measured by pension fund size. The figures show that market shares by pension fund have fallen for the largest pension fund managers through the 1990s. The largest pension fund managers have managed to retain contributors over time, but have lost some of their high earnings workers to the smaller fund managers. These trends reflect the emerging market segmentation, fuelled by the selective marketing and recruitment strategies of the smaller AFPs. This will be examined closely in the next section.

Chart 3.1
Chile: Pension funds, marketing strategy and market segmentation

1984

	Mean contributory earnings	Share of contributors	Contributors/ affiliates	Share of pension fund	Rate of return
Cuprum	145,490	0.01	0.72	0.02	2.6
Habitat	83,620	0.11	0.65	0.12	3.1
Santa Maria	80,230	0.20	0.65	0.23	2.3
Summa	76,880	0.08	0.61	0.08	2.2
Magister	71,880	0.02	0.80	0.01	4.4
El Libertador	67,000	0.01	0.46	0.01	2.7
Provida	65,410	0.29	0.57	0.28	3.4
San Cristobal	60,170	0.06	0.51	0.06	3.3
Planvital	54,060	0.02	0.46	0.02	2.8
Alameda	52,680	0.06	0.54	0.05	3.8
Concordia	52,080	0.02	0.58	0.01	1.5
Invierta	50,880	0.06	0.49	0.04	2.8

1988

	Mean contributory earnings	Share of contributors	Contributors/ affiliates	Share of pension fund	Rate of return
Proteccion	187,610	0.01	0.89	0.02	6.0
Cuprum	144,950	0.01	0.72	0.03	6.1
Habitat	83,730	0.16	0.59	0.17	4.7
Summa	81,840	0.09	0.58	0.10	7.4
El Libertador	78,920	0.02	0.56	0.02	5.1
Magister	73,800	0.02	0.71	0.02	5.4
Provida	69,050	0.29	0.57	0.27	4.6
Santa Maria	68,760	0.19	0.54	0.21	4.2
Union	61,490	0.09	0.50	0.08	5.4
Planvital	46,080	0.02	0.41	0.01	5.5
Invierta	44,350	0.03	0.41	0.02	7.0
Concordia	44,020	0.02	0.46	0.01	5.6
Futuro	16,988	0.00	0.98	0.00	*6.7

1990

	Mean contributory earnings	Share of contributors	Contributors/ affiliates	Share of pension fund	Rate of return
Futuro	201,611	0.00	0.92	0.00	19.1
Cuprum	192,569	0.02	0.75	0.06	20.4
Bannuestra	176,109	0.00	0.85	0.00	*17.7
Proteccion	162,014	0.01	0.79	0.02	19.9
Summa	94,619	0.08	0.53	0.09	20.3
El Libertador	94,601	0.02	0.53	0.02	18.8
Habitat	91,454	0.17	0.55	0.17	18.0
Santa Maria	77,904	0.19	0.51	0.19	16.7
Union	77,888	0.08	0.48	0.08	19.3
Provida	75,904	0.29	0.53	0.26	15.4
Magister	69,887	0.02	0.66	0.02	18.0
Invierta	61,681	0.02	0.39	0.02	21.6
Planvital	57,415	0.01	0.38	0.01	20.8
Concordia	49,262	0.02	0.41	0.01	18.3

Chart 3.1 Continued

	1992					1994					1996				
	Mean contributory earnings	Share of contributors	Contributors/ affiliates	Share of pension fund	Rate of return	Mean contributory earnings	Share of contributors	Contributors/ affiliates	Share of pension fund	Rate of return	Mean contributory earnings	Share of contributors	Contributors/ affiliates	Share of pension fund	Rate of return
Bansander	365,534	0.00	0.94	0.01	*4.0	378,050	0.02	0.82	0.03	18.4	419,319	0.03	0.77	0.05	6.0
Fomenta	323,415	0.00	0.98	0.00	*4.0	373,495	0.00	0.90	0.00	20.7	463,629	0.00	0.77	0.00	5.6
Cuprum	292,830	0.03	0.83	0.09	4.5	317,218	0.05	0.74	0.10	19.1	374,907	0.10	0.75	0.17	5.7
Proteccion	292,008	0.01	0.85	0.03	5.1	328,100	0.04	0.78	0.07	18.4	387,036	0.05	0.74	0.09	5.8
Futuro	263,396	0.00	0.91	0.00	5.1	313,368	0.00	0.82	0.00	16.8					
Qualitas I	263,003	0.00	0.90	0.00	*4.0	243,555	0.00	0.66	0.00	17.8					
Banguardia	249,045	0.00	0.93	0.00	*4.0	248,953	0.00	0.65	0.00	15.3					
Summa	171,165	0.07	0.59	0.10	3.9	196,828	0.00	0.54	0.07	16.7	222,821	0.06	0.48	0.07	5.8
Habitat	151,897	0.20	0.67	0.18	3.7	166,922	0.19	0.49	0.17	17.7	202,539	0.20	0.46	0.16	6.0
El Libertador	143,262	0.02	0.59	0.02	4.3	186,598	0.01	0.43	0.02	17.1					
Magister	141,356	0.01	0.75	0.02	4.0	172,238	0.01	0.58	0.01	17.8	231,403	0.01	0.54	0.01	5.6
Union	130,530	0.06	0.53	0.07	3.7	150,255	0.04	0.37	0.05	18.1	210,602	0.03	0.31	0.04	5.9
Planvital	127,711	0.00	0.48	0.01	4.6	113,934	0.02	0.27	0.02	19.5	148,823	0.03	0.22	0.02	5.7
Santa Maria	126,570	0.18	0.53	0.17	3.8	149,668	0.16	0.43	0.15	17.6	177,176	0.14	0.37	0.12	5.8
Provida	118,128	0.30	0.64	0.21	4.0	132,371	0.29	0.48	0.20	17.5	154,805	0.30	0.44	0.19	5.6
Previpan	115,865	0.00	0.83	0.00	*4.0	184,258	0.00	0.64	0.00	18.4					
Invierta	113,772	0.02	0.43	0.01	1.8										
Concordia	81,824	0.02	0.46	0.01	3.7	98,305	0.02	0.32	0.01	18.2					
Aporta						295,086	0.00	0.91	0.00	*17.8	360,158	0.00	0.81	0.00	6.6
Valora						221,792	0.00	0.76	0.00	16.2					
Armoniza						208,895	0.00	0.84	0.00	*17.8					
Genera						198,566	0.00	0.67	0.00	17.0					
Qualitas II											208,424	0.00	0.54	0.00	6.3

The Chart shows several indicators of pension fund size and performance. These include the mean contributory earnings of contributors, the share of active contributors and of pension fund value, the ratio of contributors to affiliates, and the rate of return. The pension funds have been ranked according to the mean earnings of their active contributors. The largest three pension funds are highlighted. It can be seen from the Chart that these sink to the bottom of the ranking over time. It can also be seen from the figures reported in the Chart that mean earnings of active contributors are positively correlated with the ratio of active contributors to affiliates.

Source: Superintendencia de Administradoras de Fondos de Pensiones (several issues).

Differences in pension fund managers' marketing strategy and performance

The rise in market share by contributors for the largest providers during the 1980s, and the stability during the 1990s in the face of strong competition from new entrants, points to the presence of important economies of scale and scope. Larger pension fund managers are in a better position to exploit these. At the other end of the spectrum, the survival of smaller pension fund managers, and indeed the entry of new providers in the 1990s, suggests that these may have other advantages to exploit in the market. These advantages have to do with two factors: on the one hand a strong allegiance from affiliates nurtured by links to related trade unions and other organisations; and on the other a marketing strategy aimed at capturing high earners.

This marketing strategy is based on the fact that the overwhelming proportion of the fund managers' revenue is obtained from earnings related commissions on individual retirement accounts deposits.[21] Operational costs, on the other hand, do not rise with in line with contributory earnings. In fact, to the extent that economies of scale exist in the market, average operational costs are more likely to decline in contributory earnings. Smaller pension fund managers can therefore absorb high operational costs by focusing on high earning workers. In addition, regulations on relative rates of return, and capital market constraints restrict the ability of large firms to fully exploit fund management and portfolio diversification economies of size. A selective marketing strategy allows small pension fund managers to survive and prosper in the market.

Two broad marketing strategies can be observed evolving in the pension fund management market. Firstly, there are large pension fund managers aiming to exploit economies of size in the market, and secondly, some smaller pension fund managers relying on a selective marketing strategy seeking to capture high earners and/or a loyal group of affiliates. The specialisation of pension fund managers by marketing strategy began from the late 1980s onwards, but is clearest in mid 1990s. This is illustrated in Chart 3.1 above. The Chart ranks pension fund managers by the average pensionable earnings of their contributors and reports on key market share and performance indicators. It can be observed that the larger pension fund managers gradually sink to the bottom of this ranking.

It can also be observed from the Chart that a measure of the average earnings of contributors becomes negatively correlated with the fraction of affiliates who are actively contributing. Lower earnings workers are more likely to find themselves unemployed, or inactive, and are more likely not to be actively contributing to their retirement accounts. The longevity of the larger pension fund managers is another factor, as they have thus accumulated a larger number of inactive accounts. The main explanation lies in their less selective recruitment strategy, as they attract a larger proportion of workers with irregular or informal employment relationships. Two other points emerge from the Chart. As will be noted in the next section, rates of return do not vary a great deal across pension fund managers. And for reasons that will also be discussed below, there is little correlation between the ranking and real rates of return across AFPs, apart from a period in the mid 1990s.

Profitability of pension fund managers

Figure 3.4 below shows the evolution of the after tax operational margin as a fraction of net worth for the AFPs combined. This measure of profitability shows losses in the period immediately after the introduction of the new pension scheme, due no doubt to the set up costs of the scheme. In the period between 1984 to 1988 profit rates climbed to around 25 percent, and remained there. In the next period, 1989 to 1992, profitability climbed even further upwards to just below 50 percent in 1991, encouraging the entry of new AFPs into the market in 1992. As a result of the increase in competition and marketing costs, profit levels dropped to 18 percent in 1994 recovering to 22 percent in 1995.[22]

Rates of return of the pension funds

The differences in rate of return performance across pension fund managers are not very large. As explained above, this is a consequence of the regulations applying to the pension fund managers' investment portfolios, and to their rates of return. Table 3.4 below shows the average rates of return of the pension market as a whole, for the largest three pension fund managers, and for the rest. The mean rates of return of the largest AFPs and that of the rest tracked each other reasonably well over the period. In eight years the rate of return gap between the largest three AFPs and the rest has been less than one half of one percent and in four further years it has been between 0.5 and 0.9 of one percent. Larger differences in rate of return performance can be observed in the 1989 to 1991 period. These are mainly the result of rapid equity price growth in key privatised utilities. The larger AFPs could not fully exploit these opportunities due to investment portfolio restrictions limiting the proportion of an issue (7 percent) which can be held by a single AFP (Valck and Walker, 1995).

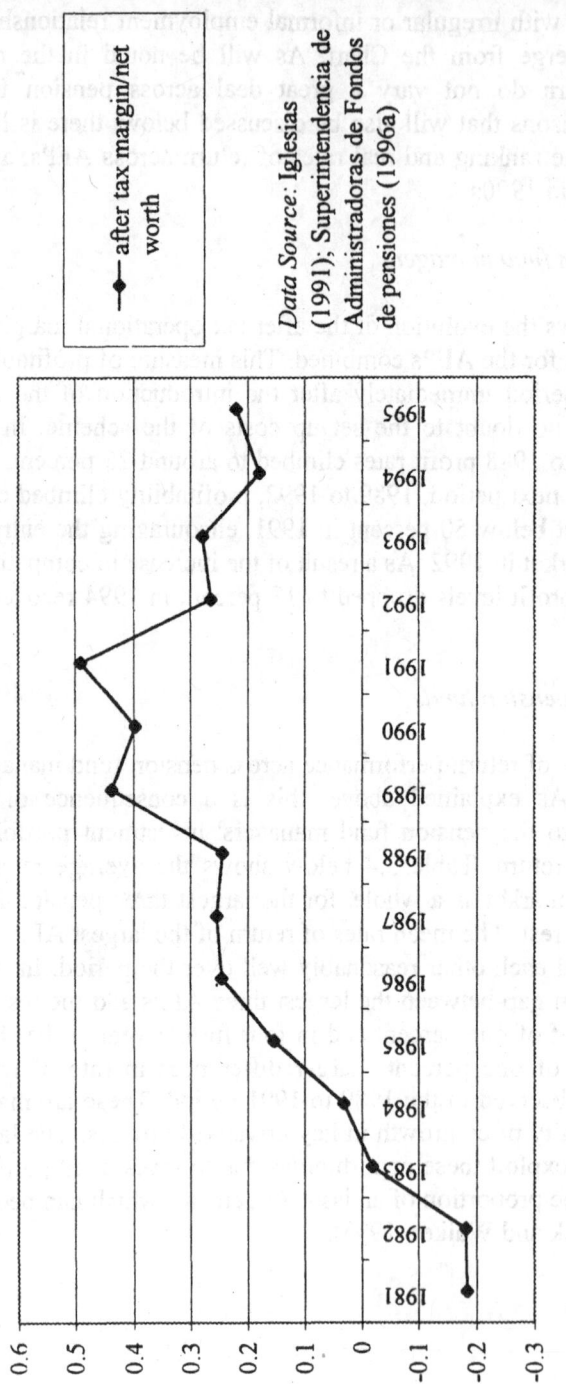

Figure 3.4 Chile: Profitability of pension fund managers 1981-1997

Table 3.4
Chile: Mean real rates of return and standard deviation

Year	1981	1982	1983	1984	1985	1986	1987	1988	1989	1990	1991	1992	1993	1994	1995	1996	1997
								All AFPs									
Average	12.8	28.5	21.3	3.60	13.4	12.3	5.4	6.5	6.9	15.6	29.7	3.0	16.2	18.2	-2.5	6.2	6.2
Stand.dev.	3.1	2.4	1.7	0.7	0.3	1.2	1.1	0.7	1.5	1.6	2.2	0.8	0.7	1.2	0.6	0.2	0.4
Minimum	5.3	23.1	18.5	2.1	13.0	10.6	4.5	5.9	4.0	13.3	25.8	0.9	14.6	15.7	-4.6	6.0	7.4
Maximum	15.5	30.3	24.7	5.0	14.3	15.5	8.5	8.7	9.5	19.4	34.3	4.2	17.0	21.1	-1.8	7.0	8.8
								Largest (L) Three AFPs									
Mean	11.9	28.4	21.8	3.5	13.2	12.0	5.2	6.2	6.4	14.6	28.7	2.9	16.0	18.0	-2.8	6.2	8.2
Stand.dev.	2.08	2.51	2.21	0.51	0.25	0.40	0.23	0.26	0.46	1.30	2.57	0.15	0.23	0.10	0.40	0.20	0.36
								Rest (R)									
Mean	12.4	26.7	21.2	3.5	13.4	12.6	5.7	7.3	7.8	17.4	31.2	3.1	16.0	18.2	-2.6	5.9	8.0
Stand.dev.	3.49	2.43	1.74	0.85	0.43	1.40	1.25	0.65	1.58	1.14	1.95	0.93	0.82	1.33	0.74	1.00	0.48
mean L - mean R	-0.52	1.70	0.60	0.06	-0.18	-0.62	-0.49	-1.16	-1.47	-2.89	-2.43	-0.17	0.03	-0.24	-0.18	0.28	0.81
Stand.dev. ratio(L/R)	0.60	1.04	1.27	0.60	0.58	0.29	0.18	0.41	0.29	1.14	1.32	0.16	0.28	0.08	0.55	0.20	0.75

Source: Superintendencia de Administradoras de Fondos de Pensiones (several issues).

Turning to differences in the standard deviation of these rates of return, again the differences across AFPs are very small. For the larger part of the period, standard deviation is smaller for the largest AFPs than for the others. In 10 out of 16 years, the standard deviation of the largest three AFPs is less than 70 percent of that of the others. Looking at the standard deviation of rates of return for individual AFPs across time, these differences disappear and the two groups are largely indistinguishable in their performance. This confirms the conclusion that general economic conditions affect AFPs similarly.

Competition and regulation in the pension fund management market

The new pension scheme in Chile was designed with a view to providing a significant role for competition in ensuring the performance of the pension fund managers. As noted, pension reform was part and parcel of a program of structural reform of the Chilean economy along neoliberal lines. At the same time, the designers understood that the special features of pension plans required extensive regulation, particularly in the initial period. In conventional markets the set of incentives generated by competitive pressures is sufficient to drive down costs, ensure efficient resource allocation, and protect consumers. There are good a priori reasons why a private pension management market may require significant regulation to achieve similar outcomes. In part this has to do with the complexity of the product traded, and its long-term horizon. These features of pension products raise significantly the costs attached to choice and decision making by pension plan contributors. In part it also has to do with the presence of economies of scale in pension provision, which encourage the concentration of pension fund managers, and consequently an increase in their market power. In addition, where participation in pension plans is compulsory, and substantial government guarantees are in place, these may significantly distort competitive forces.

Given that competitive forces may be limited in the private pension market, it becomes important to identify what is the optimal design for regulation. It is important to establish where, and what type of, regulation is likely to be effective. The long term nature of pension plans, and their interdependence with economic, financial, and labour market conditions, makes it inevitable that regulation will change over time. The dynamic nature of regulatory changes is therefore of particular relevance here. These are the issues to be examined in this section.

Pension plan participant choice, behaviour, and competition

The design of individual retirement pension plans in Chile facilitates individual choice of pension fund manager, as a means of ensuring that competitive forces prevailed in the market. In order to facilitate this choice, pension products are standard, commissions are uniform for all affiliates to a single AFP, and secondary products are closely regulated. Information flows to plan participants are also closely regulated. Government guarantees ensure that rate of return and risk differentials across pension fund managers are small and therefore not a significant factor in participant choice.

On paper, pension plan participants in Chile are expected to compare rates of return, commission levels and service quality across the different AFPs, and transfer their accounts to the one with the best deal. In practice, pension plan participants appear to be fairly insensitive to differences in these indicators across pension fund managers. This may be due to the high information costs required to make pension plan choice decisions,[23] or it may be due to that fact that as a result of regulation these differentials are too small to matter.

Empirically, participant market behaviour can be studied by analysing retirement account transfers. Table 3.5 below shows the rise in transfers and the associated rise in sales personnel. In the original legal framework, participants were given full scope to transfer their accounts in search of the best provider, and AFPs are permitted to charge commissions on transfers. In practice, administrative processes restrict the number of transfers an individual affiliate can make in a year, and very few AFPs have ever instituted commissions for transfers.

There have been some changes in the regulations applying to transfers which may have had some effect on the number of transfers. From 1982, participants wishing to transfer to another AFP had to make a request in person at a branch office. The transfer process took around three months, so that in practice four transfers a year were possible.[24] In February 1988 the regulations were relaxed to allow participants to request a transfer through a signed form. This resulted in a rapid rise in transfers, further accentuated by the entry of several new AFPs into the market in 1992 and the increase in sales personnel that followed.

The high number of transfers would appear to indicate healthy competitive forces at work, but the reality is quite different. Abuhabda (1994) studied the determinants of transfers using a panel of monthly cross sections of individual transfers across AFPs for the period April 1992 to June 1993. He regressed transfers on a range of rates of return, sales and commission variables. He found that transfers were affected by annual rates of return applying to individual retirement accounts, but that these were not affected by rates of return of pension fund units, or by rates of return over a longer time period (36 months). Transfers were also positively influenced by the number of sales personnel and negatively by the additional contribution.

Table 3.5
Chile: Individual retirement account transfers and sales personnel

	Number of transfers applied for	Number of completed transfers	Number of sales personnel (Dec.)	Transfers applied per sales personnel	Completed transfers per sales personnel
1982			1,880		
1983	15,129	14,380	1,202	12.5	11.9
1984	145,998	134,720	2,334	62.5	57.7
1985	206,920	189,163	2,415	85.6	78.3
1986	180,760	174,237	2,249	80.3	77.4
1987	185,813	181,048	2,312	80.3	78.3
1988	372,601	306,819	2,727	136.6	112.5
1989	408,754	316,763	2,615	156.3	121.1
1990	504,640	387,955	3,446	146.4	112.5
1991	670,193	500,176	4,134	162.1	120.9
1992	859,791	621,919	6,658	129.1	93.4
1993	1,260,945	875,874	10,771	117.0	81.3
1994	1,531,526	972,482	14,800	103.4	65.7
1995	1,956,980	1,328,410	15,432	126.8	86.0

Source : Superintendencia de Administradoras de Fondos de Pensiones (1996a; several issues)

All effects were predicted to be very small. He reports that a one percentage point difference in the rate of return applying to an AFP's retirement accounts increases transfers by 46 a month. A one percentage point increase in the additional contribution is predicted to reduce transfers by 2,594 a month; and an extra salesperson increases transfers by 8.96 a month. Abuhabda's findings confirm that pension plan participants are fairly insensitive to differentials in rates of return and commission level across AFPs. These results also confirm that pension fund managers would find it much more cost effective to increase market share by enlarging their sales force than by lowering commissions or obtaining higher rates of return (Abuhadba, 1994).

One possible interpretation of these findings is that they reflect optimal behaviour in the context of large information costs. There is also a great deal of evidence, supported by the results of an investigation of failed transfers and complaints by the regulator, that the rapid rise in transfers reflects rent seeking behaviour on the part of both sales personnel and affiliates.[25] Affiliates are offered presents, loans or money to apply for a transfer. Sales personnel who are likely to be paid bonuses on applications also have an interest in encouraging transfer churning.[26] Evidence reported by Abuhabdha indicates that transfers are more common among younger workers, and that they decline rapidly with the length of time an account is kept with an AFP. There is mounting concern over the rise in transfers, and the associated costs they impose on pension fund managers. The government is studying proposals to restrict transfers by requiring transferees to remain at least one year with an AFP (Superintendencia de Administradoras de Fondos de Pensiones, 1996a).

Size economies and market concentration

How competitive is the private pension market in Chile? The standard indicators of competition provide conflictive signals. The evolution in the number of pension fund managers suggests that market entry is not too difficult, and that aggressive marketing can initially secure market share. At the same time, the rapid decline in the number of providers from 22 in 1994 to 13 in 1997 demonstrates that it is difficult for new entrants to protect their market share.

In fact the private pension market in Chile remains very concentrated. The three largest AFPs accounted for 63 percent of active contributors in 1982, this share rising to 71 percent in 1990, and declining to 67 percent in 1995. Figure 3.5 below shows the Herfindahl-Hirschman concentration index computed for both active contributors and pension fund shares of AFPs.[27] Pension market concentration, measured by shares of active contributors, has remained more or less the same over the whole period. The concentration index measured by size of pension fund shows a secular decline, reflecting the fact that some of the smaller AFPs have successfully attracted higher earnings workers.

The concentration in the private pension market in Chile can be explained by economies of scale in the management of retirement accounts.[28] The general literature suggests that economies of scale are present in banking and other financial institutions. A recent survey of work on this issue concluded that the average cost curve of banking institutions shows a flat U-shape (Berger, Hunter and Timme, 1993). This survey reports that among US banks with over US $1 billion in assets, average costs appear to be lowest in the range of US $2-10 billion. In December 1995, AFPs pension fund assets ranged from US $ 152 to $5000 million. Moreover, product homogeneity generates significant economies of scale.

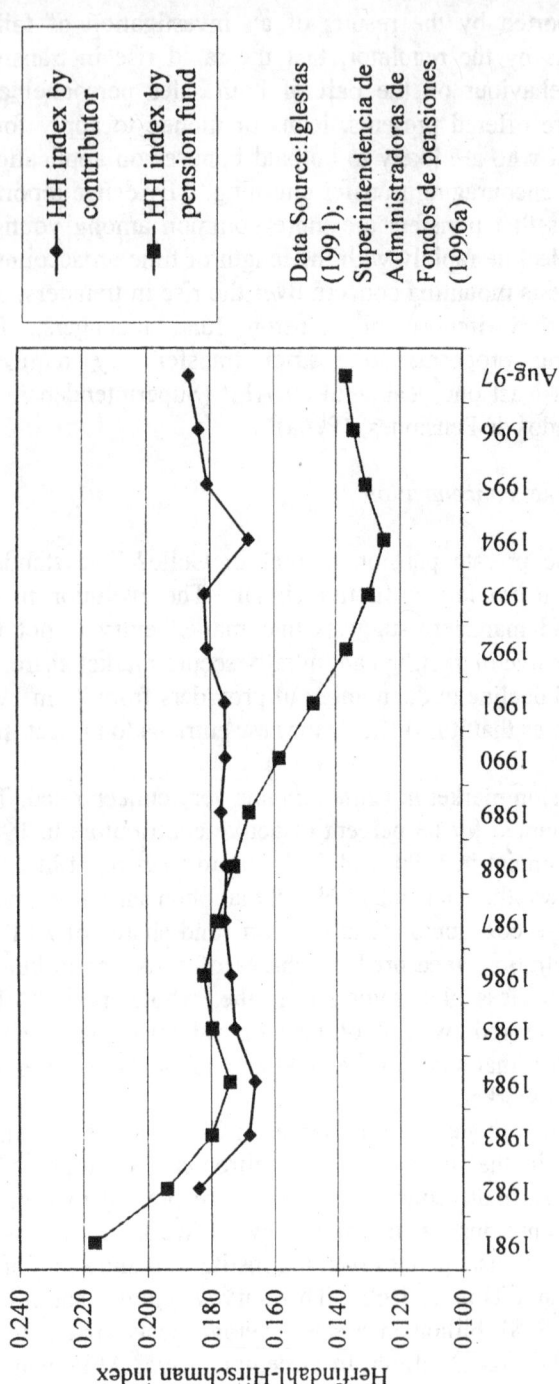

Figure 3.5 Chile: Pension fund management market concentration

Mitchell (1996) studies the cost structure of different pension saving institutions and finds significant economies of scale in pension fund provision. For employer sponsored pension plans in the USA, costs rise by 0.27 percent for every 1 percent rise in assets, and 0.8 percent for every 1 percent rise in contributors (Mitchell, 1996).[29]

Miranda (1994) measured economies of scale in the Chilean private pension market. Using a panel of pension fund manager variables for the years 1982-1993 he estimated a log cost function. He finds that for every 1 percent rise in the number of active contributors, operational costs rise in the range of 0.6 to 0.8 percent.

Furthermore, empirical investigation of economies of scope in financial institutions has shown that these may be significant (Berger, Hunter and Timme, 1993). The introduction of voluntary saving accounts in 1988, and severance saving accounts in 1990, may have created economies of scope in the Chilean pension market. The contributions made into these accounts are incorporated in the AFPs single pension fund, suggesting the existence of economies across the range of the operational costs of pension fund managers. The presence of economies of scale and scope may explain the concentration trends observed in the Chilean private pension market.

The evidence reported above suggests that a small number of pension fund managers may be able to exploit economies of scale to the full, and that further concentration is likely to take place in the medium term. It may be questioned why these trends did not assert themselves earlier. Three explanations may be advanced. Firstly, the regulations affecting the investment portfolio of the AFPs in combination with the characteristics of the Chilean capital market may generate compensating size advantages for the smaller AFPs. This is because the capital market is very concentrated and therefore illiquid, thus placing restrictions upon the portfolio management of the AFPs, but particularly so for the larger ones. Smaller AFPs may have fewer restrictions in placing their investment portfolio at a better risk-return point.[30] Secondly, differences in organisational outlook and ownership among AFPs may generate strong attachment by affiliates, as in the case of AFPs associated with trade unions, slowing down the process of increased concentration (Miranda, 1994). A third explanation refers to the impact of the marketing strategies implemented by the smaller AFPs. These aimed to compensate their cost disadvantage by segmenting the market. Existing regulations and practice in the private pension market have combined to create a wedge separating operational costs and commission revenue. Some smaller AFPs have therefore adopted a selective marketing strategy focusing on high earners. While experiencing relatively higher operational costs per contributor, they have been able to compensate for these with higher than average commission revenue.

In sum, it would appear that there are significant economies of scale in the private pension market, which limit competition. Relaxation of entry regulations has been effective in attracting new pension fund managers, but the presence of economies of scale and scope makes further market concentration likely. This trend may be weakened by institutional factors, mainly regulation and practice, which have provided smaller AFPs with the opportunity of pursuing selective marketing strategies to compensate for their size disadvantage.

Issues of efficiency and redistribution

The examination of the pension fund management market in the previous sections leads to the conclusion that competitive forces have a limited role to play in ensuring the efficiency of the market. On the consumer side, the informational requirements needed to exercise effective choice of pension fund manager are too costly for a large majority of contributors. On the provider side, the presence of significant economies of scale and scope generate pressure for market concentration and market segmentation.

It is not surprising, therefore, that effective and dynamic regulation is a necessary feature of the private pension market in Chile and, to the extent that these conditions apply to other countries, of pension reform in general. Regulation extends to the licensing and supervision of providers, the specification of standard products and performance, and the all important provision of guarantees and prudential regulation.

The mix of competition and regulation is both complex and evolving, and a very positive feature of the Chilean pension reform has been the effectiveness of the regulatory framework.[31] The mix of competition has important implications for the efficiency of the private pension market, and it generates significant redistribution for the main actors. Improvements in the operation of the Chilean pension scheme will necessarily require adjustments to this mix. The two key issues of concern here are the need to introduce a better system of incentives for reducing the costs of pension provision, and the need to improve access to, and outcomes from, the individual capitalization pension scheme for workers with low earnings and irregular employment. This section will look at these issues in the context of an overall evaluation of the Chilean pension market.

The key problem in the operation of the pension market is the misalignment of commissions charged with the costs of the services provided. As noted above, the wedge existing between commissions and costs is a product of the limited nature of competition in the pension market, the presence and design of regulation, and the rent seeking practices of both pension fund managers and affiliates. This wedge arises from two factors.

On the one hand, the presence of economies of scale and scope imply the average costs of providing services in the pension market decline with the growth of contributors and the pension fund, whilst, on the other, the majority of commission revenue comes from earnings related commission charges. In addition, marketing policies by the pension fund managers have concentrated commission charges on regular contributors to individual retirement accounts, instead of the wider universe of users. Commission charges therefore have only an indirect relationship to service costs. The misalignment of costs and commission charges leads to inefficient market outcomes, and to significant redistribution, with adverse implications for pension outcomes.

The costs of the Chilean new pension scheme

The trends in costs observed for the Chilean pension scheme can be summarised briefly here. For the AFPs operational costs per active contributor declined at first, as the set up costs were distributed across a wider contributor base, but then rose in response to the rise in marketing costs after 1988. As far as active contributors are concerned, commission charges have fallen from the very high levels at the start of the new pension scheme, but now appear to have stabilised at around a quarter of contributions. This makes the Chilean individual retirement scheme a fairly expensive one for contributors.

It is difficult to make accurate international comparisons of the operational costs of private pension schemes, as the differences in design, regulation, and practice imply wide diversity in the services offered. Differences in labour costs and capital market development also contribute to make comparison hazardous. Recent studies show that the costs of pension plans in Chile are considerably higher than those in public pension schemes in other countries in Latin America. They are also higher than those in comparable private pension schemes in the USA and Australia (Bateman, Pigott and Valdés, 1995; Mitchell, 1996; Valdés-Prieto, 1994).

The problem is to do not only with the level of costs, but also, and perhaps more importantly, with the weak incentives existing in the pension market for costs to be driven down. Since contributors are not particularly sensitive to rates of return differentials, competitive forces are too limited to pressure providers into cutting costs. The recent relaxation in entry to the pension fund management market in Chile, far from increasing competition in the market, has contributed to the upward spiral of marketing costs and the rise in transfers. The marketing strategies of all pension fund managers rely on high marketing expenditure to protect and maintain market share. Regulatory changes can be introduced which would reduce marketing costs, by restricting transfers for example, but these would only work at the expense of existing competition.

Table 3.6
Impact of sales costs on pension plan costs

Annual operational costs per active contributor under alternative assumptions concerning marketing costs	Annual costs Chile$ 1995	Change from benchmark (%)	Additional contribution[b]
Operational costs per contributor with current marketing costs (benchmark)[a]	48,288		3.0
Operational costs per contributor is marketing costs are cut by half	38,384	- 20.5	2.6
Operational costs per contributor if marketing costs are zero	28,480	- 41.0	2.1
Operational costs per contributor if costs had remained at 1988 level	36,420	- 24.6	2.5

Source: own calculations from data in Superintendencia de Administradoras de Fondos de Pensiones (1996a, 1996b). All data used are from 1995.
[a] Marketing costs include sales personnel costs and direct sales costs.
[b] Under the assumption that cost reductions are used in full to reduce the additional contribution.

The increase in marketing costs since 1988 illustrates this problem well. A high proportion of current marketing costs yield no benefits to pension plan participants, and will have a large adverse effect on their pension benefits. This is illustrated in a simulation exercise of the impact of marketing costs on the additional contribution. The results are reported in Table 3.6 above. With data from 1995, the additional contribution is simulated with marketing costs halved, or eliminated altogether, or fixed at their 1988 level. The results show that the complete elimination of marketing costs could account for a reduction of one third in the additional contribution. The other scenarios could produce a reduction of around one sixth. If these reductions applied over the full working life of an individual, they could make a sizeable difference to their retirement income.

Redistribution

The misalignment of costs and commission charges also produces significant redistribution across participants. The current practices of pension fund managers load commission charges on regular contributors to individual retirement accounts. The regular contributors are effectively subsidising the large majority of the other services provided by the AFPs. This is likely to make voluntary and severance saving accounts, but especially phased withdrawal pensions, cheaper than they actually are. For active contributors to individual retirement accounts who do not have a saving accounts as well, this practice will lower, other things being equal, their future pension benefit.

A simple simulation can illustrate the impact on commission levels of the redistribution implicit in the current cost allocation under the new pension scheme. Table 3.7 below shows annual operational costs under different charging structures. The exercise takes as a benchmark the current situation, where all operational costs are recovered on active contributors. Altering the charging structure distributes the operational costs differently. It is assumed that these alternative ways of allocating operational costs leave AFPs' profits unaffected, and the costs of transfers are not taken into account.

If the operational costs were to be charged to all affiliates, the annual operational cost on active contributors would be 44 percent lower. This is because of the large number of affiliates who are not active contributors, and are not at present charged for the management of their accounts. If operational costs were recovered across active contributors to all types of accounts, that is retirement, voluntary saving, and severance saving accounts, the operational costs for a contributor with only a retirement saving account would be 31 percent lower. If operational costs were recovered on holder of all types of accounts, irrespective of whether they are active and inactive, the operational costs for a contributor with only a retirement account would be 55 percent lower. This simulation shows clearly the significant impact that alternative ways of allocating operational costs would have on pension benefits. If the costs reductions arising from a wider allocation of costs were used in full to reduce the additional contribution, this could be as much as one third lower.

The current structure of commission charges also redistributes across active contributors. Fixed commissions are deducted from the contributor's retirement account, and have, therefore, a greater impact upon low paid workers than among highly paid workers. Commissions charged as a proportion of earnings, on the other hand, extract higher charges from higher paid workers.

Table 3.7
Redistributive impact of alternative allocations of operational costs

Alternative allocation of annual operational costs	Annual costs per head Chile $ (1995)	Change from benchmark (%)	Additional contribution[e]
Costs allocated equally to contributors (benchmark)[a]	48,288		3.0
Costs allocated equally to active affiliates[b]	26,880	- 44.3	2.1
Costs allocated equally to all active account holders[c]	33,139	- 31.3	2.4
Costs allocated equally to all account holders[d]	21,427	- 55.6	2.0

Source: own calculations from data in Superintendencia de Administradoras de Fondos de Pensiones (1996a, 1996b). All data used are from 1995.
[a] Active contributors to retirement accounts who made contributions in December 1995.
[b] All those with a retirement account who are not retired.
[c] Includes active contributors to retirement accounts plus the number of voluntary and severance saving accounts.
[d] Includes active affiliates plus the number of voluntary and severance saving accounts, plus the number of phased withdrawal pensions.
[e] This is the additional contribution to be paid by a contributor with only a retirement account on the assumption that any cost reductions are used to reduce the additional contribution.

The extent and direction of the implicit redistribution depends on the way in which costs are generated. As noted above, some services provided by the AFPs generate costs per account. These include the costs of record keeping and information provision. Other services generate costs as a factor of financial flows, such as the investment management of the pension fund and reserves. It is very likely that for the Chilean pension scheme, at present, the former are more important than the latter. This would suggest that a mixture of fixed and variable commissions might be helpful in bringing commissions in line with costs. Of these, fixed commissions will need to recover a larger portion of the operational costs than variable commissions. The latter would need to be related to the size of the pension fund, or of contributions, rather than the earnings of the participants. Variable commissions would also need to be charged to all participants with a share in the pension fund.

The analysis suggests that redistribution from high earners to low earners is quantitatively more significant, especially as fewer pension fund managers now charge fixed commissions, a change which has been welcomed by those concerned with increasing the access of low paid workers to the pension scheme.

The new pension fund management market in Latin America

As with the case of Chile, the new individual capitalization pension schemes introduced in Latin America will create new pension fund management markets. The commonality in pension design features suggests that these markets are likely to be similar across the seven Latin American countries under examination. A regulator authorizes private or social organizations to set up corporations with the exclusive purpose of providing pension fund management services. The pension fund managers concentrate almost exclusively on handling retirement and voluntary saving accounts, managing a pension fund, and calculating and paying pension benefits. The pension fund managers need to compete for affiliates. The investment portfolio of the pension funds is subject to strict prudential regulation regarding assets, risk classification, and the custody of titles. Most countries have also introduced minimum rate of return regulations to guarantee minimum performance for affiliates, and have regulated information disclosure to affiliates and the regulator. The main features of the pension fund management market in the countries under examination are presented in Table 3.8 below. A discussion of the main points follows.

As can be noted from the details in the Table, and from the discussion of Chile's experience, the performance of the individual capitalization pension schemes relies on a detailed and far reaching regulatory framework, and on market competition among pension fund managers.

To enter the market, pension fund managers must satisfy the regulators on a minimum capital. This capital is provided for by shareholders in the case of private corporations, or by social organizations where these are permitted. With the exception of Mexico and Costa Rica, pension fund managers can only operate a single pension fund for all their affiliates. In the initial stages, the requirement of one fund per manager aims to ensure affiliates are treated equally, and also to homogenize pension services so as to enhance competitive forces. As the new pension schemes develop, the need arises to provide greater choice for affiliates, and allowing pension fund managers to operate more than one fund may be the answer.

Table 3.8
Main features of pension fund management in individual capitalization pension schemes in Latin America

Country	Chile	Peru	Argentina	Colombia	Mexico	Uruguay	Costa Rica
Title	Sistema de Pensiones de Capitalización Individual	Sistema Privado de Administración de Fondos de Pensiones	Régimen de Capitalización Individual	Régimen de Ahorro Individual con Solidaridad	Régimen de Ahorro Individual	Régimen de Jubilación por Ahorro Individual Obligatorio	Régimen Privado de Pensiones Complementarias
date law	DL 3500 (4/11/80)	DL 25897 (12/1992)	Ley 24241 (1/09/1993)	Ley 100 (1/12/1993)	Ley Seguro Social (12/95)	Ley 16713 (3/9/95)	Ley 7523 (8/1995)
date start	01/05/81	06/93 relaunched 7/95	15/07/94	01/04/94	01/07/97	01/04/96	
regulatory body	Superintendencia de Administradoras de Fondos de Pensiones (SAFP); funded by AFPs	Superintendencia de Administradoras Privadas de Fondos de Pensiones (SAPFP); funded by AFPs	Superintendencia de Administradoras de Fondos de Jubilaciones y Pensiones (SAFJP); funded by AFJPs	Superintendencia Bancaria, funded by AFPs	Comisión Nacional de Ahorro para el Retiro (CONSAR); funded by AFOREs	Banco Central	Superintendencia de Pensiones; funded 80% by Central Bank and 20% by OPCs
pension fund managers	AFPs (Administradoras de Fondos de Pensiones)	AFPs (Administradoras de Fondos de Pensiones)	AFJPs (Administradoras de Fondos de Jubilaciones y Pensiones)	AFPs (Administradoras de Fondos de Pensiones)	AFORES (Administradoras de Fondos de Retiro); can run several funds SIEFOREs	AFAPs (Administradoras de Fondos de Ahorro Previsional)	OPCs, (Operadoras de Planes de Pensiones Complementarias)
public fund manager	no	no	yes	authorized	no	yes	no

Table 3.8 Continued

	Chile	Peru	Argentina	Colombia	Mexico	Uruguay	Costa Rica
pension fund managers (date)	13 AFPs (8.97)	5 AFPs (12.97)	18 AFJPs (10.97)	9 AFPs	market share of AFORE limited to 17%; raised to 20% by 2001	6 AFAPs (10.96)	
minimum capital and reserves (% of fund)	minimum capital rising with affiliates plus a 1% reserve plus fluctuations fund	minimum capital (US$207,000) plus fluctuations fund	minimum capital (US$3m) plus reserve fund (US$3m or 2% is greatest) plus fluctuations fund	minimum capital	minimum capital plus reserve (M$25m or 1% whichever the greatest)	minimum capital plus reserves not less than 2% of fund plus fluctuations fund of 2% of fund	minimum capital at least 1/4 of bank's minimum capital requirement
permitted products	retirement, voluntary, and severance accounts; plus pension benefits	retirement accounts, disability and survivor insurance	retirement accounts, voluntary saving and pension benefits	fund management and pension benefits; Fondos Voluntarios de Pensiones	retirement and voluntary accounts; fund management	retirement fund management only	retirement fund, can run more than one
permitted commission	fixed and % on contributory earnings; transfers; saving and severance accounts and pension benefits	since 1997 % of contributions only, and fixed amount on transfers set by SAPFP	fixed and % on contributory earnings; permanence discount; fixed and % on volunt. contributions; pension benefits	up to 3.5% of base salary	fixed and % of contributions and of fund balance	% of contributions; permanence discounts	% of returns up to 10% of returns; if early withdrawal up to 6% of withdrawn fund
investment regulation	upper limits by asset, issuer, and issue; insider trading; risk classification; custody of titles	upper limits by asset and issuer; risk classification; custody of titles	upper limits by asset and issuer; risk classification; custody of titles	upper limits by assets; risk classification	approved and diversified assets; foreign only if Mexican issuers; one SIEFORE in fixed interest	upper limits by asset and issuer; no foreign investment; risk classification; custody of titles	upper limits by asset; no foreign asset investment for first five years

Table 3.8 Continued

	Chile	Peru	Argentina	Colombia	Mexico	Uruguay	Costa Rica
rate of return regulation (average is weighted average returns of funds)	minimum rate of return: monthly calculation of last 12 months; (a) lowest of average minus 2% or (b) 50% of average	minimum rate of return: calculated monthly on last 12 months; lowest of (a) average minus 2% or (b) 50% of average	minimum rate of return: lowest of 70% of average or average minus 2%; in nominal terms	minimum rate of return: average adjusted by return in capital market and return of reference portfolio (last 36 months)	no	minimum rate of return: calculated monthly for last 12 months; lowest of (a) 2%; or (b) average minus 2%;	minimum rate of return: lower limit of average adjusted by risk (standard deviation)
rate of return fluctuations fund (RFF)	if rates of return higher than upper limit (greatest of 150% of average or average plus 2 %); invested in fund	0.7% of fund plus additions related to implicit risk of investment assets	if returns higher than 130% of average, or average plus 2%, whichever is the lowest; invested in fund	1% of fund	no	minimum 2% of fund; inflows if returns are higher than average plus 2 %; if RFF >3% transfer to accounts	0.5% of fund returns up to 2% of fund; and 5% of returns of OPCs
information disclosure regulations	to affiliates every four months; marketing and advertising; to SAFP on financial transact.	to affiliates; to SAFPP on financial transactions	to contributors every 4 months; to SAFJP on financial transactions	to affiliates	marketing, advertising and information flows to affiliates	to affiliates every 6 months	
government guarantees	minimum rates of return, minimum pension, annuity pension benefits	legislation includes guaranteed minimum pension but has not been implemented	minimum rate of return; annuity pension benefits; other pension benefits	minimum pension; pensions in payment; pension funds guarantee; no guarantee of rates of return	minimum guaranteed pension is 1MW at the time of the reform, then indexed by consumer prices	apply to public owned AFAPs only: minimum rate of return and pension benefits	no

110

Table 3.8 Continued

	Chile	Peru	Argentina	Colombia	Mexico	Uruguay	Costa Rica
						Banco de Previsión Social	
contribution collection	by AFPs, smaller AFPs can delegate on larger ones	by AFPs or delegated to banks	*Dirección General Impositiva*, then *Administración de la Seguridad Social* (ANSeS), then to AFJPs	by AFPs	IMSS collects contrib., then to Central Bank, then to AFOREs; centralised record keeping by CONSAR		by OPCs
transfers across pension fund managers	anytime, but restricted to three times a year due to administrative process	after 6 monthly consecutive contributions	after 4 monthly contributions, only 2 times a year		once a year; or if funds change commission or investment structure	after 6 months contributions; in person at AFAP office	after 6 months affiliation
tax treatment	contributions and returns are tax exempt		compulsory and voluntary contributions, and returns, are tax exempt	contributions and returns are tax exempt; pensions taxed if >25MW or lump sum		contributions are tax deductible up to 20% of earnings; pension fund returns are tax exempt	contributions up to 100% of pre-tax monthly earnings and returns are tax exempt
impact on insurance market	disability and survivor reinsurance and annuity pensions	AFPs cover disability or survivor insurance	disability and survivor reinsurance and pension annuities	disability and survivor reinsurance and pension annuity	pension annuity; IMSS covers disability and survivor insurance	disability and survivor reinsurance and pension annuity	voluntary insurance and pension annuity offered by OPCs

Compiled from several sources (Asociación de Organismos de Supervisión de Fondos de Pensiones, 1997; Asociación Gremial de AFPs, 1996; Bertin and Perrotto, 1997; CIEDESS, 1995; Sales, Solis and Villagómez, 1996; Superintendencia de Administradoras de Fondos de Jubilaciones y Pensiones, 1996).

In Chile, for example, there are proposals to allow pension fund managers to run two funds, one which concentrates on fixed term investment, and therefore suits workers closer to retirement; and another with a higher risk-return profile, for workers who have some time to go before retirement.

Most of the countries under examination have restricted the services pension managers are permitted to offer to the management of retirement accounts. This restriction ensures that providers are specialists. It also protects existing financial providers such as banks, from competition. A problem with this is that the full exploitation of possible economies of scope in the provision of financial services is also restricted (Shah, 1997). The Chilean experience shows, as discussed above, that there are economies of scope, and gains from product innovation, to be exploited as the pension market develops.

Pension fund managers' own capital is kept separate from the pension fund, which belongs to the affiliates. In most countries pension fund managers must have a reserve fund, usually a proportion of the total fund, and a rate of return fluctuations fund. These are used to supplement the pension fund wherever its performance falls below the minimum acceptable level.

As regards commissions, the general situation is that the incidence of commissions is closely regulated, but their level is left for the providers to decide. There is also a common requirement that commissions charged are the same for all affiliates, which is intended to restrict discriminatory practices by providers. In Argentina and Uruguay the regulations allow for lower commissions to be charged to affiliates with longer permanence. Similar proposals are under discussion in Chile as a means of reducing transfers. But the same discounts must be offered to all affiliates in the same situation.

Permitted commissions are a fixed amount, and/or variable as a proportion of contributions. The variable charges vary in their incidence across the countries under study. In Chile and Argentina, variable commissions are charged as a proportion of contributory earnings. In Colombia these are calculated as a fixed proportion of base salary. In Peru, Mexico, and Colombia commissions are calculated as a proportion of contributions paid. In Costa Rica commissions are charged as a proportion of returns.

Neither of these commission structures is optimal, since they are unlikely to reflect the cost structure of the services provided. As noted earlier, studies of costs in the finance and insurance sectors show that these decline quite significantly in fund size. There are fixed costs attached to the handling and investment of retirement accounts that would best be recovered through a fixed commission on fund balances. Fixed charges affect workers with low earnings or inactive contributors more strongly. This led Peru to abandon fixed charges as from 1997. Earnings related commissions introduce cross subsidies from high to low earners, and from inactive contributors to active contributors, and ceteris paribus weaken incentives for cost reductions by pension fund managers. Whether commissions are discounted from the pension fund, or from the contributions paid, will have different effects upon inactive contributors.

Regulations aimed at protecting affiliates include minimum rate of return and minimum pension benefit guarantees. With the exception of Mexico, all other countries have a minimum rate of return guarantee in place. These ensure that the performance of individual pension fund managers does not fall below a minimum level. In Argentina the minimum rate of return is calculated in nominal terms, while most other countries do so in real terms. The minimum level is in most cases defined by reference to the weighted average of rates of return in the previous 12 months. Exceptions to this are Colombia which has a more sophisticated minimum rate of return definition taking into account capital market returns, and Costa Rica which has a minimum rate of return including some adjustment for risk. It is also noteworthy that the period of time used in the calculation of the minimum rate of return is very short, twelve months for all except for Colombia at 36 months. The guarantee operates by requiring that pension fund managers operate a fluctuation reserve that is used to supplement the pension fund where performance falls below the minimum. In most cases, where this fluctuation reserve fund is not sufficient, normal reserves are used. And if these prove insufficient, government guarantees take their place, the pension fund provider is liquidated, and the affiliates moved to a different provider.

Investment portfolio regulations have the objective of protecting the pension funds from risky investments by enforcing some minimum diversification. They also have the objective of facilitating government debt management and other objectives. If the experience of Chile is replicated in other countries, these regulations will be gradually relaxed reflecting the development of the capital markets. There are also regulations requiring that pension funds are invested in assets which have a risk classification and are traded in secondary markets. Other portfolio regulations include rules to prevent insider trading, to secure custody of titles, and to ensure transparency in the reporting of financial transactions.

The pension fund managers compete for business by offering higher returns, lower commissions, and better service. Affiliates must assess the advantages of different providers and transfer to the one offering the best deal. In theory, competition will ensure that efficient providers will grow at the expense of the inefficient ones, and that affiliates secure a good return on their contributions. Regulations are therefore aimed at homogenizing products, procedures, and information disclosure as far as possible. Most countries have introduced regulations detailing the minimum levels and format of information flows to affiliates.

Allowing affiliates to transfer from one pension fund manager to another is a key feature of the new pension schemes in Latin America, and an essential factor in encouraging market competition. While transfers are an integral factor in enhancing competitive forces, they are also very costly to administer. In the initial stages of the new individual capitalization pension scheme, pension fund providers aim their marketing efforts at affiliates to the old pension scheme and to new entrants to the labour market. Later on, growth in market share is dependent on attracting contributors from other pension fund managers. Transfers may be a consequence of marketing and sales strategies by pension fund managers, and may not therefore reflect optimizing behaviour on the part of affiliates. Controlling transfers through minimum stay periods, or through entry and/or exit fees, is an effective means of reducing these costs.

Other regulations are aimed at controlling and reducing the *sui generis* administrative and marketing costs arising form the individual capitalization pension scheme. Argentina, Mexico, and Uruguay, have introduced central collection of contributions, and a central body can perform this function least costly. In the context of Latin American labour markets, the enforcement of compulsory pension scheme affiliation and contribution can be done more effectively by a government body with access to employer databases. Mexico has gone further in locating record keeping with the same body.

It is likely that individual capitalization pension plans will make a significant contribution to the development of the life insurance market in these countries. In most cases the private insurance market will handle the provision of annuity pensions, and reinsure the disability and survivor risks covered by the pension fund managers. Mexico, however, has opted for concentrating disability and survivor insurance within the *Instituto Mexicano de Seguro Social*.

The success in the establishment of the pension fund management market is essential to the future of pension reform in Latin America. In the next section the pension fund management markets in Chile, Argentina and Peru will be examined with a view to assessing their likely development and performance.

The evolution of the pension fund management market in Chile, Argentina and Peru

This section attempts a comparison of the development of the pension fund management market in Chile with those in Argentina and Peru. This will help clarify to what extent the trends and issues identified with the Chilean experience are common to other individual capitalization pension schemes.

The new pension fund management market began in Peru in June 1993, while in Argentina the start date was July 1994. This is a very short time span to evaluate their evolution and performance. Nonetheless, some useful points emerge from this comparison.

Pension fund growth and operational efficiency

As was the case in Chile, the initial period after the establishment of the pension fund management market is dominated by fast growth. This is because workers switching from the old pension scheme provide a rapid boost to the number of affiliations. In Chile, the number of individuals affiliated to the new pension scheme grew from 1.4 million in December of 1981 to 2.28 million in December 1985, after which the rates of growth in the numbers of affiliates begins to slow down. In Peru there were 0.62 million affiliates in December 1993, rising to 1.1 million by December 1995. In Argentina, the new pension scheme began with 2.2 million affiliates in August 1994 doubling to 5.4 million in December 1996. This suggests that initial efforts by pension fund managers to capture market share are very important to their future prospects.[32]

The pension funds also grew very fast. As shown in Table 3.9 below, pension fund value as a proportion of GDP rose in Chile to 5 percent in the first two years, and to 1.1 and 1.5 in Argentina and Peru respectively. Naturally, growth in the pension fund will be slower for Argentina given a lower rate of retirement account contribution. Another factor is the slower growth in affiliation of the labour force in both Argentina and Peru than in Chile.

In terms of the balance sheet of the pension fund managers, the initial period after the start of the new pension scheme is dominated by the large set up costs involved. These are associated with the initial investment in capital equipment, marketing and personnel, but especially by the large initial expenditures in promotional and sales personnel required to secure market share. It is not surprising that the pension fund managers' accounts show significant operational deficits in the first two years of the new scheme. This is shown in Table 3.9 below by the ratio of returns to asset, and operational surpluses to assets. In the case of Peru, only in 1996 did some of its AFPs begin to generate positive returns. Perhaps as a result of the Chilean experience, the initial growth rate in affiliates was overestimated in Argentina and Peru, resulting in temporary overcapacity. As a result, further capital injections, and some reduction in branches and personnel, took place in the first two years. In Peru these reductions were fairly drastic (Barúa, 1995). This also helps explain the reduction in the number of pension fund managers in these two countries observed in the initial period.

Table 3.9
Indicators of pension funds growth, and of pension providers costs, returns and efficiency

	Chile				Argentina			Peru	
	1982	1983	1994	1995	94/95	95/96	96/97	1995	1996
Pension Fund/GDP (%)	3.2	5.8	40.9	40.0	0.4	1.1	2.2	0.7	1.4
Returns/Net Assets[a] (%)	-141.8	-11.6	15.8	18.7	-49.1	-2.7	8.9	-58.2	-16.3
Operational Surplus/Net Assets[a] (%)	-69.3	-75.0	25.8	26.8	-36.6	17.1	22.6	-54.5	-13.2
Operational Costs/Pension fund (%)	12.1	5.8	1.81	1.74	45.5	27.1	17.5	12.9	5.9
Operational Costs/Affiliates (US$)	77.8	60.1	86.3	83.2	115.5	135.4	175.9	63.7	35.5
Commissions/Operational Income (%)	86.2	86	87.3	90.3	98.1	98.3	97.4	96.2	96.1
Personnel Costs/Pension Fund (%)	3.0	1.7	0.41	0.38	17.2	10.6	7.7		
Personnel Costs/Operational Costs(%)	25.1	29.2	22.6	21.5	38.0	39.3	43.8		
					1994	1995	1996	1993	1995
Commissions/Mean covered earnings[b]	5.1[c]	8.2[c]	2.27	2.36	1.6	2.6	2.6	0.7	1.9

a. Net Assets are Assets net of deferred costs.
b. This is a measure of the costs to participants of the services provided by the pension fund managers. For Chile and Argentina, Pension Costs is a measure, for an individual retirement account, of all commissions and charges net of disability and survivor insurance premiums. This is a weighted measure of commission and charges across pension fund managers. For Peru, the value shows the variable commission only. A fixed commission was charged until 1997.
c. for these years only a gross measure of pension costs is available, which includes insurance premiums.

Source: (Superintendencia de Administradoras de Fondos de Jubilaciones y Pensiones, 1996; Superintendencia de Administradoras de Fondos de Jubilaciones y Pensiones, 1997).

The rapid rise in both the number of affiliates and the pension fund help to improve efficiency in the operation of pension fund managers. A range of indicators included in Table 3.9 shows this. Operational costs fall as a proportion of operational income, and also as a proportion of the pension fund. These indicate the pension fund managers were able to achieve an efficient level of operation very soon after the start of the pension schemes, and may also indicate the existence of significant economies of scale

Commissions and costs

Commissions provide by far the main source of income of the pension fund managers. In all three countries marketing costs are high and account for an increasing share of operational costs. Expenditure on marketing and on sales personnel account for around one half of total expenditure, followed by administration and computing costs. In Peru marketing costs accounted for over 50 percent of total costs in June 1996. Clearly the marketing costs associated with the individual capitalization pension scheme are high, and point to one of the key weaknesses of the new pension schemes. It can be observed that operational costs per affiliate showed a declining trend in Chile in the first two years of the new scheme, but a rising trend in the 1990s. These costs also show a rising trend in Argentina, although a declining one in Peru. The share of personnel costs in total costs is more or less stable in Peru, but rising in Argentina. In all three countries, sales personnel costs show a tendency to rise, with the costs attached to administrative personnel rising more slowly if at all.

Commission income per contributor has increased in all three countries, ensuring high returns for the pension fund managers. A measure of pension costs net of disability and survivor insurance premiums shows a rising trend in all three countries. This may not be immediately apparent to pension scheme contributors. Insurance premiums are high at the start of the new pension scheme, but show a tendency to fall later on. This is due to a more accurate estimation of risk probabilities, and the fact that, as individual retirement accounts build up, the covered liabilities fall. With the costs of this insurance cover falling, there should be room for reducing the charges and commissions to pension scheme participants.[33] Yet pension fund managers have on the whole retained these, or even increased them as in Peru. As a result, commission income per contributor has risen strongly.

Pension fund managers, market entry and concentration

The number of providers at the start of the new pension scheme was 12 in Chile, 25 in Argentina and 8 in Peru. There is some considerable variation in the number of pension fund managers since 1981 in Chile. During the

1980s the number of AFPs fluctuated between 12 and 14, then rose to 22 in 1994, and declined to 13 in August 1997. As discussed above, in large part the rise in the number of market providers in the early 1990s was a consequence of regulatory changes relaxing entry restrictions. In Peru, the number of providers began at five, but immediately rose to eight, only to decline later to 5 again. In Argentina, there has been a process of mergers that has reduced the number of providers to 18 by December 1997. This seems to indicate that while entry into the pension fund management markets is not difficult, retaining market share is much harder.

Table 3.10
Indicators of market concentration for Chile, Peru and Argentina

Chile	1982	1986	1993	1994	1995	1996	1997
Number of AFPs	12	12	18	19	16	13	13
HH[a] contributors	18.4	17.3	18.2	18.1	18.4	18.4	18.7
HH pension fund	19.4	17.9	13.0	12.5	13.1	13.4	13.7
Peru							
Number of AFPs				8	6	6	[b]6	5
HH contributors				20.3	19.6	19.6	[b]19.5	20.5
HH pension fund				20.5	21.5	21.5	[b]21.2	22.2
Argentina							
Number of AFJPs					25	24	22	18
HH contributors					8.8	9.4	10.3	9.4
HH pension fund					8.9	9.6	10.4	12.0

a. The Herfindahl-Hirschman index is the sum of the square of the pension fund managers' market share, measured by number of active contributors, and by size of pension fund. It is reported as a percentage. Data refer to December of each year.
b. May 1996.
Source: (Superintendencia de Administradoras de Fondos de Jubilaciones y Pensiones, 1996; Superintendencia de Administradoras de Fondos de Jubilaciones y Pensiones, 1997; Superintendencia de Administradoras de Fondos de Pensiones, 1996a; Superintendencia de Administradoras de Fondos de Pensiones, several issues; Webb and Fernández, 1995).

Despite the variation in the number of providers, measures of concentration have remained more or less stable in Argentina, and have declined only marginally in Chile and Peru. The Herfindahl-Hirschman measure of concentration is shown for the countries concerned in Table 3.10 above. The levels of concentration in the pension fund management market are high and highlight the existence of significant economies of scale. As in Chile, some smaller pension fund managers have succeeded in Argentina in pursuing a market segmentation strategy in focusing on high earning workers (Bertín, 1997).

Investment portfolios, and rates of return

The investment portfolios of the pension fund managers across the three countries involved have focused strongly on government debt. In Chile this was due to the fact that equity investment by the pension funds was not permitted until 1985, and in Argentina it was a consequence of the 1994 'tequila effect' from the Mexican crisis. These restrictions also help facilitate government debt management. Equity investment picked up in Chile after 1985 and also in Argentina after 1995. Some modernization of capital markets is needed for them to absorb pension fund investment, and as Chile's experience shows, this takes some time to materialise.

The rates of return secured by the pension funds across the three countries have been high, as shown in Table 3.11 below. This is a very short period of time for proper evaluation of these. Two important points need to be taken into account. The rapid growth of the pension funds raises demand for a restricted number of financial instruments, and is likely to have some price effects. And secondly, that there is significant variance in rates of return across the range of pension fund managers within the countries under examination.

In sum, the evolution of the new pension fund management markets in Argentina and Peru share many similarities with the early development of the new Chilean pension scheme. This results from all three countries having similar design features as regards their pension fund management. On the positive side, the pension fund managers can rely on a fast growth in affiliates and funds, and can approach relatively effective levels of operation within a short period of time. After two years in Chile and Argentina, and three in Peru, pension fund managers were in a position to secure positive returns. This greatly facilitates entry to the market. There is a high level of concentration in the pension fund market across the countries examined. At the same time there is evidence that market strategies aimed at securing high earning affiliates were successfully pursued by some of the smaller pension fund managers.

Table 3.11
Real annual rates of return in Chile, Peru and Argentina
(December of each year)

Chile	1982	1986	1993	1994	1995	1996	1997
Mean	28.8	12.3	16.2	18.2	-2.5	3.5	8.1
Maximum	16.5	15.5	17.0	21.1	-1.8	4.1	8.8
Minimum	5.3	10.6	14.6	15.7	-4.6	2.9	7.4
Peru							
Mean			ᵃ11.7	8.5	5.5	5.8	11.1
Maximum			ᵃ14.0	10.6	6.0	7.4	11.8
Minimum			ᵃ9.8	7.4	5.3	4.6	10.5
Argentina							
Mean				ᵇ13.1	19.7	19.8	14.7
Maximum				ᵇ17.0	25.6	25.7	19.2
Minimum				ᵇ9.1	13.8	13.8	10.3

a. Year to August 1994.
b. Year to July 1994.
Source: (Superintendencia de Administradoras de Fondos de Jubilaciones y Pensiones, 1996; Superintendencia de Administradoras de Fondos de Jubilaciones y Pensiones, 1997; Superintendencia de Administradoras de Fondos de Pensiones, 1996a; Superintendencia de Administradoras de Fondos de Pensiones, several issues; Webb and Fernández, 1995).

On the less positive side, it is clear that the individual capitalization design of the pension schemes absorbs a great deal of resources. The costs to participants of the new pension scheme are fairly high and, more worryingly, show a rising trend. The costs of marketing and sales personnel account for a large proportion of total costs, at over 50 percent. Moreover, the indications are that in the new pension scheme there are no strong incentives operating to reduce costs, and to pass cost reductions on to affiliates. The influence of competitive forces is muted, and if anything operates to increase costs through sales and marketing expenditure.

Conclusion

This chapter has examined the pension fund management market in Chile, and in the other Latin American countries in some detail. The centrality of the pension fund management market to the success of the new pension schemes in the region justifies this. A private pension fund management market will be created anew by the reforms. It will have a significant impact upon the financial sector in these countries, and through them it will influence future economic growth. At the same time, the future income of the retired population will depend on whether the new pension fund managers become effective pension fund managers.

The twin forces of competition and regulation will determine the evolution of the new pension fund managers in Latin America. The reforms establish pension fund managers, which will compete for affiliates. The provision of standard pension products, and the exercise of choice of manager by affiliates, is expected to encourage market competition. At the same time, the designers of the new pension schemes were aware of the possibility of market failure in the provision of financial products. Government, although withdrawing from a direct role in pension provision, still retains a function as a provider of last resort. Supervision and regulation are in place to ensure that the risks taken by the pension fund managers, and the returns they secure for affiliates, have acceptable variance.

Chile was the first of the Latin American countries to implement pension reform, and has the longest experience with the new pension fund management market. A close examination of the evolution of this market in Chile yields both positive as well as negative expectations of the future course of pension reform in Latin America. Chile did manage to establish a pension fund management market from scratch. The new pension fund managers operate in a well regulated environment, and have secured more than adequate rates of return for their affiliates. The pension fund managers have developed structures that are sound and have performed reasonably successfully under different circumstances, and they have also introduced product innovations giving workers access to financial services.

At the same time, a number of negative features have emerged that point to weaknesses in the design of the new pension schemes. Pension fund managers have high costs, both in comparison to others countries, and over time. There are large marketing costs associated with the operation of the new schemes that may reduce, to a significant extent, the welfare of future pensioners. Affiliates appear to be relatively insensitive to the key parameters affecting their retirement saving, suggesting that competition is weak in the private pension fund market. More importantly, the pattern of incentives facing pension fund managers is such that these have not succeeded in cutting costs, nor in passing lower insurance costs on to affiliates.

These trends are not peculiar to Chile, as comparison with trends in Argentina and Peru shows. Although at the very early stages of their evolution, pension fund managers in these countries also exhibited large and rising costs, as well as market concentration and segmentation. Despite some efforts by pension designers and regulators in Peru and Argentina to avoid some of the problems observed in the Chilean pension reform, it is clear that many of these are structural, and that possible solutions are finely balanced.

A reasonable conclusion from extensive examination of the new pension fund management markets in Latin America is that these, in common with financial markets, can only be expected to work imperfectly. The effectiveness of the supervision and regulation of these markets will provide the key to the future course, and success, of the new pension schemes in Latin America.

Notes

1. There are a number of good sources on the private pension fund management market (Baeza and Margozzini, 1995; Diamond and Valdés-Prieto, 1994; Iglesias and Acuña, 1991; Superintendencia de Administradoras de Fondos de Pensiones, 1996a).
2. There is a proposal currently being discussed to allow AFPs to create a second pension fund to be invested in fixed interest instruments which could be safer for affiliates near retirement.
3. The *Unidad de Fomento* or UF is an inflation adjusted unit of account introduced by the government during the high inflation period of the late 1970s. Its value is set, and published, daily by the Chilean Central Bank. It has become the main denomination unit for inflation proof contracts. Life annuity contracts, for example, are set in UFs. Once in operation, the minimum capital requirement rises with the number of affiliates to UF 10,000 for 5,000 to 7,499 affiliates; UF 15,000 for 7,500 to 9,999 affiliates; and UF 20,000 for AFPs with 10,000 or more affiliates.
4. This reserve, or *encaje*, was initially 5 percent of the pension fund. It plays a role in stabilizing the rates of return of the pension funds. See below.
5. A disaggregated analysis of pension fund managers follows in the next section, and a discussion of issues of competition and concentration will be found in the section that follows.
6. Where an account has not registered any changes in the last year, information on the balance of the account is required to be sent annually.
7. It must include information on the rate of return applying to the individual retirement accounts at five different levels of earnings, and of the rate of return applying to the pension fund unit, for the last 12 and 36 months. These rates of return must be calculated using a standard formula.
8. Before 1 January 1994, withdrawals were in theory subject to wealth tax. In practice this seldom applied given the high thresholds of this tax. Currently capital gains tax applies only to withdrawals equivalent to capital gains of more than 30 UTM (*Unidad Tributaria Mensual*, inflation adjusted units of account used for tax purposes), providing account holders receive income solely from labour earnings or from profits of microenterprises.

9   One of the objectives behind the introduction of severance saving accounts was to attract non-affiliated workers into the pension scheme.
10 For this purposes contributory earnings have a ceiling of 90 UF.
11 Pension benefits provided by the new pension scheme are discussed in chapter 6 below.
12 In February 1997, seven out of thirteen AFPs did not charge fixed commissions on deposits.
13 In February 1997 only one AFP, Planvital, charged a fixed commission for withdrawals under the phased withdrawal and deferred life annuity retirement pensions.
14 The form is called F.E.C.U. (*Ficha Estadística Codificada Uniforme*).
15 The rates of return regulations have been criticized on two counts. Firstly, because they are defined in relative terms, they enforce a 'herd like' behavior among pension fund managers. Secondly, because they are focused on 12 months periods, they encourage short rather than long term horizons in investment decisions. Proposals for reform currently in Parliament would extend the calculation period of these regulations from 12 to 36 months.
16 Valck and Walker show that for the five year period 1990 to 1994, equity holdings by AFPs averaged 23 percent of their combined investment portfolios, but contributed close to 60 percent of the returns (1995).
17 In the event pension funds exceed their investment limits due to asset price changes, they are not forced to sell these assets.
18 See Superintendencia de Administradoras de Fondos de Pensiones (1996c).
19 These issues will be explored in more detail in chapter 4 below.
20 In 1983 the required reserves were lowered from 5 percent of the pension fund to 1 percent, and in 1987 the minimum starting capital was reduced from 20,000 UF to 5,000 UF.
21 For the market as a whole nearly 95 percent of commission income came from this source in 1995.
22 Pablo (1991) finds that profit rates in the private pension market are higher than in comparable financial sectors. In 1992, for example, profit rates were 26.4 percent for the AFPs as a whole, while only 20 percent for banks (1991).
23 See Valdés-Prieto (1992) for a discussion of the complexity of the information required, and Diamond (1993) for a more general discussion of market failure in the context of insurance markets.
24 Individual affiliates had to notify the transfer request to their AFP and their employer 30 days in advance. Until recently, individual affiliates had a folder which provided a record of their contributions and which needed to be checked and physically transferred from one AFP to another. The plan AFP2000 aims to introduce microfiche record keeping and electronic transfers across AFPs, and since 1995 exchanges of information relating to transfers are made electronically.
25 In November 1997 a new regulation was introduced by the regulator requiring the presentation of the last account balance, and of copy of identity cards for transfer applications. This led to violent demonstrations and a hunger strike by AFPs sales personnel. Representatives of sales personnel

claimed that this measure could result in 25 thousand redundancies (La Epoca 14 November 1997).
26 Valdés-Prieto (1995) reports that sales personnel received a bonus of 12 percent of the monthly income of the transferee.
27 The Herfindahl-Hirschman index is calculated by summing the squares of the market shares of all firms in the market. Values for the index range from zero to one, the latter indicating full concentration. The inverse of the computed value for the index shows the number of equal sized firms which would have generated the same index value (Ferguson and Ferguson, 1994). For the active contributor concentration measure in 1997, this value could have been generated by 5.3 equal sized firms.
28 Strictly, these are economies of size rather than economies of scale. In financial institutions size differences normally involve more than a simple scale factor, and include output, as well as input, efficiency gains (Berger, Hunter and Timme, 1993; Lewis and Davis, 1987).
29 These include defined benefit and defined contribution pension plans.
30 This was confirmed by econometric evidence in Walker (1993a; 1993b).
31 Shah (1997) in a recent paper has examined the regulation on pension funds in Chile and Peru and finds that regulation has had adverse effects upon competition and efficiency. The paper suggests changes to the existing regulatory framework to enhance the freedom of pension fund managers to invest their assets, and to encourage competition from other financial intermediaries.
32 A study for Argentina confirms the findings for Chile reported above to the effect that sales personnel and marketing expenditure are the main determinants of transfers (Grushka and de Biase, 1997).
33 In Argentina, the commissions are deducted from the pension scheme contributions, and the remainder is capitalized. Rofman (1997) simulates the impact on capitalization of the reductions in the disability and survivor insurance premiums in the period July 1994 to December 1995 being passed on in full to affiliates. He estimates that fall in insurance premiums would have reduced commissions from 3.5 percent of earnings to 2.2 percent. The residual contribution rate left for capitalization would have risen from 7.5 percent of earnings to 8.8 percent.

4 Pension reform, saving and capital markets

One of the key objectives of pension reform in Latin America is to raise savings and improve the operation of capital markets. The expectation that pension reform could meet these objectives is founded on the view that social insurance had detrimental effects on saving, and that the new individual capitalization pension schemes would not only eliminate these, but also enhance saving incentives.

The growing financial deficits of pay as you go pension schemes in Latin America led to high contribution rates, and low or negative rates of return on contributions. These may have contributed to low saving rates. The replacement of an unfunded pension scheme with individual capitalization pension plans was expected by the proponents of the reform to have positive effects on saving, especially as it provided improved saving instruments and incentives. At the same time, a strong case was made that diverting pension saving through the financial markets was likely to encourage their growth and modernization. Providing these expectations materialise, pension reform could make a significant contribution to economic growth in Latin America. The purpose of this chapter is to assess and evaluate the impact of pension reform on saving and capital markets.

The next section briefly reviews the possible saving effects of pension reform. It finds that the case for pension reform having a strong impact on saving is ambiguous at the theoretical level, and cannot be confirmed by the available empirical evidence. This is in line with the findings emerging from the debate on the impact of pension instruments on saving in the USA (Gravelle, 1991). An assessment of the likely impact of pension reform on saving in Latin America would need to focus on the empirical evidence. This is undertaken in the section that follows. Of all the countries that have introduced pension reform in Latin America, only in Chile has the reform had a sufficiently long span to permit an assessment of this issue. The empirical evidence from Chile is mixed, but does not support the view that pension reform has had significant effects on saving.

A related argument is that pension reform could contribute to economic growth through its impact upon capital markets. A further section examines this claim. In so far as pension reform creates a new pension fund management market, and a larger life insurance market, it can spearhead a modernization and development of capital markets. The development of capital markets can in turn introduce greater efficiency in financial intermediation and corporate control, leading to improvements in productivity and economic growth. Since the introduction of pension reform at the beginning of the 1980s, but particularly since the mid-1980s, the Chilean capital market has experienced a remarkable boom. While pension reform has made an important contribution to this growth, other factors are also important. These include the privatization program, a comprehensive overhaul of the legal and regulatory framework of financial markets, and the sustained growth of the economy. Section four provides a brief discussion of the experience of Peru and Argentina, which complements and extends the discussion on Chile. A final section concludes.

Pension reform and saving

Proponents of pension reform argue that it may have significant effects upon household saving. These effects result from replacing an existing saving instrument with a more efficient one, thus encouraging household saving.

In the context of Latin America, it is argued that the public pension schemes in place before the reform had developed financial deficits that rendered them less effective as saving instruments. The rise in contribution rates and the reduction in the promised pension benefits combined to lower the implicit rates of return on contributions paid. Affiliation to the social insurance pension schemes became less attractive, and rates of pension scheme coverage declined. Other things being equal, these result in a drop in household saving.

Pension reform that introduces a more effective saving instrument could help reverse this trend. It is claimed that the new individual capitalization pension plans provide an improved saving instrument with better saving incentives. Under the new pension schemes, there is a closer and more transparent correlation between contributions and benefits, which encourages saving. The new pension plans are also deemed more efficient vehicles for pension saving accumulation. These features of the new pension schemes introduced by pension reform are expected to improve household saving incentives.

A rise in saving rates could have an important positive impact upon economic growth. It raises the funds available for investment, and reduces the Latin American economies' dependency upon foreign capital inflows. Higher investment leads to economic growth, which itself generates higher saving. Pension reform, the argument goes, pushes an economy towards a virtuous circle of economic growth. This is why pension reform was given a key role in securing the success of the structural adjustment programs implemented in the region, especially after foreign capital inflows dried up after the early 1980s debt crisis.

It is important, therefore, to assess whether pension reform is capable of delivering these objectives. This is not clear cut from the analysis of life cycle models of consumption and saving. The Chilean experience with pension reform will be studied in order to test this claim empirically.

Predicting the impact of pension reform on saving

Pension reform may influence saving behaviour by offering a more efficient saving instrument, that is an instrument generating higher future income for a given amount of present saving. Taking for granted the improved efficiency of individual capitalization plans[1], the impact of pension reform on saving cannot be predicted with certainty from theoretical models. This is because an individual's response to the introduction of a more efficient saving instrument is twofold. On the one hand, saving is now better rewarded than before, making it a more attractive proposition. Individuals may thus be persuaded to substitute a fraction of their current consumption for future consumption, and saving will rise. On the other hand, the improved pension scheme provides a more efficient means of transferring income from work to retirement, and therefore the individual would need to save less today to generate the same target pension benefit in the future. The income effect resulting from a successful pension reform supports the expectation that saving will fall, while the substitution effect suggests the opposite will happen. The income and substitution effects of a more efficient saving instrument operate in opposite directions, and are likely to neutralize each other (Munnell, 1982). The net impact of pension reform on saving is therefore difficult to predict with certainty.

A more clear cut prediction can be generated from these models if it is assumed that individuals were, prior to the pension reform, frustrated in their attempts to save due to the unavailability of effective saving instruments. Pension reform, by making available just such instrument, would allow individuals to raise their savings to their desired level. Introducing this assumption does help predict a positive effect of pension reform on saving, but fits uneasily with the compulsory nature of the new pension schemes. After all, if the Latin American countries had a large number of repressed savers, why is it necessary to make the new pension schemes compulsory?

The compulsory nature of pension plans saving bears some further analysis. In a situation where individuals own a portfolio of assets, the introduction of a mandatory pension plan may not change aggregate saving, but simply the distribution of savings across different assets. Individuals are likely to respond to the mandatory pension contributions by reducing their savings elsewhere. In this situation, the mandatory nature of pension plan contributions is not binding. In this context, the introduction of a new pension saving instruments that is more efficient is likely to produce a fall in aggregate saving.

Making some further restrictive assumptions can help identify potentially positive effects of pension reform on saving. Some households may be forced to save more as a result of the introduction of a compulsory pension plan. These can be organised into two main groups. One group who may now be forced to raise their saving consists of individuals who failed to save because they are myopic or suffer from weakness of will. For these workers, the introduction of mandatory pension plan membership imposes welfare enhancing time-consistency. A compulsory pension plan would, for this group, raise both aggregate saving and welfare.[2]

Another group for whom mandatory pension contributions will be binding consists of non-savers. Individuals who did not save before the pension reform, and have therefore no other discretionary saving assets, are now forced to save. It may be possible for this group to borrow on their forced saving, thus restoring their optimal consumption plans, but if individuals are credit constrained, this possibility is closed. This group will be forced to reduce their current consumption against their wishes. Aggregate household saving will rise following pension reform, but welfare will be adversely affected.

Workers who find themselves in this situation typically include the young, who are unlikely to have accumulated other saving assets and who are likely to be credit constrained, and the poor. This suggests that while saving rates will rise in the aggregate for the economy, welfare may decline in as far as these workers have consumption levels below their preferred ones. Providing that saving does result in output enhancing investment, economic growth would increase at the expense of the welfare of poor or inexperienced workers. Furthermore, in the context of Latin America, informal sector employment may allow workers in this situation to avoid the compulsory pension contributions. At the same time, the expansion of a low productivity informal sector will have adverse effects upon the economy.

In sum, the net effect of pension reform on saving cannot be safely predicted from life cycle models of consumption and saving, and must be identified empirically. The discussion that follows reviews the empirical evidence for Chile.

Pension reform and saving in Chile: trends in saving rates

There are considerable difficulties involved in isolating the saving effects of pension reform in Chile from the broader effects of structural adjustment and other macroeconomic conditions. Furthermore the effects of pension reform on saving will only become apparent some time after the implementation of the reforms. The strategy pursued in this section will be to examine the broad trends in saving arising from national accounts data, then to review evidence from econometric studies, and finally to compare pension saving trends before and after the reform.

Saving rates from national accounts provide a useful starting point. It is important to note that in the national accounts saving measures are generated as a residual. Gross domestic saving is the residual of gross domestic product minus consumption. By definition gross domestic saving plus foreign saving, the balance of the current account of the balance of payments, equal gross investment. Gross domestic saving represents the sum of public saving and private saving. With a measure of public saving derived from the government accounts, it becomes possible to identify a residual that represents private saving. Private saving is therefore a residual of a residual. It is apparent from this description that there are significant data quality problems associated with national accounts saving data.

Moreover, it is household, rather than private, saving that would best capture any pension reform effects. Private saving can be analytically decomposed into corporate saving, that is the undistributed profits of corporations, and household saving, the excess of household income over household expenditure. For Latin American countries this decomposition is not implemented in official data sources.

The evidence on domestic saving rates in Chile since 1960 is shown in Figure 4.1 below. The values reported are for gross domestic saving as a proportion of GDP. The trend shows a sharp fall associated with the early 1980s crisis, a recovery from 1985 onwards, and a sustained rise around the 25 percent level in the mid-1990s. The sustained rise in saving rates since the mid-1980s has received a great deal of attention, as it would appear to confirm the success of the structural adjustment program. It has also been taken to indicate that Chile's economy is on a par with the South East Asian economies as regards the conditions needed for 'take-off' (Agosin, Crespi and Letelier, 1996; Edwards, 1995; Marfán and Bosworth, 1996; Morandé, 1996).

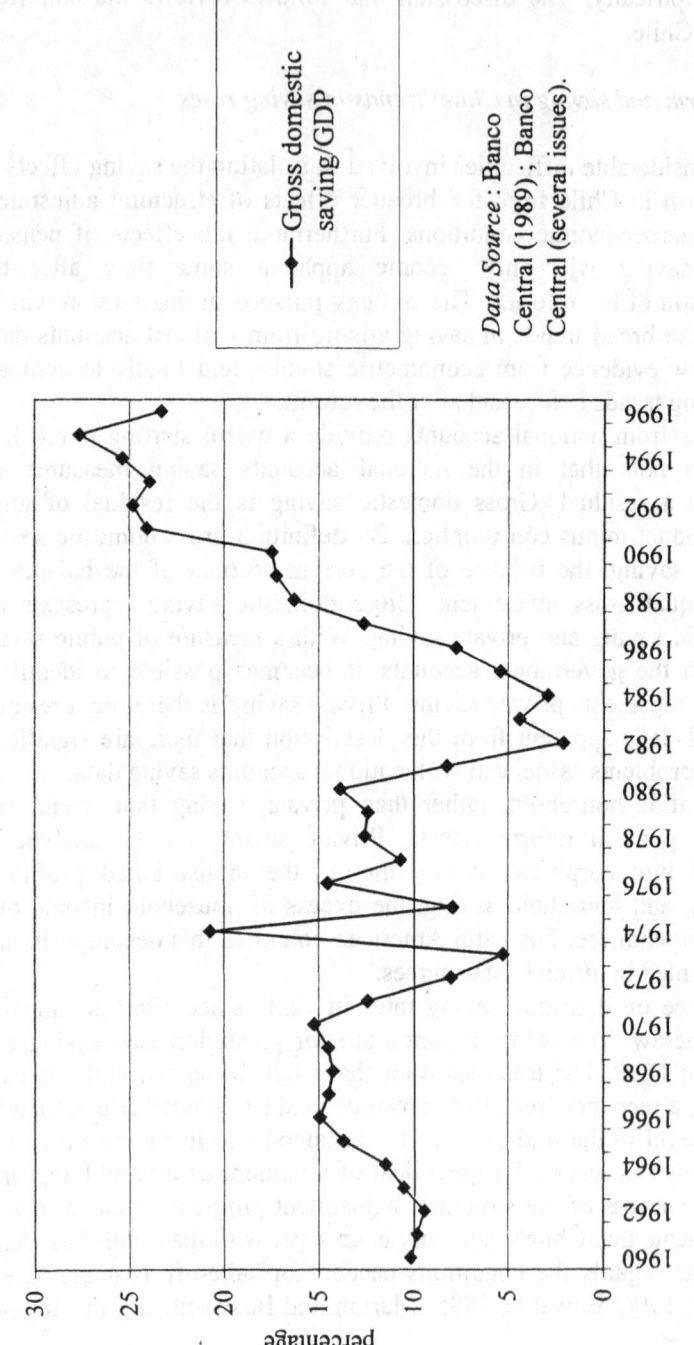

Figure 4.1 Chile: Gross domestic saving as a proportion of GDP

Data Source: Banco Central (1989); Banco Central (several issues).

In attempting to explain the sustained rise in the saving rate in Chile from mid 1980s many commentators have focused on pension reform. The growth in the pension funds in the same period is taken to confirm, by implication, the impact of pension reform on saving. This evidence is, however, largely circumstantial

To arrive at this conclusion, it is necessary to investigate further the behaviour of private and household saving rates. This requires a decomposition of gross domestic saving into its public and private components. As noted by Marfán and Bosworth (1996) there are considerable problems in performing this decomposition for the period we are interested in. This is because of the second wave of privatization in mid 1980s, which reclassified firms, and therefore their undistributed profits, from the public to the private sector.[3] Figure 4.2 below shows alternative measures of private saving. These include reported figures from Marfán and Bosworth (1996), which are adjusted for the impact of the privatization program. The figures reported in Agosín et al. (1996) are also included. Three findings should be noted. Firstly, there is evidence of a significant rise in the private saving rate since mid 1980s. Secondly, the values reported in the Figure also show clearly that the rise in private saving is largely responsible for the rise in gross domestic saving. Finally, comparison of these alternative measures of private saving show that the upward trend in private saving over the late 1980s and early 1990s is exaggerated by the privatization program.

As noted, many commentators have suggested that the rise in the private saving rate in Chile is to a significant extent a direct consequence of the success of pension reform. The evidence for this claim comes from observing the growth in the value of the pension funds. Pension saving flowing into the new individual retirement accounts has risen steadily after 1981, and in 1991 accounted for around 3 percentage points of the domestic saving rate, and around 15 percent of total gross domestic saving (Superintendencia de Administradoras de Fondos de Pensiones, 1992b). While it is undeniable that the new individual capitalization pension plans make a positive contribution to private saving, the evidence suggests this contribution is marginal.

The central issue is whether as a result of the introduction of the new pension scheme households are saving a higher proportion of their income than before, or whether there are households that are now saving where previously they did not. In this context, pension saving becomes a "net concept" (Engen, Gale and Scholz, 1996), and focusing solely on the inflow of new pension scheme saving will not grasp this. If, for example, the rise in retirement account saving simply displaces social insurance saving, or other forms of household saving, the net impact of pension reform on saving may be nil.

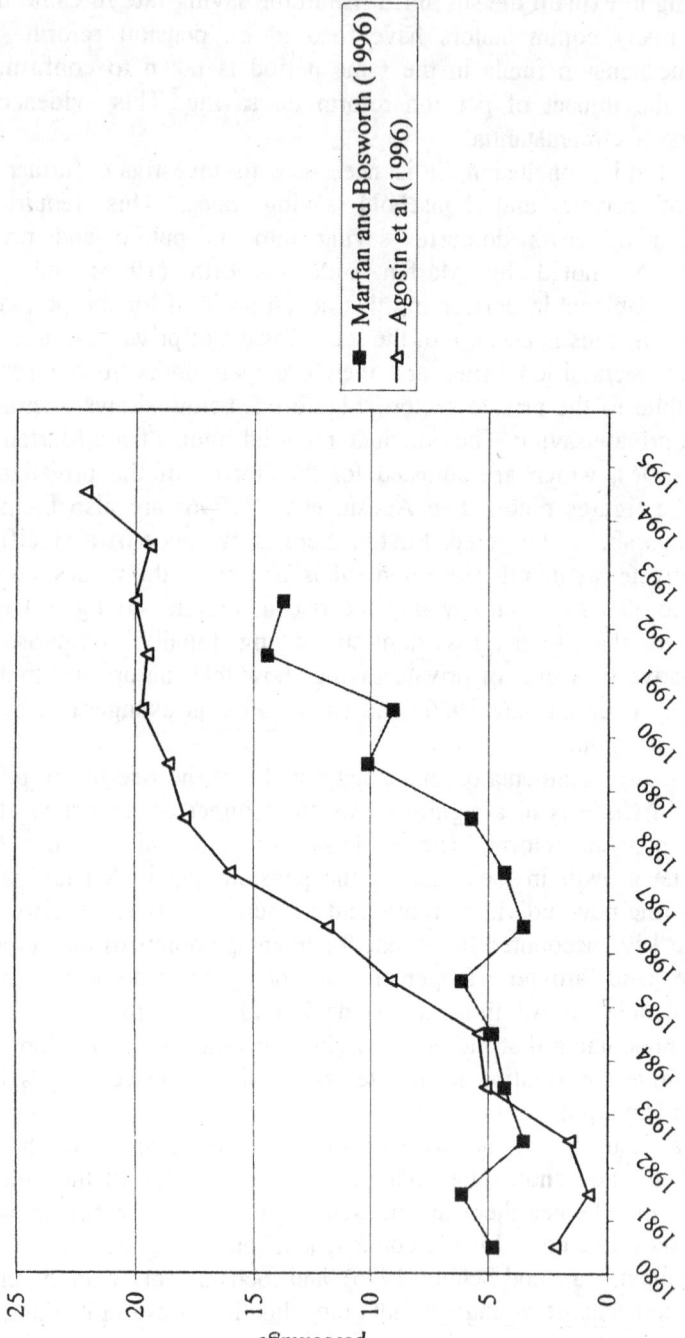

Figure 4.2 Chile: Alternative measures of private saving as proportion of GDP

Agosín et al. (1996) carry out a decomposition of private saving into corporate and household saving, and are also able to decompose household saving into pension and non-pension household saving components. Figure 4.3 below shows the relevant trends. A number of important conclusions emerge from this decomposition. First, the rise in private saving is dominated by the rise in corporate saving, particularly since the late 1980s. It is largely corporate saving, as opposed to household saving, which is responsible for the sustained rise in private saving. Secondly, the estimated household saving is negative for all years except 1985, 1992, and 1993.[4] It is therefore unlikely that the pension reform effects on household saving could have been large and significant. And thirdly, the measured contributions to the pension funds show a steady, and unremarkable, rise over the period, with the non-pension households saving component being the more volatile element.

In sum, the evidence on saving from national account data indicates that Chile experienced a steep rise in gross domestic saving from mid 1980s. This rise in domestic saving is largely driven by a rise in the private saving rate which climbed to just over 27 percent in 1995. The remarkable rise in the private saving rate is, however, exaggerated by the reclassification of a large chunk of the economy following the 1980s privatization program. The rise in the private saving rate is largely explained by a steep rise in corporate saving. Throughout the period households were net dissavers. A steady rise in pension saving can be observed, although once the public sector pension saving and dissaving is taken into consideration, the impact of pension reform is marginal (Agosin, Crespi and Letelier, 1996).

Pension reform and saving in Chile: econometric evidence

The evidence on the savings effects of pension reform emerging from econometric analysis of aggregate data is mixed. This is because it has proven difficult to isolate, with these data, the saving effects of pension reform from those arising from concurrent macroeconomic changes. Corsetti and Schmidt-Hebbel (1997) estimate an aggregate consumption equation and find an inverse relationship between private consumption and a measure of private pension funds value as a proportion of GDP. They conclude that the rise in private pension fund value accounts for around one half of the decline of the private consumption in the period 1980 to 1992. As they acknowledge, the measure of pension saving value "is highly correlated with other structural and policy changes that took place during the 1980s and early 1990s in Chile" (Corsetti and Schmidt-Hebbel, 1997). In addition, this measure reflects to a larger extent the accumulation of pension saving, rather than household saving.

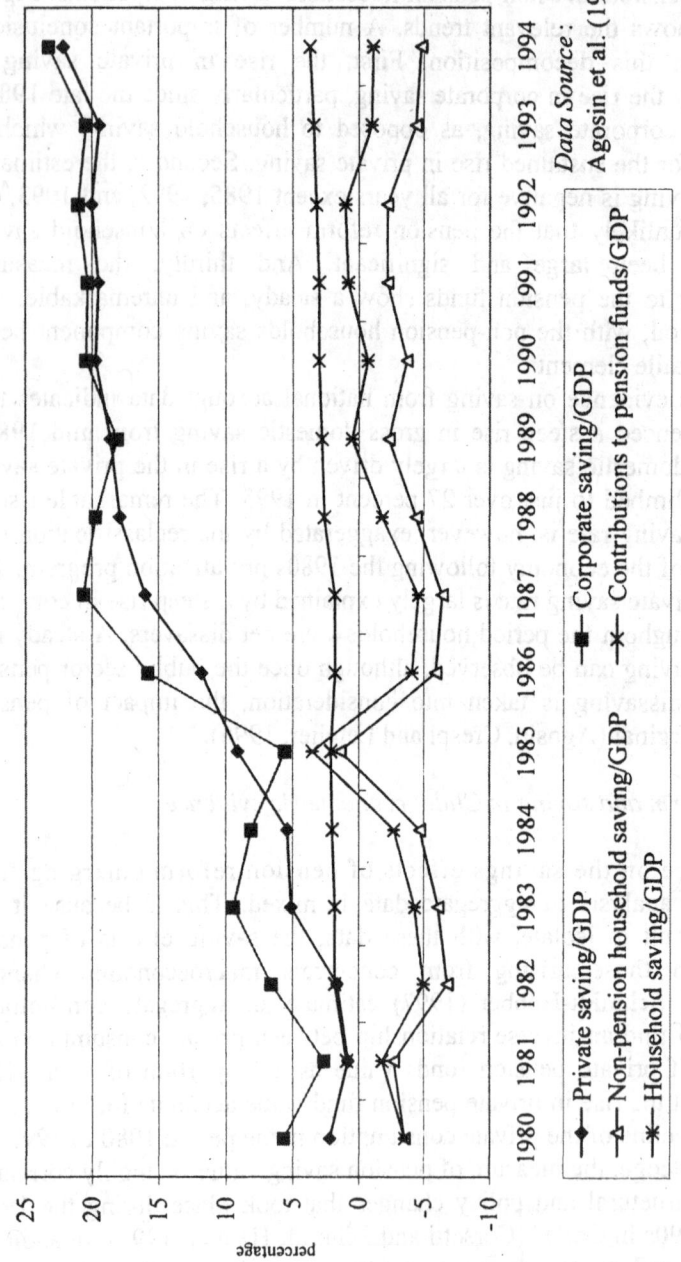

Figure 4.3 Chile: Private saving and components as a proportion of GDP

Similar problems beset other studies. Morandé (1996) estimated a model of domestic saving in Chile using national accounts data for the period 1960 to 1995. A dummy variable taking the value of 1 for the period 1986 to 1995 is included to capture the impact of the growth in the private pension funds on saving. The year 1986 is chosen in preference to 1981, because this marks the relaxation in the regulations on pension fund investment portfolio allowing equity investment. Morandé finds that this variable shows a positive and statistically significant effect on domestic saving. As was the case with Corsetti and Hebbel's analysis discussed above, it is not possible to isolate the pension reform effect from the impact of many other concurrent changes.

On the other hand, Agosín et al (1996) conclude that the net effect of pension reform on saving is marginal, once the impact on both government and household saving are considered (Agosin, Crespi and Letelier, 1996).

This conflictive evidence for Chile echoes the prolonged and exhaustive debate on the saving effects of the introduction of Individual Retirement Accounts in mid 1970s in the USA, and of other pension instruments since then. After two decades of debate in the USA, no firm conclusion has been reached, except that the impact of the introduction of pension instruments on savings is likely to be, at best, marginal (Engen, Gale and Scholz, 1996; Gravelle, 1991).

Pension reform and saving in Chile: pension saving trends

The existence of a positive and significant impact of pension reform on saving could be tested at the micro level by comparing private pension saving with pension saving in the old pension scheme prior to the reform. Figure 4.4 below shows, for selected years, measures of pension saving in the old scheme, and in the new one. The construction of the series for the old pension scheme needs some explanation. For the three main social insurance funds (*Servicio de Seguro Social, Caja de Empleados Particulares* and *Caja Nacional de Empleados Públicos*), a measure of pension saving was constructed by taking the product of the number of active contributors, employer and employee contribution rates, and average covered earnings.[5] This measure is computed as a fraction of GDP. Pension saving data for the new pension scheme come from published data (Superintendencia de Administradoras de Fondos de Pensiones, 1992b). The Figure shows that, aside from cyclical fluctuations, there is no significant change in the ratio of pension saving to GDP before and after pension reform in 1981.

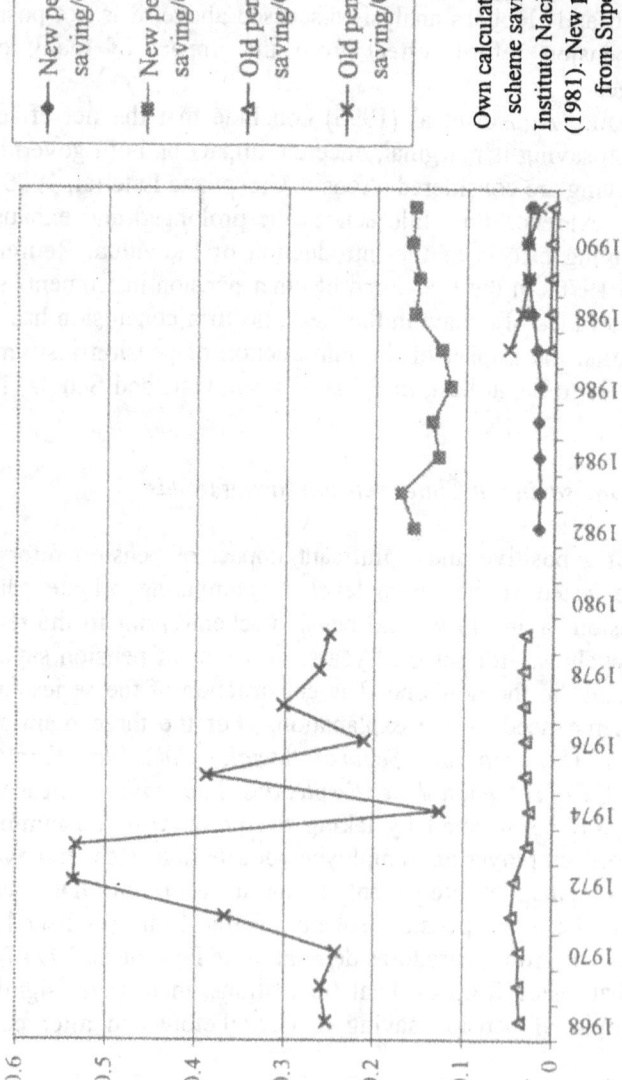

Figure 4.4 Chile: Pension saving under the old and new pension schemes

In conclusion, there is no compelling evidence to show that the introduction of individual retirement accounts in Chile has directly resulted in a rise in household saving. Explanations for the rise of private saving in Chile must be found in the growth of corporate saving, and more broadly in the sustained growth experience by the Chilean economy since the second half of the 1980s.[6]

Pension reform and capital markets

The conclusions of the previous section suggest pension reform in Chile has not had a significant impact upon saving. Pension reform can still make an important contribution to economic growth if it is capable of developing and modernising capital markets. The link from pension reform to economic growth is established in a different way. The impact of pension reform on saving was supposed to enlarge the available funds for investment, and raise capital accumulation. The pension reform impact on capital markets operates by improving the efficiency with which investment funds are allocated, and corporate control (Holzmann, 1997). A more efficient allocation of available investment funds raises productivity, and therefore economic growth. This section examines to what extent pension reform in Latin America will generate these effects.

Pension reform and the development of capital markets

There are at least four ways in which pension reform can help to improve the efficiency of capital markets. Firstly, pension reform, which replaces pay as you go public pension schemes with private pension plans, redirects pension saving away from government and towards capital markets. This has the effect of enlarging the capital markets, capturing possible gains from economies of scale and scope. Secondly, the involvement of new large institutional investors could accelerate the modernization of the institutional framework of capital markets, and improve its effectiveness in discharging its investment fund allocation and corporate control functions. Thirdly, the growth of pension funds could lead to the deepening of capital markets by encouraging securitisation, and by generating demand for longer-term instruments to match their longer term liabilities. Finally, pension reform may facilitate and attract foreign investment. If some, or all, of these developments do take place, pension reform could produce a significant improvement in the efficiency of financial markets, and could therefore improve the allocation of investment funds. The boost to capital markets could be felt over the long term, as pension fund accumulation takes place over a long period. This boost could be sustained even after pension schemes mature, with the development of the insurance annuity market. These could make a significant contribution to economic development in the region.

The rapid growth of the pension funds in the countries that have implemented pension reform show the size of the potential boost to capital markets. In Chile the value of private pension funds reached just over 40 percent of GDP by 1995. Their equity investment accounts for around a third of the funds. The growth in the pension funds is expected to continue in the future fuelled by growth in contributions and by rises in asset values. Projections of the future growth of private pension funds in Chile based on conservative estimates of future rates of accumulation suggest they could reach 80 percent of GDP at the turn of the century (Superintendencia de Administradoras de Fondos de Pensiones, 1992a). Similar projections for Argentina predict private pension funds could reach 46 percent of GDP by the year 2050 (Rofman and Stirparo, 1997).

The experience of developed countries with a substantial private pension sector, such as the UK and the USA, shows that pension funds account for a large part of stock market capitalization. It also shows that the development of a pension fund management industry, with the emergence of large institutional investors, has qualitative effects upon capital markets. These come to have an important effect upon the organisation and operation of these markets, and of the participating firms.

The view that pension reform, of the type that Latin American countries are implementing, has the potential to significantly improve the operation of capital markets is widely accepted. There is much less consensus on the likely impact the potential development of capital markets will have on economic development, and on the policies that need to accompany pension reform to ensure this impact is both significant and wholly beneficial.

The superiority of capital markets in allocating investment funds is strongly disputed, and particularly so for developing countries. Stiglitz (1989) makes the point that the public good properties of information ensure that information flows will be less than optimal in financial markets, leading financial institutions to invest in projects that are too risky, or engage in fraudulent practices. These problems are aggravated in developing countries with financial markets that lack the counterweight of an effective supervisory and rule enforcement framework. In this situation, investment fund allocation by the banking system or government may be preferable. The general tenor of Stiglitz argument is that capital market allocation may be less than optimal in developing countries. On a different level, the experience of developed countries shows that equity finance has not been an important factor in their own economic development (Mullin, 1993), nor has it been a key factor in the success of the Asian tigers (Edwards, 1995).

Since the 1970s an important body of literature has sought to establish the positive contribution that financial liberalization and the development of capital markets could make to economic growth. The argument is that financial liberalization is likely to improve the efficiency with which investment funs are allocated by improving the flow of information and the mechanisms for their evaluation. In this context, capital markets could play a key role in improving economic efficiency and therefore productivity growth.[7]

The growth of capital markets in Chile

The capital markets in Chile before the 1980s were shallow, concentrated and highly illiquid.[8] This is a common feature of developing countries. The success of the structural adjustment of the Chilean economy required, especially given its emphasis on market resource allocation, the modernization and enlargement of the capital market. Financial liberalization and capital market modernization were an important precondition to the success of the privatization program, pension reform, and the reallocation of resources following economic and trade liberalization. Financial liberalization was therefore a key component of the structural adjustment program in Chile. Pension reform made an important contribution to these. As the same time, the success of pension reform required the modernization of capital markets.

The initial steps taken to liberalize the operation of financial markets date from mid 1970s, with the liberalization of interest and exchange rates, and the relaxation of entry requirements to the financial markets. The first wave of privatization, which began soon after the military takeover in 1973, encouraged the formation of large financial groups who bid for the large number of financial and corporate institutions that were being transferred to the private sector. Financial and banking deregulation fostered these new fast growing financial groups, and was responsible for the banking and financial crisis of the early 1980s.

The acute crisis in 1982 led to acceleration in the pace of structural adjustment. In the sustained economic recovery and growth that followed the early 1980s recession, the capital market has expanded in line with the growth of pension funds and insurance company reserves, as shown in Figure 4.5 below below. The stock market capitalization as a proportion of GDP has risen since 1988 from 32 percent of GDP (a similar level to that of 1980 before the crisis) to 125 percent in 1994. A large part of this growth reflects the performance of stock prices. This factor also helps to explain the growth of pension fund value from 18 percent of GDP in 1988 to 40 percent in 1994, and the growth of insurance companies reserves from 5 to 9 percent of GDP in the same period.

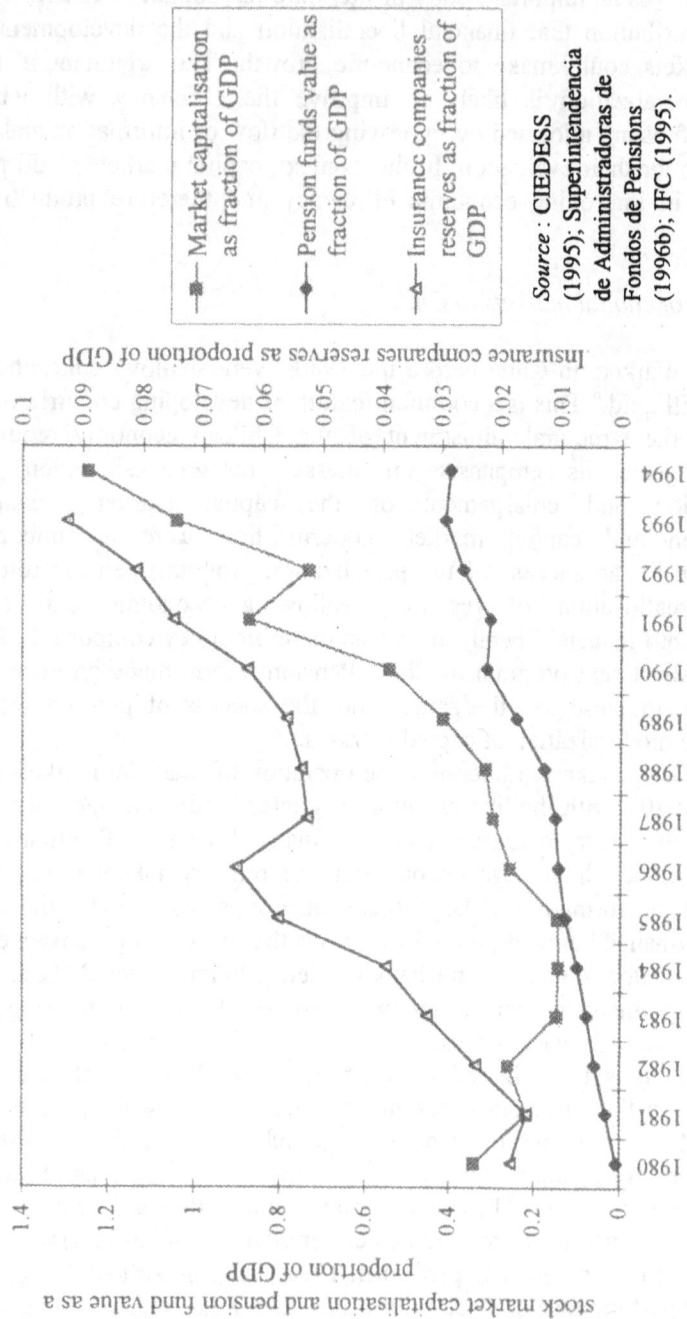

Figure 4.5 Chile: Growth of stock market, pension funds and insurance reserves

A number of factors are, in addition to pension reform, responsible for the rapid development of the Chilean capital markets. These include the second wave of privatization in the mid 1980s. This included the privatization of large public utilities. Another important factor has been the willingness shown by the government in providing an effective regulatory and supervisory framework for the financial sector.

Privatization. The concentration of the capital markets did not provide sufficient scope for the pension funds' equity investment at first, but the privatization program helped cover this gap. The flotation of public utilities in this second wave of privatization supplied deconcentrated stocks in which pension funds could safely and profitably invest. The equity investment of the private pension funds developed rapidly. The privatization of large public utilities in the mid-1980s gave a boost to the size and liquidity of the capital market (Larroulet, 1996), and provided the AFPs with a relatively safe and very profitable investment outlet.[9]

The growth in equity investment by private pension funds. The investment regulations of the pension funds sets limits to the proportion of the investment portfolio of the pension funds that could be invested in a given set of instruments. The objective of this regulation is to reduce the exposure of the pension fund to risk. The Chilean pension reform was implemented in 1981, but the pension funds were only permitted to invest in equity in 1985. Initially, the regulations limited total pension fund equity investment to 30 percent of the fund. This limit was increased to 37 percent following the May 1995 Capital Market Law.[10] Within this limit, the regulations require that pension fund investment is restricted to shares from open corporations, that is from those that can fulfil minimum standards of ownership deconcentration and governance and have a continuous risk classification.

The regulations also limit the proportion of the shares of a corporation that can be held by a pension fund (7 percent [11]), as well as the proportion of the fund that can be invested in a specific instrument (5 percent [12]). As shown in Figure 4.6 below, equity investment by pension funds has risen to around 27 percent of the combined pension funds, and accounts for just above 10 percent of total market capitalization. Pension funds clearly make an important contribution to capital markets in Chile. Before the 1995 changes to the regulations, pension funds came close to their maximum permitted equity investment, and it is expected that regulation changes will continue to gradually raise these limits, as well as broaden the range of instruments they can invest. Comparison with developed countries shows that pension funds have the potential to increase their investment portfolio share of equity investment to twice the current level in Chile (Barrientos, 1993).

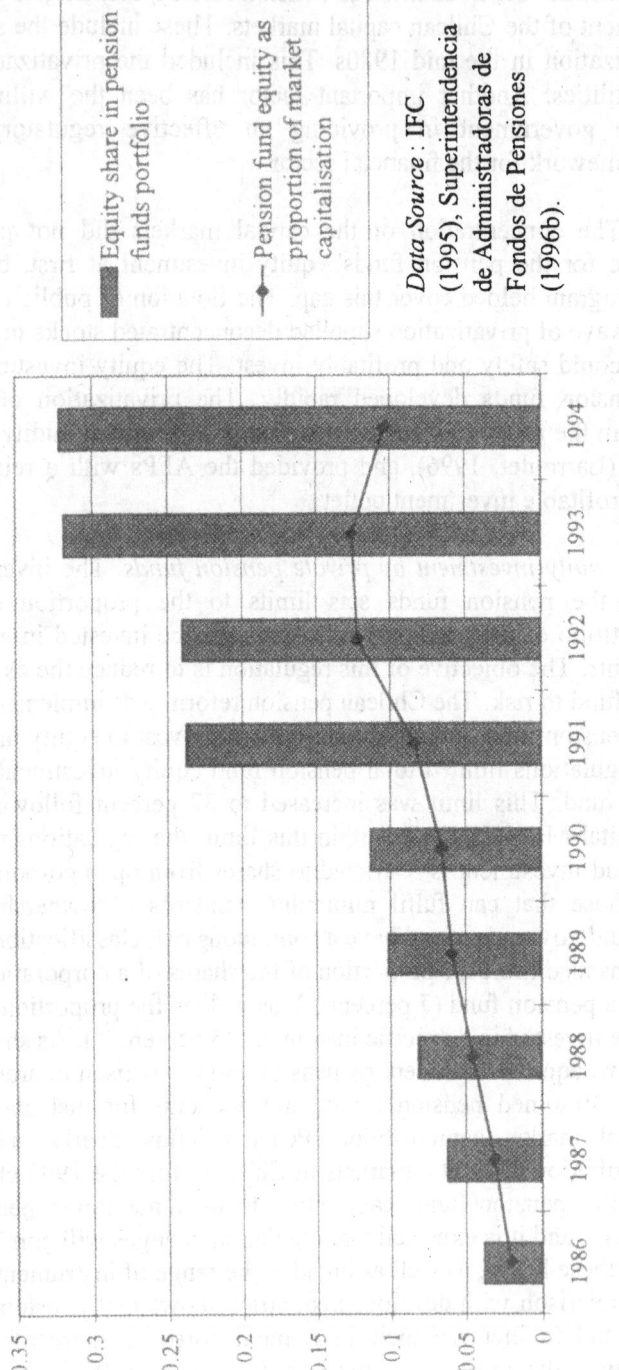

Figure 4.6 Chile: Pension fund equity investment and stock market capitalization

Data Source: IFC (1995), Superintendencia de Administradoras de Fondos de Pensiones (1996b).

The regulation and supervision of the financial sector. The financial crisis in 1982 left over 60 percent of the banking sector under government intervention (Larroulet, 1996). This strengthened the view that financial liberalization had gone too far, and accelerated a change to a more proactive approach to the supervision and regulation of the financial sector.

From 1980 onwards substantial pieces of legislation helped provide the institutional framework in which financial markets could modernize (Arrau, 1994; Paul, 1995).[13] In 1980 the *Superintendencia de Valores y Seguros* was created and was entrusted with the supervision of capital markets and insurance companies. In 1981 the powers of the *Superintendencia de Bancos e Instituciones Financieras* were extended. In 1981 corporations are given a new legal structure and rules regarding governance; and in the same year legislation is put in place regulating stock market trading and participants.

The crisis in 1982 led to a significant tightening up of financial sector regulations. In 1985, regulations on insider trading and own-account trading by company directors were set in place. In 1986 a new Bank Law reforms bank information practices and restricts concentration. In 1987 a new Risk Classification Commission headed by the banking, capital markets, and pension regulators is established. This Commission has the main role of providing continuous risk evaluation for traded securities. In 1989 new legislation creates investment funds and share title custody. And in 1995 a new Capital Markets Law updates and tightens up the regulatory framework of capital markets (for example, it specifies the obligations of pension fund managers with respect to the companies their funds are invested in).

The existence of an effective regulatory framework has made a major contribution to the development of capital markets, and is a fundamental pre-requisite to the success of the reforms.

It is unlikely that without either the privatization of utilities or the improvement in the supervision and regulation of the financial sector, pension reform and the modernization of capital markets would have been successful. This brief review of the development of capital markets in Chile leads to the conclusion that pension reform played an important role in this. At the same time, pension reform is only one among a number of factors responsible for the development of capital markets in Chile. And it is only the combination of pension reform, privatization of public utilities, and effective regulation, against the background of very favourable macroeconomic conditions, than can explain the rapid development of capital markets in Chile.

Pension reform and the efficiency of capital markets

The entry of large institutional investors into the capital market may have also contributed to an improvement in the efficiency of capital markets. This can be observed in the reduction in commission costs, the improvement in market practices, and greater competition (Larrain, 1995; March, 1995). In the Santiago Stock Exchange transactions are subject to brokers's commissions and a market charge. The expansion of the market has led to a decline in transaction costs. March (1995) reports that charges for a regular monthly US$ 1 million trade in shares have fallen from 0.5 percent in 1985 to 0.22 percent in 1991. Transaction costs on fixed interest instruments are close to 0 percent.

Other important changes in the operation of the capital markets include the development of new products and general securitization, and the more accurate identification of risks associated with the functioning of the Risk Classification Commission. The expansion of pension funds has produced a spread of securitization and an increase in the supply of longer-term financial instruments.

Pension funds are restricted in their investment to assets of corporations older than five years that have a good risk classification and are continuously traded in the secondary markets. Three new types of investment trusts have developed to open up investment opportunities for pension funds. The Real Estate Investment Funds (*Sociedades de Inversiones Immobiliarias de fines específicos*), deal in real estate purchases and rentals. Investment Funds (*Fondos de Inversión*) are unit trusts investing in a range of assets that pension funds are not permitted to invest directly, such as corporations younger than five years. Finally the Corporate Development Funds (*Fondos de Inversión de Desarrollo Empresarial*, or FIDE) are venture capital unit investment funds.

What these new types of investment funds have in common is that they help securitize assets to permit pension fund investment, and are a direct consequence of the development of pension funds. As pension funds demand for investment assets expands, new products will need to be developed to absorb it. Along the lines of the investment funds mentioned here, a new law has opened the way for the development of Leasing Funds, that will support the expansion of housing on leasing terms for low income households. Similarly, new legislation in 1996 allows Investment Funds to invest abroad.

The expansion of the capital markets has encouraged the entry of participants. The numbers of market participants has increased from 145 in 1985 to 207 in 1993. Stock Exchange brokers more than doubled from 31 to 73 in the same period. And the numbers of pension and investment funds also show a large rise.

Capital markets and the success of pension reform in Chile

While the expansion of pension funds equity investment has made an important contribution to the modernization of capital markets, the latter has in turn had positive effects upon the consolidation of pension reform. The modernization of capital markets has helped absorb the flow of pension saving generated by the reform. The privatization program provided a crucial factor facilitating these reforms. The Chilean experience has changed perceptions about the need to have a well functioning financial market as a precondition for pension reform. It is now argued that pension reform could succeed if implemented alongside capital market reform and privatization (James, 1997a).

An important issue is whether the modernization and development of capital markets can secure the success of the new pension scheme in Chile in the medium and long term. The recent growth of pension funds cannot be projected linearly into the future. It is a design feature of funded pension schemes that initially, while the fund is growing, the demand for financial assets rises. This rise in demand for financial assets may, given market conditions, be responsible for pulling share prices upwards. When the pension scheme matures and the settlement of pension liabilities becomes significant, pension funds become net sellers of financial assets. With given market conditions, this stance is likely to depress share prices.

The returns to equity investment have been largely responsible for the high returns experienced by the pension funds since mid 1980s. E. Valck (1995) shows that for the period from January 1991 to December 1993, equity investment was around one third of the pension funds portfolio, but contributed two thirds of the pension fund returns. Moreover, privatized utilities accounted for 90 per cent of the pension funds equity returns.

At the same time, the volatility, concentration, and low liquidity of capital markets may have adverse effects upon the performance of pension funds in the future. Equity investment returns are in large part responsible for the recent volatility of pension fund returns. This is to be expected as equity investment has a higher risk-return point than fixed interest instruments. Pension funds' rate of return volatility may be aggravated by the concentration of pension funds equity holdings on privatized utilities. Investment in privatized utilities provided the main source of investment for pension funds initially, and ensured the success of the privatization program. It has been very profitable in the recent past, but may pose problems for the future. Poor returns experienced by the electricity sector in 1995 ensured negative returns for the pension funds in that year. The long term performance of the pension funds will depend on their capacity to diversify more widely, and on the capacity of the capital markets to develop new products and to reduce share ownership concentration.

The issue of liquidity is also important. While the Chilean capital market has shown remarkable growth, liquidity has not improved at the same pace. Market liquidity indicators reflect the ability of investors to move to a different set of assets. A standard measure of liquidity is the turnover ratio, that is the annual traded value over the average market capitalization in the same period. This is shown in Figure 4.7 below. The Figure shows that the turnover ratio, while improving, is still well below 10 percent. This figure is low compared to other Latin American countries.

The potential constraints upon pension fund investment arising from market liquidity can be highlighted by measuring the ratio of pension fund equity holdings over stock market traded values measured for the same year. Figure 4.7 also shows this. The Figure shows a rise of the ratio of pension fund equity holdings over traded values over the period, but a fall in 1994. Both these measures suggest that, aside from the restrictions arising from current investment regulations, pension funds would face considerable restrictions in their capacity to alter their equity portfolio. It would take a long time for pension funds to change, or dispose, of their equity investment given current market traded values. This also applies to fixed interest instruments which are traded in the secondary market (Valck and Walker, 1995).

In sum, pension reform had an important part in the expansion and modernization of capital markets in Chile. In turn, capital market modernization played an important part in the success of the pension reform, mainly by contributing to the high rates of return experienced by the pension funds. Two other developments were key to these reforms: the legislative efforts setting up an institutional framework within which modernization of capital markets could take place; and the extension of privatization to large utility corporations. While market capitalization has grown dramatically, market liquidity and deconcentration have not grown apace. Pension fund investment is heavily concentrated in privatized utilities, thus enhancing the impact of market volatility on pension fund investment performance. The concentration of pension fund investment combined with the illiquidity of the capital market may become an important issue when the pension scheme matures. These are likely to pose some constraints upon pension fund investment strategy and performance in the longer term. Pension fund investment diversification, continued financial product innovation, and improvements in the liquidity of capital markets are needed to avert these risks.

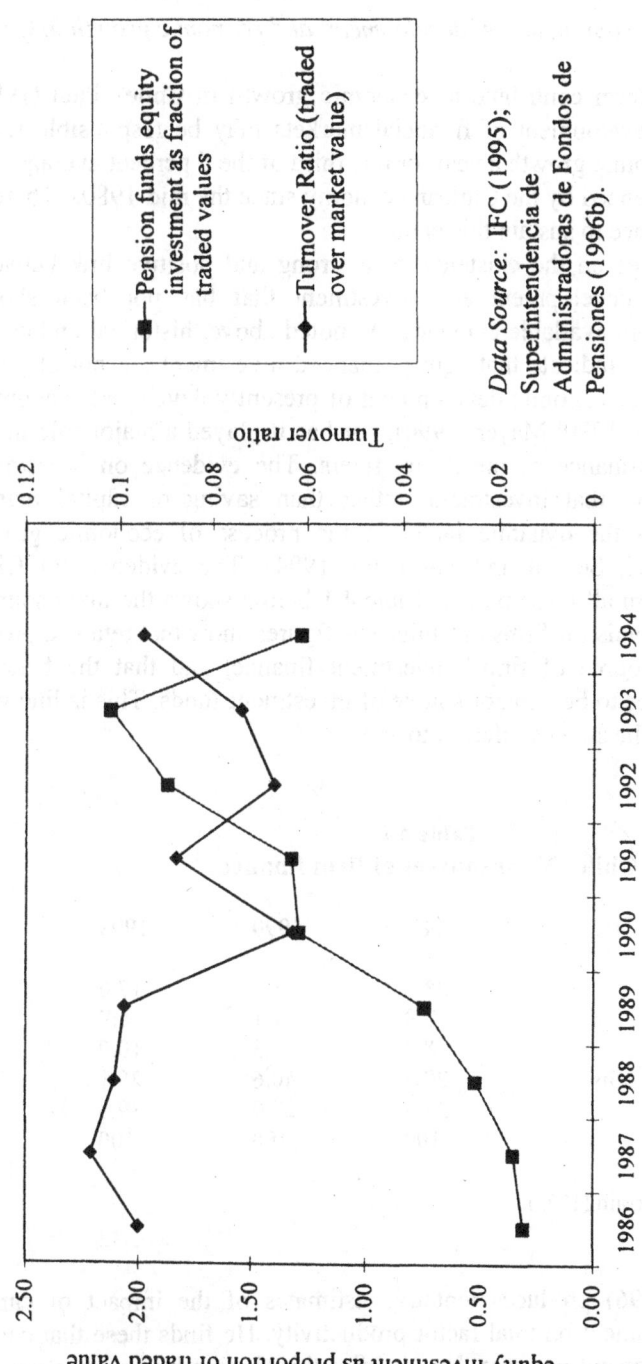

Figure 4.7 Chile: Capital market liquidity and pension fund investment

Did pension reform contribute to economic growth in Chile? Paul (1995) suggests that development of financial markets may be responsible for 2 percent of economic growth a year, or one third of the 6 percent average rate of return experienced by the Chilean economy since the mid-1980s. There is no strong evidence to sustain this claim.

The claim relies on the existence of a strong and positive link between capital market development and investment that has not been shown conclusively from available evidence. As noted above, historical and cross-country evidence indicate that equity financed investment did not played a major role in the economic development of presently developed economies (MacKie-Mason, 1990; Mayer, 1990), nor has it played a major role in the economic performance of the Asian tigers. The evidence on investment behaviour shows that investment, rather than saving or capital market development, is the dynamic factor in the process of economic growth (Schmidt-Hebbel, Serven and Solimano, 1994). The evidence for Chile seems to confirm all these points. Table 4.1 below shows the main sources of investment funds for firms in Chile. The figures show that retained profits are the main source of firms' investment finance, and that the banking system continues to be a major source of investment funds. This is line with the findings in the studies referred to above.

Table 4.1
Chile: Main sources of firm finance

	1987	1990	1993
Equity	28.5	5.1	17.6
Bonds	2.9	7.1	6.9
Banks	8.0	23.3	10.9
Retained Profits	29.3	40.6	25.1
Other	31.3	23.9	39.5
Total	100	100	100

Source: Larrain (1995)

Holzmann (1996) produces tentative estimates of the impact of capital market development on total factor productivity. He finds these that can be as large as 1 percent per year. He qualifies this finding by pointing out that this estimate may be contaminated by other factors correlated with financial market development such as trade and exchange rate liberalization.

Impact of pension reform on insurance markets

The new pension scheme in Chile has also provided a boost for the life insurance sector, another important institutional investor. As shown above, insurance companies' reserves rose to 9 percent of GDP in 1994, and in large part this reflects the growth of the life insurance sector. The insurance companies participate in the new pension scheme in Chile in two ways. Firstly, the AFPs reinsure their liabilities for disability and dependant pension benefits with insurance companies. Secondly, workers have the choice at retirement of using their accumulated pension fund to contract a pension annuity from an insurance company. The expansion of the individual capitalization pension scheme will be accompanied by a growth in the life insurance sector. And as large institutional investors, the life insurance companies will also contribute to the development of the capital markets.

As in most developing countries, the life insurance sector in Chile was relatively undeveloped. Tight controls on product, prices and entry were in place to ensure the solvency of the sector. In Chile, these controls allowed only domestic insurance companies in the market, and closed it completely to foreign ones. The Insurance Law (*Ley de Seguros*) of 1980 aimed to open up the sector to competition both foreign and domestic, lifted price controls and product restrictions, and enforced the indexation of both policy premia and benefits (Iglesias and Acuña, 1991). The liberalization of the insurance sector was of great importance to the pension reform implemented in 1981. Subsequent changes in the regulatory framework of insurance companies have facilitated the expansion of the life insurance sector in response to the development of the new pension scheme.

In the initial period after pension reform, the AFPs reinsurance of their disability and survivor pension liabilities made up the largest portion of the insurance companies new business. The insurance companies benefited from large margins. The AFPs usually contract cover for these contingencies with an insurance company for periods of one or two years. In the event of disability or death by an affiliate, the insurance company covers the difference between the pension entitlement and the accumulated fund in the individual's retirement account. Initially, the AFPs were required to transfer an individual's pension saving to the insurance company who then delivered the pension benefit. Changes were introduced in 1987 encouraging greater competition among insurance companies. The changes in the regulations reverse the transfer of funds in the event of an insured contingency materializing. Insurance companies now provide the AFPs with any required additional funds, and the beneficiaries of disability or dependant pension benefits could now opt for a pension annuity from any of the insurance companies in the market. This attracted new entrants to the annuity market.

From the late 1980s the value of the premiums being paid to insurance companies by the AFPs has shown a tendency to decline. As a proportion of contributory earnings, the cost of reinsurance to the AFPs as a whole has fallen from 2.05 percent in 1987 to 0.66 percent in 1995 (Martínez, 1996). This has been a consequence of a number of factors. The numbers of contributors to the new pension scheme have increased, and their associated liabilities are better known. There have also been a number of changes made to the disability and survivor pension benefits that have had the effect of reducing liabilities. A more effective certification of disability was introduced in 1988 leading to a reduction in the volume of disability pensions awarded. The disability and survivor pension benefits are now calculated on the basis of the average of 120 months of contributory earnings, as opposed to the 12 months instituted in the original legislation. Entry of new life insurance providers has also exercised downward pressure on reinsurance costs. And there is increasing scope for some of the AFPs to take on a greater proportion of their disability and survivor liabilities, and therefore to reinsure only a fraction of these.

The factors behind the fall in insurance premia have been strong enough to overcome opposite trends arising from the expansion of pension benefits, and therefore liabilities. In 1988 the insurance for disability and dependant pension benefit was extended to the unemployed for a period of twelve months. And a new partial disability pension benefit for workers who lose one half to two thirds of their capacity to work was introduced in 1990. Other things being equal, this expansion of benefits would have increased insured liabilities, and therefore reinsurance costs, but these have in fact fallen.

The annuity pension business growth was initially very gradual as few workers near to retirement joined the new pension scheme. The rise in the take up of annuity pension benefits originated in the 1988 legislation facilitating early retirement. In 1995 pension annuity premiums accounted for just over 71.3 percent of the total premiums received by the life insurance sector. And early retirement pension annuities accounted for around 85 percent of total pension annuity premiums. The pension annuity business will continue to increase steadily over the next three decades, but its rate of growth has more recently stabilized at around 12 percent a year.

The expansion of the life insurance sector accompanying the expansion of the new pension scheme in Chile has been made possible by the modernization of the regulatory framework of the life insurance market. Three measures implemented in the late 1980s are particularly important. Firstly, the new regulations introduced in 1987 on the investment portfolios of insurance companies, which encouraged diversification.[14] Secondly, the relaxation of regulations on insurance companies' reserves in 1988, which led to lower capital requirements and hence facilitated entry of new life insurance providers. Thirdly, the requirement, introduced in 1988, that insurance companies comply with risk classification regulations.

These changes to the regulatory framework of the life insurance sector, together with the growth in demand originating from the pension reform, have created the conditions for the rapid modernization and growth of the sector. The number of life insurance companies offering pension annuities doubled from 8 to 16 between 1988 and 1990, and has further risen to 22 in 1995 (out of a total of 30 life companies). With increased competition, market concentration and margins in the sector have fallen. The largest three insurance companies controlled nearly two thirds of the business in 1988, but only one third in 1995 (Martínez, 1996).

The charges of insurance brokers, however, show a marked upward trend.[15] It is important not to lose sight of the fact that the government guarantees pension annuities in full up to the minimum pension levels, and by 75 percent of amounts up to 45 UF. These guarantees may be scaled down with the further development and modernization of the life insurance sector.

Pension reform and financial markets in Latin America

It is too early to determine what effect pension reform is likely to have on economic growth in the region. On the basis of the Chilean experience with pension reform, it can be tentatively suggested that the saving effects of pension reform are likely to be marginal, but that pension reform could have a large and positive impact upon financial markets. It remains difficult to assess whether the modernization and development of capital markets in other Latin American economies can achieve levels similar to Chile's, and it is harder to assess what effect capital market modernization could have on economic growth. This section provides some cross-country comparisons, and speculates on likely developments.

Saving in Latin America

Low saving rates were identified as an important factor in explaining the poor economic performance of Latin American countries in the late 1970s and 1980s, a point highlighted by comparison of the Latin American economies with the fast growing economies of South East Asia (Agosín, 1994; Edwards, 1995). A key objective set for pension reform in Latin America is to raise private saving, which in turn makes possible higher investment rates and economic growth.

The discussion of Chile's experience points to the fact that pension reform by itself is unlikely to raise saving rates significantly. Sustained economic growth, favourable tax structures, and especially public saving, are more likely to lead to higher saving rates.

Capital markets and pension reform

The development of capital markets in Chile following pension reform raises the issue whether the latter will also give a boost to the capital markets in the other Latin American countries. In common with other emerging markets, capital markets in Latin America have experienced dramatic growth and volatility since 1980. Table 4.2 below provides information on the size and liquidity of capital markets for the countries under examination. Figures for stock market capitalization as a proportion of GDP in Panel A show that these fell from 1980 to 1984 as a result of the economic crisis, but recovered in the second half of the 1980s, and then grew rapidly in the 1990s. The Chilean capital market is, in proportion to the size of the economy, the largest in Latin America. By 1994 stock market capitalization in Chile amounted to 130 percent of GDP. Before the 1994 crisis, Mexico's stock market had reached 54.5 percent of GDP. Colombia and Peru also show a sustained growth of their stock markets to between 20 and 25 percent of GDP by 1995. The contrast of these countries with Chile shows the enormous potential for capital market development.

The expectation that pension reform will provide a significant boost to capital markets in Latin America as it did in Chile is broadly correct, but other relevant factors need to be taken into account. The second wave of privatization in Chile followed after pension reform, and was key to the large and positive impact the latter had on capital markets. Most of the Latin American countries that have followed Chile's pension reform had in fact gone some way in their privatization program before it. It will be more difficult for these countries to exploit the synergies from implementing pension reform, capital market modernization, and privatization of major utilities, at the same time.

The figures in Panel B show traded values over market capitalization and provide a liquidity indicator. These figures indicate that liquidity in the Chilean stock market shows sustained improvement over the whole period, rising from 6.8 percent in 1980 to 12.1 percent in 1996. Despite this marked improvement, the Chilean capital market is much less liquid than those in Mexico, Peru, or Argentina, if a longer period of time is considered. This comparison of the turnover ratio shows the Chilean capital market has some way to go to achieve regional standards of liquidity and deconcentration.

Table 4.2
Indicators of capital market development in selected Latin American countries

Panel A. Market capitalization as a proportion of GDP

Country	1980	1984	1988	1992	1993	1994	1995
Argentina	2.5	1.5	1.6	8.1	17.1	13.1	13.4
Chile	34.1	11.0	28.4	69.3	97.8	130.7	109.8
Colombia	3.9	2.0	2.9	11.7	16.7	20.9	23.5
Mexico	6.7	1.3	8.0	41.6	54.6	34.5	36.3
Uruguay	2.1	0.2	0.3	3.2	1.8	1.0	1.0
Peru			3.1	1.0	6.3	12.5	16.3	20.5
Costa Rica			4.6		7.1		

Panel B. Turnover Ratio

Country	1980	1984	1988	1992	1993	1994	1995	1996
Argentina	27.0	15.5	28.0	83.9	33.0	28.1	12.3	10.6
Chile	6.8	2.0	10.1	6.7	7.4	9.5	15.3	12.1
Colombia	11.2	5.8	5.3	11.4	9.8	18.9	7.0	8.1
Costa Rica		0.2		2.8	2.4	4.8		3.5
Mexico	26.0	84.8	51.7	37	36.8	44.5	33	42.5
Peru		5.6		19.3	43.8	46.8	39.3	31.5
Uruguay		4.4	6.0		4.7	5.7	2.7	1.7

Source: IFC (1995, 1997).

Pension reform and the life insurance sector

As regards the impact of pension reform on insurance markets, this was significant in Chile. Table 4.3 below provides some indicators for the life insurance market in the relevant countries. Chile is well ahead in terms of the size of the life insurance market, and it also shows a steady increase through the 1980s. Providing the other countries follow the example of Chile in designing, and implementing, an appropriate regulatory framework for the life insurance market, there is a strong likelihood that their life insurance companies will receive a significant boost.

Some countries have sought to restrict the scope for private life insurance. Mexico, for example, will continue to rely on the IMSS to provide disability and dependant insurance. This will in all probability restrict the development of their life insurance sector. As noted above also, the development of the life insurance sector is vitally necessary to the success of pension reform.

Table 4.3
Life insurance market indicators for selected Latin American countries

	Gross premiums as % of GDP				Gross premiums per head in US$			
	1984	1986	1989	1996	1984	1986	1989	1996
Argentina	1.39	0.46	ᵃ0.10	0.44				38.6
Chile	1.00	1.00	1.30	2.19	12.9	14.1	23.5	106
Colombia		ᵇ0.33		0.60		ᵇ11.8		13.9
Costa Rica	0.19	0.21	0.22	0.12	2.7	3.4	3.8	3.1
Mexico	0.21	0.33	0.49	0.54	15.4	11.9	17.3	19.2
Peru	0.11	0.03		0.14	9.3	12.4		3.5
Uruguay	0.09				18.0			

a. 1988
b. 1987
Source: (UNCTAD, 1994); and Asociación de Superintendentes de Seguros de América Latina (ASSAL) (Chile Finanzas, 1997).

Conclusion

This chapter has focused on the impact of pension reform on saving and capital markets. Pension reform is expected to play an important role in raising private saving and in developing and modernizing capital markets. Raising saving rates could have potentially positive effects on the levels of investment in the region. On the other hand, the development of capital markets could lead to a more efficient allocation of investment funds, with consequent improvements in productivity. Pension reform could contribute to sustained economic growth in the region, reversing the disappointing performance of the last three decades.

The evolution of pension reform in Chile was studied in some detail to shed light on these claims. It was concluded that the sustained rise in private saving in Chile since mid 1980s is in the main explained by a rise in corporate, rather than household, saving. The new individual capitalization pension plans have made a contribution to the rise in household saving. The net impact of pension reform on household saving is neither large nor significant, especially after the impact of pension reform on public saving is taken into account. The findings from econometric studies are mixed. These studies have not distinguished between the different components of private saving, nor has it been possible to isolate the effects of pension reform from the other significant structural economic changes that accompanied it. In short, the net saving effect of pension reform is, at best, marginal.

On the other hand, pension reform in Chile has had a significant impact on the development and modernization of financial and capital markets. Pension reform diverts a large measure of saving through the financial markets, and as such provides a large boost to the financial sector. Closer examination of the Chilean pension reform shows that two other factors played at least as large a role in the development of capital markets. These are the second wave of privatization which from mid 1980s transferred to the private sector a large number of firms, including key public utilities, and the radical overhaul of the legal and regulatory framework of the financial sector. It was the combination of all these that created the conditions needed for the rapid growth of the capital market. It remains difficult to assess whether the development of the capital market in Chile will make a significant contribution to economic growth.

Comparison of Chile's capital market and life insurance sectors with the other Latin American countries under study indicate that pension reform could potentially have a large impact on these. By the middle of the 1990s Chile is leading other countries in Latin America in terms of market capitalization and life insurance sector development, both measured as a proportion of GDP. Pension reform can make a significant contribution to the rapid development of these sectors in Latin America, with significant gains for their economies.

Notes

1 The greater efficiency of the saving instruments introduced by pension reform should not be taken for granted, and will depend on the detailed features of both the new and the old pension schemes. For instance, where the new pension scheme lowers contribution rates, savings will be lower in the aggregate, although this may be compensated for by voluntary additional saving.
2 This outcome requires the further assumption that these workers are credit constrained. It is important to note that it is very difficult to identify this group empirically.

3   Larroulet (1996) reports that the public enterprises involved in this second wave of privatization had a value of around 14 percent of GDP.
4   Agosín et al (1996) use independent estimations of household net saving produced by the Chilean *Banco Central*, and corporate saving is therefore a residual. The authors point out that household dissaving may be overestimated in the figures.
5   The data came from several sources Instituto Nacional de Estadísticas (1981); Superintendencia de Administradoras de Fondos de Pensiones (several issues).
6   Evidence on private saving aggregate behaviour in Latin America and other developing countries suggests that economic growth, via changes in income levels, is the main factor behind variations in the saving ratio (Schmidt-Hebbel, Serven and Solimano, 1994). In particular, saving models estimated for Latin American countries have concluded that households are classically keynesian, with a powerful and stable relationship of income and saving. Key elements of this characterisation are restrictions which operate on households ability to smooth consumption over the life cycle due to poverty, and credit and human capital acquisition constraints. In this context, rapid and sustained economic growth, such as Chile's in the late 1980s and 1990s, can provide a sound explanation behind the recent rise in the private saving rate.
7   This contrasts with the earlier literature which focused on the impact of financial liberalization on financial repression and capital accumulation (Edwards, 1995).
8   Edwards explains this by reference to the financial repression associated with import substitution strategies (Edwards, 1995).
9   The pension funds are prevented from investing in equity of concentrated companies. Given the high levels of concentration prevailing in the Chilean capital market, the privatization of utilities has provided most the equity investment opportunities for the AFPs.
10 The Capital Market Law set a band for pension funds' maximum aggregate equity investment of 30 to 40 percent of the fund. The Central Bank then fixed, via regulation, the maximum at 37 percent.
11 This figure is adjusted by a concentration factor, and a by company liquidity factor (see chapter 3 above). Investment in equity of Financial and Property Corporations is subject to lower limits.
12 See previous footnote.
13 These include the 1981 legislation on capital markets and limited liability corporations; the 1986 modification of banking law; the 1987 legislation on continuous risk classification; the 1989 legislation on investment funds; and the 1995 reform of capital markets.
14 The regulations on the investment portfolio of life insurance companies mimic the framework set in place for pension fund investment. The net result is that the investment portfolio of insurance companies is very similar to the pension funds', but has, as expected, a longer term (Iglesias and Acuña, 1991).

15 Martínez (1996) calculates that in 1995 the charges of insurance brokers averaged close to 5 percent of premiums, while the administrative costs of the five largest insurance companies were around 2 percent of reserves.

5 Pension scheme coverage

Pension reform is expected to have a significant impact upon the operation of labour markets in Latin America. There are close links existing between pension schemes and the labour market. On the one hand, the accumulation of pension entitlements is, in most cases, tied up with participation in paid employment. Pension scheme participation and future pension benefits, are normally determined by work and occupation status. As a consequence, labour market conditions will have important effects on the performance of pension schemes. This link played an important role in the financial imbalances developed by pay as you go pension schemes in Latin America. The deterioration of labour market conditions in the 1980s was a dominant factor in the crisis of social insurance in Latin America. On the other hand, pension schemes have important effects upon the labour market, through their influence upon labour market incentives. Pay as you go pension schemes in Latin America, it was argued, had adverse effects upon the pattern of incentives for labour supply, and occupational choice. Pension reform aims at eliminating these adverse effects, and introducing instead incentives for labour market flexibility and mobility. It is to be expected that pension reform will impact on the operation of the labour markets in Latin America, and also that conditions in the labour market will influence the evolution of the reformed pension schemes. This is the subject of this chapter.

Proponents of pension reform in Latin America have argued that pension reform will make a significant contribution to labour market efficiency. In the first place, pension reform will eliminate some of the distortions in labour market incentives that pay as you go pension scheme introduced. The new individual capitalization pension schemes are expected to reduce pension scheme contributions, bring individual contributions and benefits closer in line with each other, make pension benefits dependent upon full working lives, and enhance worker mobility. The first section outlines and evaluates this argument. One of its key conclusions is that studying pension scheme coverage rates may provide a test of whether these are likely to be the outcomes of pension reform.

The definition of pension scheme coverage is slightly more complex in individual capitalization pension schemes than in social insurance ones. Pension scheme coverage rates provide information on the extent to which a population is covered against relevant risks, such as the risk of having longer, or shorter, lives, or having shorter working lives. Longevity risks are covered by old age and retirement pensions. In individual capitalization pension plans coverage is a function of the density of contributions and the success of pension fund managers in securing adequate returns. Disability and survivor risks, on the other hand, are treated differently in the new reformed pension schemes in Latin America. Coverage against these risks depends upon a worker's contribution status immediately before disability or death. The second section discusses these issues and identifies appropriate measures of pension scheme coverage.

The evolution of pension scheme coverage rates and the determinants of pension take up in Chile are the subject of the next section. Chile has the longest experience with individual capitalization pension schemes. As a result, the evolution of pension scheme coverage rates can be observed more clearly. The section complements the analysis of aggregate pension scheme coverage rates with a disaggregated analysis of household data. These two levels of analysis are used to identify the determinants of pension scheme take up in 1994.

A further section compares the findings for Chile with the evolution of pension scheme coverage rates in other countries in Latin America, and especially Peru and Argentina. It explores common trends and discusses the likely course of pension scheme coverage, and the longer term impact of pension reform upon the labour market. A final section provides some conclusions.

Pension reform and labour market efficiency

Pension reform in Latin America is expected to make an important contribution to labour market efficiency. This is another key objective of pension reform. There is some degree of consensus in the view that many features of the pay as you go pension schemes in Latin America introduced important distortions in the operation of the labour market. High payroll pension contributions, for example, reduced labour supply and forced workers and employers to operate in the non-covered sector. An important objective of pension reform was to reduce the level of payroll contributions. Pension reform was also intended to facilitate the changes in the labour market required by structural adjustment. The change in the orientation of the economy to an export led growth strategy necessitated large transfers of resources and employment, for example, from non-tradeables to tradeables. Pension reform was intended to facilitate structural change by enhancing labour market flexibility and worker mobility, thus contributing to greater efficiency in the operation of the labour market.

Pay as you go pension schemes and labour market distortions

In chapter 1 above, it was noted that some design features of social insurance pension schemes discouraged continued contribution to pension schemes, with consequent adverse effects upon labour supply, sectoral attachment, and job mobility. The harsh economic conditions of the 1980s further intensified these effects, and led to the current wave of pension reform in the region.

The design of pay as you go pension schemes allows for redistribution both within and across cohorts. The accelerated implementation of pay as you go pension schemes, which occurred in most countries in the region, enforces redistribution from future to current generations of pensioners. Schwarz (1993) finds that this is by far the most substantial redistribution generated by pay as you go pension schemes.[1] There is also redistribution within cohorts which arises, in large part, from the pattern of benefits provided by pay as you go pension schemes. These secure pension benefits for the remaining life of retirees, and their dependants. These pension benefits redistribute from the short-lived to the long-lived, and from those retiring late to those retiring early. Both types of pension scheme redistribution introduce a wedge between individuals' contributions and benefits.

Looked at from the perspective of individual contributors, and ignoring insurance motivations, the pension benefits in pay as you go schemes depend mainly on the scheme rules, and only partly on contributions. It is therefore likely that workers will alter their labour supply and/or occupational choices in an attempt to maximise benefit entitlement from their contribution flows.

If contributions do not result directly in benefit entitlements, or are expected not to do so, these are perceived by workers as a 'pure tax', which they will be keen to avoid.[2] In social insurance pension schemes sizeable gaps in employment or contributions, dependent on when they occur, may have little or no effects upon workers pension benefits. This will have important implications for labour supply. Remuneration levels directly determine labour supply. If pension entitlements are taken into account as remuneration, and the wage is assumed to be constant over an individual's working life, work at different points in someone's working life will be therefore remunerated at different levels. Workers will adjust labour supply to these different levels of remuneration. Workers can avoid the 'pure tax' element of payroll pension contributions by failing to work or contribute for portions of their working lives, or by underreporting earnings for the contribution purposes. In addition, where pension benefit rules encourage early retirement, the labour supply incentives of older workers will be affected.

In the social insurance pension schemes in Latin America avoidance and evasion of social insurance contributions were widespread, and especially so after the deterioration in labour market conditions in the 1980s. The key problem with pension design in this context is the narrow window of contribution experience needed to secure full entitlement to pension benefits. Access to pension benefits required typically between 5 and 15 years of contributions, and the pension benefit was calculated on the basis of the last 2 to 5 years of earnings. These design features meant that workers had strong incentives to make only minimum contributions for the qualifying period, and full contributions only in the short period leading to retirement that was used for the benefit calculation. Given the inadequate enforcement of labour and social insurance regulations, and the spread of informality in employment relationships, neither workers nor employers in the private sector faced sufficiently steep penalties for evasion.

Furthermore, where it is not feasible to alter labour supply to avoid the 'pure tax' contributions, employment shifts between formal and informal sectors may provide an alternative mechanism.

With deteriorating labour market conditions in the 1980s, and the gradual impact of demographic trends, contribution rates climbed rapidly, compounding the financial problems of social insurance schemes. The higher the pension contribution rates, the greater the labour market distortions they produced. A vicious circle developed in the 1970s and 1980s in which the number active contributors to pay as you go pension schemes declined due to unemployment or informality, leading to higher contribution rates for those that remained, in turn leading to fewer active contributors, and so on.

To the extent that pension schemes were fragmented and heterogeneous, as was the case in most Latin American countries until the reforms, pension scheme affiliation placed important restrictions on worker mobility. Workers who attempted to move across jobs covered by different pension schemes faced significant pension entitlement losses. In most pension schemes pension benefits are calculated as a fraction of final salary. This implied that workers, identical in every respect except for job changes, could receive significantly different levels of pension benefit. The absence of pension scheme integration effectively penalises workers who move jobs, restricting flexibility and mobility in the labour market.

Pay as you go pension schemes had adverse effects upon life cycle labour supply, worker mobility, and sectoral employment choice. In the context of standard models of labour demand, it is also likely that high payroll pension contributions may have pushed some employers towards more capital intensive technologies, and other employers towards the informal sector. When supply and demand effects are put together, it is likely that pay as you go schemes may have been responsible for significant distortions in the operation of labour markets.

The impact of pension reform on labour market

Pension reform is expected to reverse some of the negative features observed in pay as you go pension schemes. The new pension schemes in Latin America are designed to ensure a closer correlation between pension contributions and benefits for individual workers. Three key design features ensure this. These are the absence of redistribution, individual pension fund accumulation, and the pension benefit dependence on lifetime, as opposed to final, earnings. A closer correlation of contributions and benefits can be expected to reduce or eliminate the 'pure tax' element of pension contributions and therefore generate stronger incentives for workers to contribute throughout their working life. These features could help reverse or eliminate some of the distortions generated by pay as you go pension schemes.

It is also claimed that private individual capitalization pension schemes may result in greater efficiency in the administration of pension funds, which is likely to reduce administration costs, and consequently contribution rates. This would further reduce labour supply and demand distortions.

Pension reform also transfers responsibility for pension arrangements from government and employers to workers. This switch allows greater flexibility in workers life cycle work and consumption decisions, although this is somewhat restricted by mandatory fixed contributions.

The new pension schemes are integrated, homogeneous, and fully portable, so that worker mobility is not affected by membership of a pension plan. It is important to note that measures aimed at increasing worker mobility may have adverse effects upon human capital acquisition. Long term tenure and long term contracts have been found in the literature to encourage firm specific training (Gustman, Mitchell and Steinmeier, 1994).

Overall, pension reform is expected to encourage employment in general, and more specifically in the formal sector. Pension reform is also expected to improve labour supply incentives, and to reduce labour market segmentation. It is expected to reduce or eliminate any existing capital-intensive bias on the labour demand side, which results from high employer pension contributions. It is expected to facilitate labour market adjustment by encouraging worker mobility, and by eliminating employer pension liabilities. Pension reform thus could provide a significant boost to labour market efficiency in Latin America.

These expectations have been encouraged by the findings from some studies simulating the impact of pension reform. Corsetti and Hebbel (1997) use an overlapping generations model with endogenous growth to simulate the impact of payroll contributions on a hypothetical economy. Their focus is on the impact of payroll pension contributions on the size of the formal and informal sectors. Assuming that the informal sector is labour intensive, and therefore has lower productivity, a diversion of employment to the informal sector is consistent with lower growth rates. The authors simulate different payroll tax scenarios, and find that rising payroll taxation is consistent with a larger informal sector, and lower economic growth. For example, assuming that pension payroll contributions are perceived in full as a 'pure tax' by workers, an increase in the contribution rate from 10 to 20 percent is consistent with the informal sector rising from 15 to 47.5 percent of the labour force, and growth rates declining from 3 to 1.8 percent in the steady state.

It is, however, more difficult to find empirical support for these claims. Corsetti and Hebbel (1997) and Holzmann (1996) argue that broad labour market and pension coverage trends in Chile after pension reform in 1981 provide some empirical support for the argued for pension reform effects. Corsetti and Hebbel (1997) suggest that the reduction in pension contributions brought about by pension reform in Chile, roughly 10 percentage points, may be associated with a fall in the share of independent workers in the labour force, and with a slight rise in activity rates.[3] Holzmann (1996) argues that supporting evidence can be found in the rise in pension coverage for dependent workers after the pension reform, in the stability of the ratio of active contributors to those in employment, and in the fact that the self-employed have generally stayed out of the new pension scheme. These claims need to be examined very closely against the available evidence.[4]

There is conflictive evidence on this issue. As noted, the claim that pension reform has positive effects on labour market efficiency is premised, to a large extent, upon workers viewing their pension contributions as a 'pure tax', rather than as deferred compensation. To take the alternative scenario, if workers perceive their pension payroll contributions fully as deferred compensation, pension reform that replaces a pay as you go pension scheme with individual capitalization plans would have marginal effects upon labour supply, or on the sectoral composition of employment. Gruber (1997) analyses data from a panel of manufacturing firms in Chile and finds that pension reform raised workers earnings,[5] but had no significant impact upon employment. This would appear to indicate that the distortionary impact of payroll taxes was not particularly significant.[6] Gruber concludes that "the shift in financing of social insurance in Chile in the early 1980s did not have important consequences for labor market efficiency" (1997, p.S99).

The preceding discussion suggests that an examination of trends in pension scheme coverage, and in sectoral employment, could provide an appropriate test of whether the labour market effects of pension reform materialised. This will attempted in the following sections.

Pension scheme coverage: definitions and policy issues

At the outset it is important to define what is meant by pension scheme coverage. It would be useful to make reference to the insurance function of pension schemes discussed in chapter 2. Pension schemes insure participants against a range of contingencies that may affect the consumption of workers and their dependants. Longer than expected lives give rise to the risk that an individual may outlive his or her resources. Longevity risks are insured against by old age and retirement pension benefits. Shorter than expected lives give rise to the risk that an individual's dependants may have low consumption levels. Similarly, shorter than expected working lives will impair the consumption levels of a worker and his or her dependants. These are insured against by the provision of disability and survivor pension benefits. Pension scheme coverage refers to whether an individual, group, labour force, or population is effectively insured against these risks.

Pension scheme insurance cover depends largely on participants satisfying entitlement requisites. Where insurance cover is dependent on individuals being active contributors to the pension scheme, the pension scheme coverage rate is usually defined as the proportion of a population that is contributing to a pension scheme. Under the social insurance schemes, it was common that contributions to the scheme entitled contributors and their dependants to available benefits. Coverage rates can be defined, in this case, as the proportion of the labour force who are active contributors, or alternatively as the proportion of the population entitled to benefits.

In the context of the Latin American pension reform, the situation is slightly more complex. The introduction of individual retirement pension plans separated out old age and retirement pensions (covering longevity risk) from disability and survivor insurance (covering shorter life and working life risks). Entitlement to old age or retirement pension benefits simply requires that workers make contributions to a pension plan and reach retirement age. Old age and retirement pension coverage rates could then be measured as the proportion of the labour force who are affiliated to a pension plan. However, this is not satisfactory, as the proportion of retirement consumption that would be covered by the pension benefit depends, in the individual capitalization pension scheme, on the size of the accumulated fund at retirement.[7] A more appropriate measure of pension scheme coverage is the proportion of the active labour force that contributes regularly to a pension plan.[8]

Access to shorter life insurance also depends on whether a worker is contributing to a pension plan, but the contribution requirements are more stringent.[9] Usually workers must have been contributing at the time of death or disability to be entitled to a disability or survivor pension. A definition of pension coverage rate in this case needs to take account of these more stringent requisites.

A key indicator of the success of pension reform in Latin America will be the extent to which it succeeds in raising pension scheme coverage rates. International comparisons of pension scheme coverage rates show that these are closely related to economic development, conditions in the labour market, and pension plan design. Developed countries have succeeded in securing almost universal pension scheme coverage. Developing countries, by contrast, lag far behind, with participation in pension plans often restricted to public sector workers and high earnings workers in the private sector.

The proportion of the labour force participating in a pension scheme in Latin America in the 1960s and 1970s was, by developing country standards, relatively high. This was mainly a result of rapid industrialisation and the expansion of social insurance schemes. Figure 5.1 below shows the trends in coverage for the Latin American countries under examination. With the exception of Uruguay and Chile, the expansion of coverage continued through the 1970s. From the early 1980s a number of factors conspired to produce a decline in pension scheme coverage rates. These included: the economic crisis and stagnation of the early 1980s, the liberalization of the labour market and the growth of the informal sector, the financial problems affecting social insurance schemes, and government retrenchment. Colombia provides the only example of a sustained rise in pension scheme coverage.

In this context, the introduction of individual capitalization pension schemes in many countries in Latin America has given rise to expectations that they would be able to stem the decline in coverage. Proponents of pension reform in Latin America claim that the introduction of individual retirement pension plans are likely to make regular participation in pension plans more attractive to workers, and are therefore likely to raise pension scheme coverage rates.

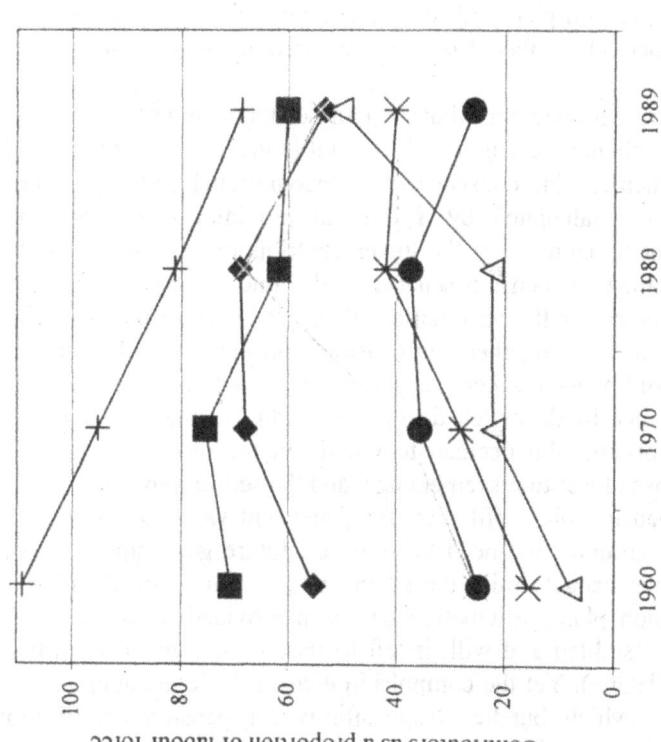
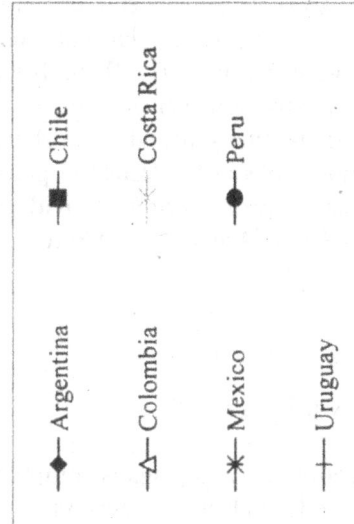

Figure 5.1 Social insurance and pension scheme coverage for selected Latin American countries

In individual retirement pension schemes, workers have incentives to make accurate contributions throughout their working lives, but particularly earlier on given the pattern of accumulation of the fund. The flexibility and transparency of the new individual capitalization pension plans was expected to prove more attractive to the self-employed and to workers in non-standard employment. The next section looks at the trends in pension scheme coverage in Chile, with the subsequent section providing a comparison of pension scheme coverage in Chile, Argentina and Peru.

Pension scheme coverage in Chile

Compulsory and voluntary participation in pension plans

Affiliation to the new individual capitalization pension plans is compulsory for dependent workers, and voluntary for independent workers. As regards dependent workers who were members of the old social insurance pension schemes, these were given the choice of remaining in their schemes or joining the new pension plans. All dependent workers who have joined the labour force since December 1983 are required to affiliate to the new pension plans.[10]

Civilian workers who had contributed to any of the insurance funds under the old pension scheme were given a financial inducement to switch to the new pension scheme. This consisted of a Recognition Bond, representing past contributions, calculated by a formula providing generous terms. Further inducements came from the lower contribution rate under the new individual capitalization pension scheme, and a one off salary increase to compensate workers for the termination of employer contributions. These financial inducements, together with rising concern with the financial viability of the old pension scheme ensured the majority of active members of the old insurance funds switched to the individual capitalization pension scheme. The workers who decided to remain in the old pension scheme were mainly those closer to retirement age, and the self-employed.

Compulsory pension plan affiliation for dependent workers was justified on paternalistic grounds, the need to minimise future government pension liabilities, and the need to raise the saving rate. A strong justification for mandating pension plan participation has been provided by the view that workers are shortsighted and will, if left to themselves, undersave for old age (Diamond, 1996a). Yet the compulsion element looks incongruous in a pension scheme which bundles responsibility for pension contributions wholly onto workers, and seeks to maximise individual choice in pension arrangements. Mandating pension plan participation for dependent workers, providing it is adequately enforced, does have the effect of reducing future government financial liabilities associated with providing minimum income programs for the old. More importantly, forced pension saving is the most likely source of new pension saving, especially where workers are not able to reduce saving elsewhere. This is especially relevant to younger workers with few saving assets (Barrientos, 1996b).

Participation in pension plans is voluntary for independent workers. This is justified by the considerable administrative complexities involved in determining earnings and contribution levels for those workers. There is also the expectation that some of these workers, professionals in particular, may be in a better position to organise pension arrangements for themselves. Many independent workers invest in capital and property assets that may provide them with an income in old age, and may not therefore be interested in contributing to a pension plan instead. There will be a substantial proportion of independent workers for whom these justifications may not apply. The liberalization of the labour market in Chile and other countries in Latin America has resulted in a sizeable informal or flexible sector where workers are in a variety of employment relationships providing little protection. The fact that participation in pension plans is voluntary for independent workers may encourage the growth of informal sector employment.

Evolution of affiliates and contributors over time

For the purposes of analysing the new pension scheme coverage it is important to distinguish affiliates from active contributors. Affiliates are those who have joined the new pension scheme by opening a retirement account with an AFP at any point since the inception of the scheme, and have not yet retired. Active contributors, on the other hand, are those who make regular contributions to a retirement account. Figure 5.2 below tracks the rise in the labour force and employment, the number of affiliates, and the number of active contributors, to the old and new pension schemes.

The Figure shows the number of workers in the pension schemes against the backdrop of the large rise in the labour force and employment in the period. Both the labour force and employment rose by around two million in the period from 1980 to 1992. There is greater variation in the number of workers in employment. The 1982 acute economic crisis was responsible for a significant fall in employment to just below 3 million. Employment recovered strongly with the sustained growth in the Chilean economy from 1984. The growth in employment levelled off in the period 1993 to 1995.

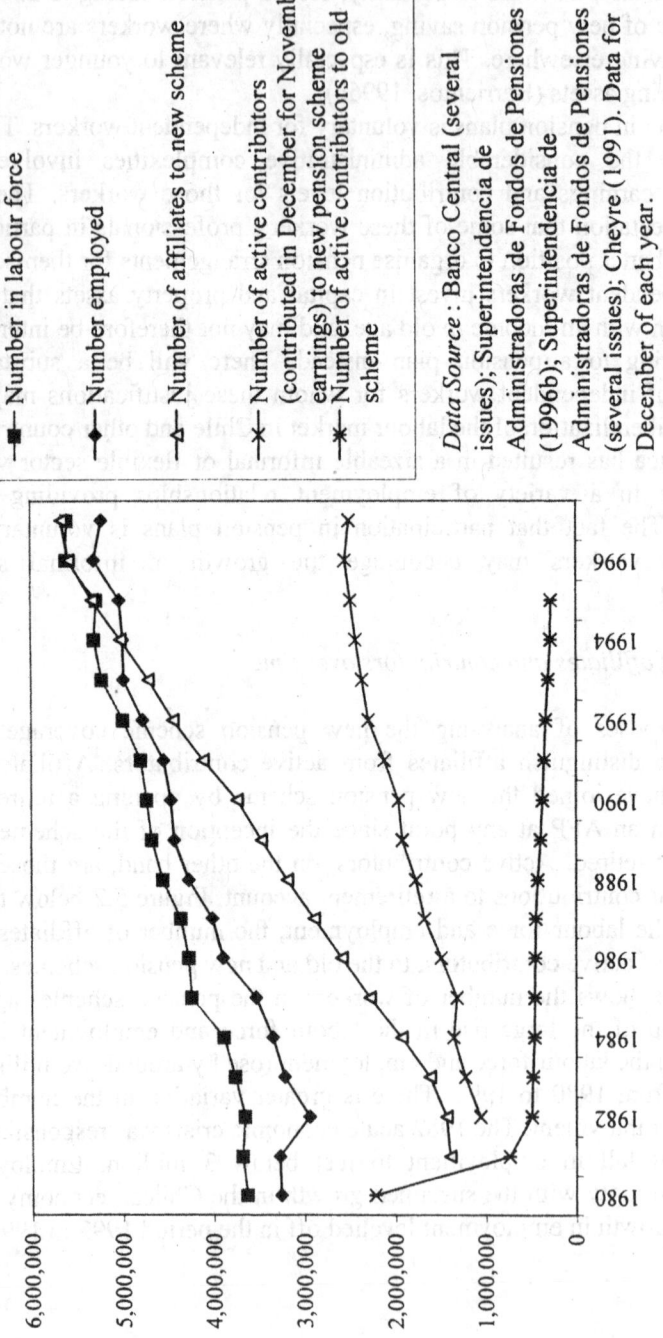

Figure 5.2 Chile: Labour force and pension scheme membership 1980-1997

The number of those affiliated to the new pension scheme shows a remarkable growth from 1.4 million at the end of 1981 to 5.6 million in June 1997. From the implementation of pension reform in 1981, the number of affiliates rose rapidly, reflecting at first the large number of workers switching from the old pension scheme to the new one, and later on the growth in the labour force. The former can be observed in the steep decline in the number of contributors to the old pension scheme between 1980 and 1982. After mid 1980s, the rise in the labour force and employment sustained the rise in affiliates. By 1995, the number of affiliates begins to exceed the numbers employed, and in 1996 the numbers in the labour force.

The number of active contributors also shows growth over the period, from just over 1 million in 1982 to 2.5 million in 1997. The growth in the number of active contributors is far less dramatic than the growth in affiliates, with the consequence that the gap existing between these two series widens over time. This is a consequence of the considerable flexibility characterising the Chilean labour market. The liberalization of the labour market in Chile since mid 1970s contributed to facilitate transitions between economic activity and inactivity, and between formal and informal employment.[11] There is a significant flux in labour market status, which impacts directly on the numbers affiliated. The numbers of affiliates most probably include a large number of people who are inactive, and underlines the inappropriateness of using affiliation as a measure of pension coverage.[12] The proportion of affiliates that actively contribute to the new pension plans has fallen from 73 percent in 1982 to 52 percent in 1990, and 44 percent in June 1997.[13]

The evolution of the number of active contributors tracks closely the trend in employment. It shows signs of stagnation in the aftermath of the early 1980s crisis, and the slow down in the growth of employment in the late 1980s and mid-1990s.

The *Superintendencia de Administradoras de Fondos de Pensiones* releases two measures of active contributors. One measure simply adds the numbers of affiliates who contributed in a particular month. Normally contributions are registered into an account on earnings corresponding to the previous month. However, in some cases delays in registering contributions (where, for example, employers are slow in passing on contributions collected to the respective AFP, or where there are administrative delays in the AFP) mean that contributors are entered for several months' earnings. This results in double counting of contributors and will therefore overstate the number of active contributors. To avoid this double counting a second measure is provided. This adds the number of affiliates who contributed on a particular month covering earnings received the previous month. This measure avoids double counting, but may understate the numbers of active contributors where there is a delay in registering contributions. The true figure for active contributors will be somewhere between these two measures.

Figure 5.3 shows the evolution of the two measures of active contributors. The gap between these two measures widens over time, perhaps reflecting the rise in the absolute number of contributors. At the end of 1982 active contributors were 1.06 million, by March 1997 they had risen to 2.56 million if the narrower measure of active contributors is used, but to 3.18 million if the broader measure is used. The gap becomes wider in the period since 1995, especially as the more restrictive measure of pension scheme coverage declines in line with the changes in the number employed. This suggests that, especially towards the end of the period being studied, the narrower measure of pension coverage is the more reliable. In the discussion that follows, it is this more restrictive measure of pension coverage that will be used.[14]

Figure 5.4 shows the trends in pension scheme coverage rates in Chile. It traces the proportion of the labour force who are affiliated to the new pension scheme, and the proportion of the labour force who are active contributors to the new and old pension scheme.

The Figure shows that the aggregate pension coverage rate (including active contributors to both the old and new schemes) has remained very steady during the whole period (the blip in 1981 is due to the implementation of the reform). It was 52.6 percent in 1982 and rose to 55 percent in 1995, the last year for which figures for active contributors to the old pension scheme were available. These figures are well below the coverage rates of the late 1960s and early 1970s at over 70 percent.[15]

It should also be born in mind that employment was unusually depressed in 1982 as a consequence of the economic crisis, an that it therefore is a poor benchmark against which to assess growth in pension coverage. When disaggregated by pension scheme, the proportion of the employed labour force covered by the old pension scheme has declined, while the proportion covered by the new pension scheme has risen from 38 percent in 1982 to 48 percent in 1997.

With regard to the evolution of disability and survivor insurance coverage, this may differ from the retirement pension scheme coverage. Strictly, the former only covers those who are contributing at the time of the event leading to the insurance claim. This applies to both dependent and independent workers. From 1998 cover for disability and survivor was extended for unemployed dependent workers for up to 12 months from the last contribution paid, providing they contributed for at least six months in the year prior to the start of the unemployment spell. This means that coverage rates for disability and survivor insurance may be higher than the proportion of active contributors in the labour force.

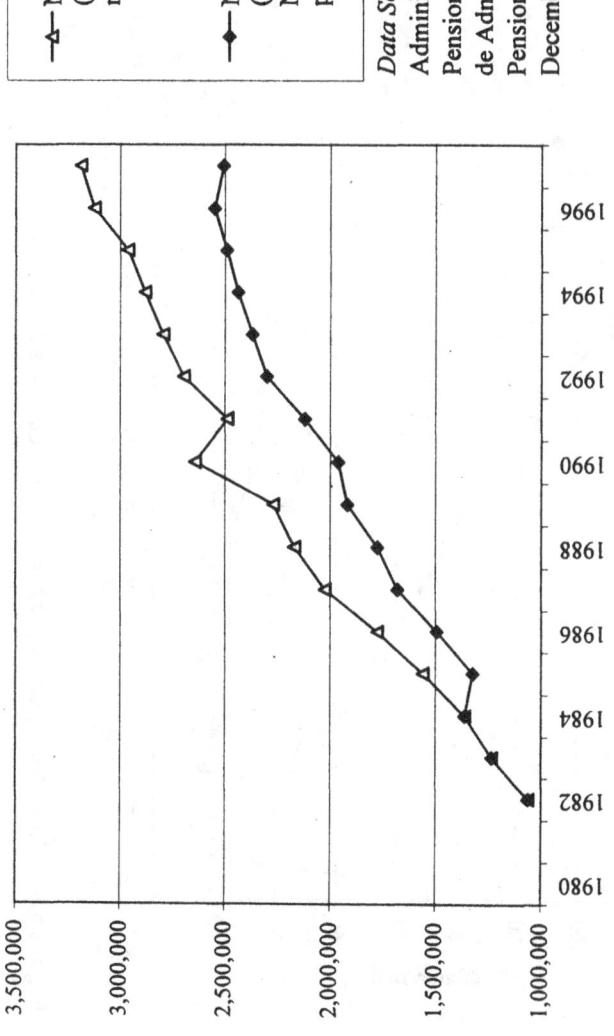

Figure 5.3 Chile: Alternative measures of active contributors to the new pension scheme

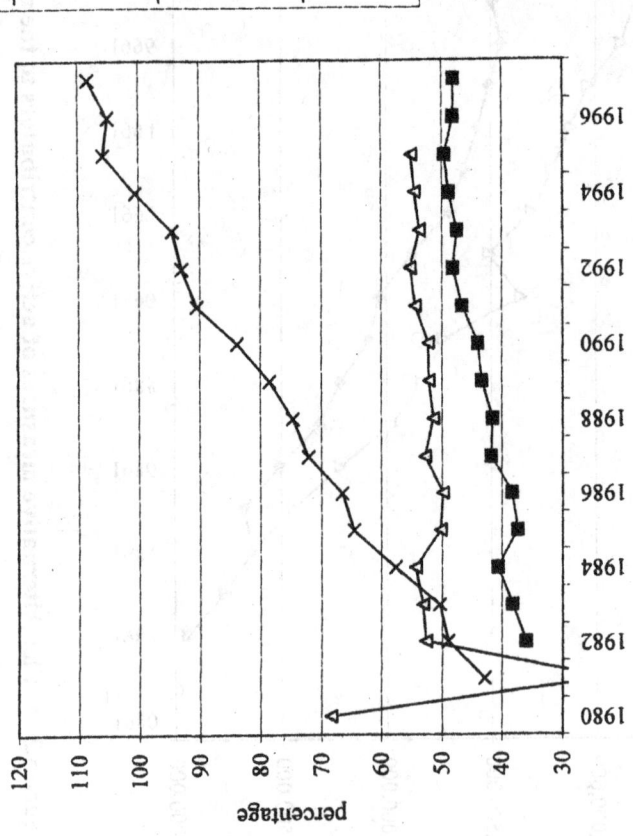

Figure 5.4 Chile: New pension scheme coverage rates 1982-1997

It is not possible to distinguish accurately the unemployed from all other affiliated workers who have stopped contributing for other reasons (e.g., inactivity, move to informal sector, etc.). Figure 5.5 below shows the cumulative number of affiliated workers who have not registered movement in their retirement accounts for the specified length of time. As expected, the number of affiliates not contributing rises through time. The number of affiliates who have not contributed for a period of 12 months or less could provide an upper limit to the extra numbers potentially covered by disability and survivor insurance. For June 1997, for example, around 1.2 million non-contributing affiliates could be covered by this insurance in addition to the active contributors.

Gender dimension of pension scheme coverage

Developed countries with a significant private pension sector have lower rates of private pension scheme coverage among female employees than for male employees. Even and Macpherson report that in the USA in 1988 private supplementary pension plans covered around 55 percent of the male labour force, but only 45 percent of the female labour force (Even and Macpherson, 1990; Even and Macpherson, 1994). In the UK, where until recently the main form of private supplementary pension provision consisted of employer-run occupational pension plans, these covered 64 percent of male employees, but only 36 percent of female employees (Ginn and Arber, 1993).

As pension entitlements are in most cases obtained through employment, this gender gap in private pension coverage is in large part explained by women's labour market experience. Women are more likely to have employment gaps associated with household responsibilities, and are more likely to be subject to employer discrimination as regards recruitment, training, and pay. In the UK, for example, the gender gap in occupational pension coverage is strongly associated with the fact that a large proportion of women work on a part-time basis, and are more likely to change jobs than males. Occupational pensions with a defined benefit formula are designed to benefit full-time workers with long tenures, and this places women at a disadvantage.

A remarkable fact about pension coverage in Chile after the reform is the absence of this often observed gender private pension gap (Barrientos, 1998). Figure 5.6 below shows trends in coverage for men and women in Chile. In fact the proportion of women in employment who actively contribute to an individual retirement pension scheme is 2 to 3 percentage points higher than men's. This is in contrast to the situation prior to pension reform, where pension coverage was lower for men than for women.[16]

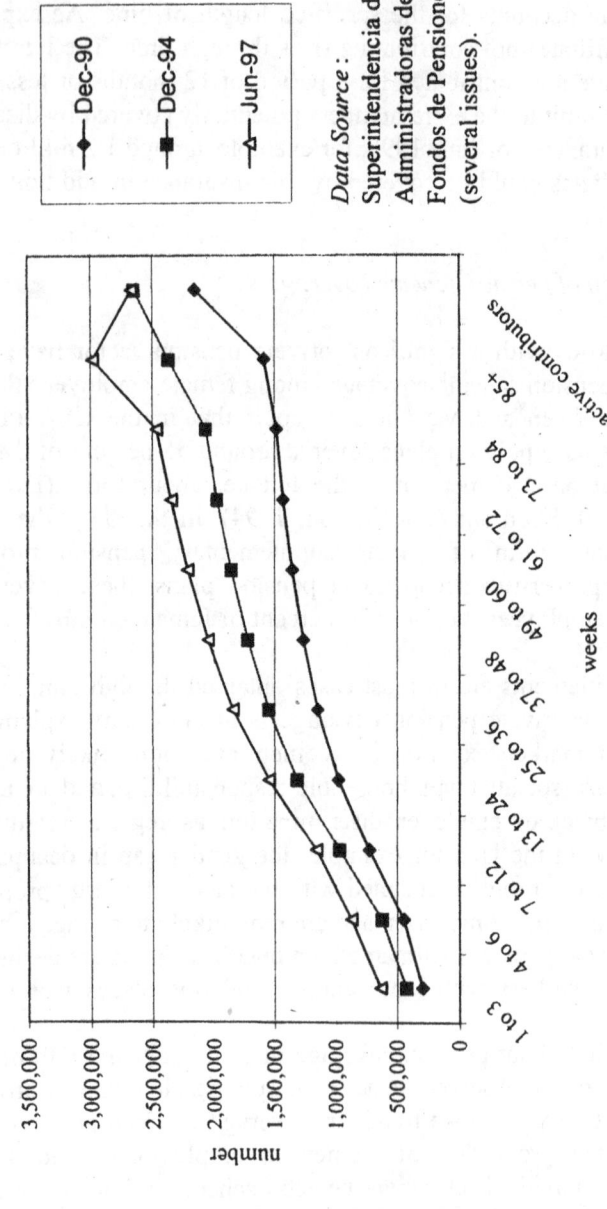

Figure 5.5 Chile: Cumulative number of affiliates without contributions to their retirement accounts by length of time

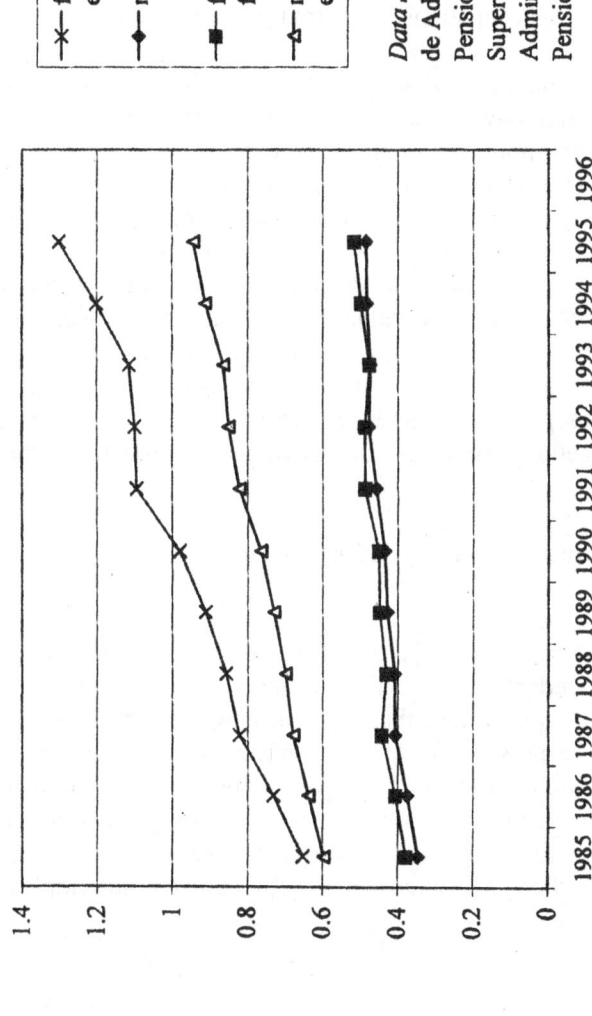

Figure 5.6 Chile: New pension scheme coverage rates by sex

What explanations can be offered for the higher rate of pension scheme coverage among women employees in Chile? Firstly, women active in the labour market are likely to be a more selected group than men, who have higher activity rates. There have been important changes in the labour market attachment of women in this period. Activity rates for women climbed steadily over the 1980s, and by the end of 1993 around 45 percent of women between the ages of 20 and 44 were active in the labour market. The growth in employment since mid 1980s in Chile has concentrated on the sectors traditionally associated with women's employment. There has been an important growth in women's employment in the managerial, and managerial support, occupations that traditionally have high coverage rates.[17]

Secondly, demographic and social changes have raised life cycle risks for women. Fertility rates have declined while life expectancy has risen. And families look much more fragile in their capacity to provide insurance against economic risks. The proportions of women who are separated, and those who are heads of household, have risen substantially in the same period. These changes are likely to strengthen the need for women to participate in pension plans that provide some measure of insurance.

Thirdly, the introduction of individual retirement pension plans may raise coverage among women as employers have less influence over pension arrangements, and women are freer to exercise their pension preferences. Women employees pension preferences provide the main explanation for the absence of a gender private pension coverage gap in Chile (Barrientos, 1998).

Pension scheme coverage of independent workers

Affiliation to the individual capitalization pension plans is voluntary for independent workers. The new pension scheme has features that should be attractive to independent workers. Two of these features are the portability of the new pension plans, and the fact that contribution gaps, especially towards the end of a person's working life, have less damaging effects upon pension benefits than under pay as you go pension schemes. In practice, the coverage of independent workers by the new pension scheme in Chile has remained very low. Figure 5.7 below shows the trends in pension coverage for independent workers, measured as the self-employed plus employers.

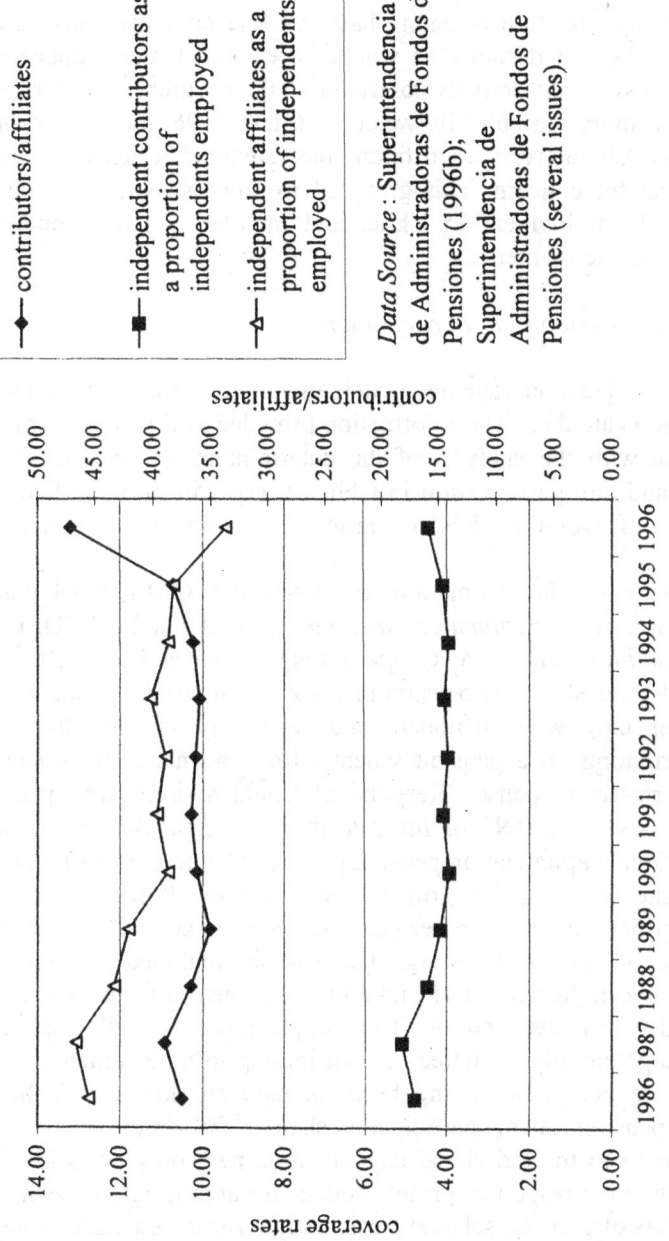

Figure 5.7 Chile: New pension scheme coverage rates for independent workers

The Figure shows that the proportion of independent workers affiliated to the individual capitalization pension plans in Chile have oscillated around 10 percent for the last decade. As would be expected, the proportion of independent workers who actively contribute to their retirement accounts is both lower and more variable. Between 1986 and 1996, the proportion of independent workers actively contributing has remained at below 5 percent. This is a matter for concern. This group of workers account for around a quarter of total employment in Chile, and includes a large number of especially vulnerable workers.

Determinants of Pension Plan Participation

The evidence on pension scheme participation rates examined so far has focused on aggregate data. The information provided will be complemented in this section with the analysis of the determinants of pension scheme participation and non-participation in Chile. These will be identified from the estimation of probit models of participation using household survey data.

The data used in the estimation are from the CASEN 94 Survey (*Caracterización Socio-Económica Nacional*) carried out by MIDEPLAN (*Ministerio de Planificación y Cooperación*) in November 1994.[18] The Survey included questions on pension plan participation. Respondents were asked whether they were affiliated, and separately whether they were actively contributing, to a pension scheme. Respondents could select one from five alternative responses. Respondents could register participation in the old pension scheme (INP or *Instituto de Normalización Previsional*) , the new individual capitalization pension plans (AFP), in CAPREDENA the pension scheme covering the Armed Forces and the Police, an OTHER category covering a variety of other pension schemes; and NONE, for those not affiliated, or not contributing. The sample included all employed individuals between the ages of 15 and retirement age (60 for women and 65 for men) with valid observations. The sample represents all respondents who could be potentially affiliated or contributing to a retirement account, as these require being, or having been, in paid employment. Table 5.1 describes the pension scheme participation share in the sample.

As participation in the individual capitalization pension plan is identified from a dichotomous response, probit models are appropriate to estimating the probabilities of pension scheme participation associated with a range of demographic, occupation, job status, education and experience variables.

Table 5.1
Chile: Pension scheme coverage rates from CASEN94 data

	Full sample	Employed only	
Pension Scheme Status	percentage affiliated	percentage affiliated	percentage contributing
INP (old pension schemes)	6.0	6.6	4.6
AFP (new pension scheme)	38.3	60.1	54.1
CAPREDENA	0.8	0.9	0.8
Other pension schemes	0.5	0.5	0.4
None	54.4	31.9	40.1
Total	100	100	100
Number of respondents	110,567	59,629	59,629

Underlying the probit model of participation are assumptions about pension scheme participation behaviour by individual workers, and about availability of pension choices. On the demand side, it is assumed that workers will choose the pension status that will maximise their life cycle consumption taking account of their risk preferences, and available information on the probabilities that the contingencies covered by pension schemes materialise. Workers who are, for example, likely to have long lives or who have dependants they care for, are more likely to participate in a pension scheme. Workers who have made a substantial investment in their human capital, which is intrinsically illiquid and risky, are more likely to seek to join a pension scheme that protects them from large variations in consumption. On the supply side, it is assumed that employers offering jobs that require productivity enhancing financial incentives are more likely to make membership of pension schemes available to their workers. Thus, for example, large firm employers are more likely to offer pension scheme membership to their workers than small firm employers. The results from the probit models of participation can be interpreted as reflecting a reduced form pension participation model.

Determinants of affiliation and active contribution to the new pension plans

The probabilities, that an individual is affiliated or is actively contributing to an AFP, associated with a range of demographic, occupation, job characteristics, and region variables, are presented in Table 5.2 below.

Table 5.2
Results from probit models of affiliation and contribution to individual capitalization pension plans

	Affiliated to AFP		Contributing to AFP		
Variable	Parameter[a]	t-stat	Parameter[a]	t-stat	Mean
Constant	-0.478 *	-19.39	-0.693 *	-24.31	
Personal Characteristics:					
Female Married	-0.048 *	-6.09	-0.064 *	-7.38	0.13
Graduate	0.036 *	3.24	0.025 **	2.16	0.09
Head of Household	0.057 *	9.12	0.024 *	3.43	0.53
Numbers In Household	0.001 *	1.14	0.002	1.93	4.63
Potential Experience	0.005 *	7.47	0.005 *	6.53	22.44
Potential Experience sqrd.	-0.0002 *	-16.77	-0.0001 *	-14.20	689.10
Employment Status:					
Self employed	-0.214 *	-29.41	-0.298 *	-35.58	0.23
Permanent	0.150 *	12.15	0.266 *	17.69	0.68
Temporary	-0.083 *	-7.76	-0.130 *	-10.79	0.05
Fixed Term	0.194 *	10.85	0.232 *	11.67	0.03
Piecework	0.070 *	4.85	0.070 *	3.96	0.06
Seasonal	0.030 **	2.26	0.064 *	3.99	0.17
Place of Work:					
Homeworker	-0.082 *	-10.98	-0.114 *	-13.46	0.14
Ambulatory	-0.007	-0.76	-0.031 *	-2.92	0.08
Unionisation & Training:					
Union member	0.030 *	2.80	0.047 *	4.14	0.07
Trained in last year	0.024 *	2.77	0.028 *	3.12	0.12
Hours of Work:					
Weekly Hours	0.009 *	14.61	0.011 *	15.05	48.9
Weekly Hours Sqrd.	-0.00007 *	-12.82	-0.00009 *	-13.29	2580
Establishment Size:					
Size 2-5	-0.015 **	-2.25	-0.023 *	-3.08	0.23
Size 6-9	0.061 *	5.92	0.068 *	6.01	0.06
Size 10-49	0.155 *	18.70	0.169 *	18.88	0.22
Size 50-199	0.225 *	21.53	0.247 *	22.34	0.10
Size 200+	0.146 *	13.49	0.190 *	16.38	0.10

Table 5.2 continued

Variable	Affiliated to AFP Parameter[a]	t-stat	Contributing to AFP Parameter[a]	t-stat	Mean
Occupation:					
Manager & Administrator	-0.103 *	-7.34	-0.093 *	-6.09	0.05
Professional	0.067 *	5.09	0.091 *	6.55	0.10
Sales	-0.024	-1.83	-0.023	-1.65	0.06
Personal Service	0.049 *	3.40	0.059 *	3.90	0.04
Agriculture	-0.043 *	-3.29	-0.049 *	-3.50	0.09
Skilled manual	0.082 *	6.90	0.072 *	5.67	0.13
Unskilled manual	0.011	0.99	0.014	1.22	0.34
Transport & Communication	0.065 *	5.01	0.065 *	4.75	0.08
Health Program:					
PublicHealth	0.358 *	63.39	0.424 *	68.91	0.35
PrivateHealth	0.017 **	2.21	-0.014	-1.60	0.10
ISAPRE	0.464 *	55.32	0.518 *	58.20	0.20
Region :					
Region 1	-0.087 *	-5.29	-0.127 *	-7.06	0.02
Region 2	0.004	0.30	-0.027	-1.87	0.04
Region 3	0.038 *	2.72	-0.003	-0.21	0.03
Region 4	-0.038 *	-3.55	-0.053 *	-4.57	0.06
Region 6	0.048	3.39	-0.005	-0.34	0.03
Region 7	-0.040 *	-4.50	-0.074 *	-7.55	0.11
Region 8	-0.025 *	-3.14	-0.025 *	-2.78	0.18
Region 9	-0.037 **	-2.53	-0.044 *	-2.72	0.03
Region 10	-0.046 *	-3.62	-0.071 *	-5.06	0.04
Region 11	0.044 **	2.26	-0.038	-1.77	0.01
Region 12	-0.036	-1.95	0.003	0.15	0.01
Metropolitan Region	-0.024 *	-3.13	-0.028 *	-3.38	0.25

N=59,629

LogL = -27,044.8   LogL = -24,949.06
RlogL = -40,096.4 RlogL = -41,129.21
LHS = 0.601   LHS = 0.541
PredLHS= 0.645   PredLHS= 0.554
ZM = 0.596   ZM = 0.642

a. Parameters are the partial derivatives of the probit coefficients evaluated at the mean of the regressors. They can be interpreted as the change in the probability of affiliation, or active contribution, associated with a unit change in the RHS variable.

* means significant at the 1 % level.
**means significant at the 5 % level.

To facilitate the evaluation of the findings the independent variables have been grouped, and the parameters reported are the partial derivatives of the estimated coefficients evaluated at the mean of the regressors. These parameters have the advantage that they can be interpreted as the change in the probability of affiliation, or being an active contributor, to an individual capitalization pension plan resulting from a unit change in the relevant variable.

Beginning with personal characteristics, the results suggest that married women are less likely to be affiliated to a pension plan than men or single women. This is a consequence of the impact of household responsibilities on women's labour market experience. Another explanation is contributed by gender discrimination in the design of the new pension scheme. In particular, survivor benefits are provided for all female spouses of pension plan contributors, but only for males spouses who are disabled. Women married to a contributing spouse may have, to this extent, weaker incentives for affiliating, or being an active contributor to the new pension scheme.

Higher levels of human capital investment are more likely to lead graduates to seek to join a pension plan. Similarly, heads of household are more likely to join a pension plan as it provides a range of insurance cover for other household members. Potential experience, a variable constructed by subtracting years of schooling from the age of the respondents, exhibits a non linear relation in pension plan participation. The probability of pension plan participation rises with years of potential experience, but at a declining rate. This reflects the fact that older workers were more likely to have participated in the old pension scheme and were less likely to join the new pension scheme. The age pattern of pension plan affiliation and contribution will change over time as those in the old pension scheme retire, and the scheme is wound up.

Employment status is an important determinant of individual pension plan contribution. The self-employed are less likely to be active contributors to an individual retirement account. For dependent workers, affiliation to an individual pension plan is much less likely for those in temporary jobs, and to a lesser extent for those in seasonal and piecework jobs, than for those in permanent or fixed term employment. Comparing the parameters from the affiliation model with those of the contribution model shows only one change in sign. Temporary work is negatively and significantly associated with active contribution to a pension plan.

As expected, the effects of employment status are stronger in the contribution model. It is likely that lower quality jobs may have a detrimental effect on the availability of pension plans as well as the demand for them. This is because employers offering low quality jobs have lower rates of pay, and are less likely to be prepared to incur pension scheme contribution collection costs (this point is discussed below in the context of firm size). Employment status variables capture key dimensions of the employment relationship, although the latter is also captured by place of work, unionisation and training variables. Working at home, or in a workshop next to the home, and working on the streets or at customers' homes are all strongly and negatively associated with being affiliated or an active contributor to individual capitalization pension plans. These are indicators of lower job quality. By contrast, being a member of a trade union or receiving training at work indicate better quality jobs, and are positively associated with both affiliation and active contribution.

As regards weekly hours of work, their impact upon probabilities of affiliation or contribution to pension plans is non-linear. Probabilities are concave in hours worked. This is because very long hours jobs are of poor quality. This applies especially to domestic work.

The estimated parameters associated with establishment size provide useful information. Likelihood of pension plan participation is negative for small establishments, rises with establishment size, and then declines for the largest size of establishment. It is likely that supply side factors are important here. There are costs for firms associated with collecting and depositing workers' pension plan contributions. It is very likely that there exist economies of scale in this activity. Therefore, pension contribution collection costs should be lower for larger firms that have more effective administrative and payroll departments. By contrast, smaller establishments may well find the costs associated with workers pension plan participation to be large, and will therefore discourage workers from participating. Employers are under a legal obligation to collect these contributions, which is enforced by an agency under the Labour Ministry (the *Dirección del Trabajo*). The probabilities of being inspected, and fined, are bound to be positively associated with firm size. At the lower end of establishment size there are also demand side factors at work in that workers who wish to avoid paying pension plan contributions may find it easier to do so by seeking employment in these establishments.

As regards Occupation, three occupational groups have negative probabilities of affiliation and active contribution: Managers and Administrators, Agriculture and Sales (although this last one is significant only at 10 percent). Of the rest, there is evidence of some association between skill levels and pension plan affiliation and active contribution.

The process of pension reform in Chile was accompanied by a reform of health provision, the other key program within social insurance. Health reform made it compulsory for dependent workers to participate in a basic health insurance program. Workers pay 7 percent of their earnings to finance their basic health insurance premium. They have the choice of arranging their health insurance with an autonomous public provider (*Fondo Nacional de Salud* or FONASA), or with new private providers (*Institutos de Salud Previsional* or ISAPRES). Some workers with alternative arrangements are grouped as Private Health. Membership of FONASA or ISAPRES is associated with a strong positive probability of being affiliated or actively contributing to a pension plan.

The broad picture provided by this analysis is that affiliation and active contribution to an individual capitalization pension plan is positively correlated with job and worker quality, and is to a large extent determined by the nature of the employment relationship. Affiliation and active contribution is more likely for skilled workers in medium to large size establishments, and in more secure and stable employment.

Determinants of non-affiliation and non-contribution

The figures in Table 5.1 indicate that just over 30 percent of employed workers are not affiliated to any of the pension schemes, and that 40 percent are not contributing to any to any of these. It is important to establish what reasons explain their non-participation.

A number of factors can explain why workers are not participating in pension schemes. Workers who are unlikely to collect pension benefits, for example because they are unlikely to work for the minimum period to access the pension benefit floor, have few incentives to affiliate to a pension scheme. Workers with high intertemporal discount rates may be reluctant to affiliate to a pension scheme. This may be due to impatience, but also to poverty. Workers with large stocks of financial or property assets may not be attracted to taking up a pension plan. Workers who belong to large household groups where contingencies may be more easily and cheaply insured against may also have few incentives to join a pension scheme. These points suggest that, non-participation in a pension scheme is likely to associated with, on the demand side, poor employment prospects, poverty, large families, and ownership of alternative assets.

There are also supply side reasons for workers not participating in pension schemes. As discussed in the previous section, non-participation may be a consequence of employers discouraging workers from joining a pension scheme.

Table 5.3 below shows the results of estimating a probit model of the probability of non-affiliation for a sample of employed workers. Given the high coverage rates of the new pension schemes, the analysis of non-affiliation and non-contribution should provide a mirror image of the results in the previous section.[19]

Table 5.3
Results from probit models of non-affiliation and non-contribution to pension schemes among employed workers

Variable	Not affiliated		Not Contributing		
	Parameter	t-stat	Parameter[a]	t-stat	Mean
Constant	0.254 *	12.43	0.538 *	20.20	
Personal Characteristics:					
Female Married	0.083 *	12.31	0.100 *	11.88	0.13
Graduate	-0.041 *	-4.02	-0.034 *	-2.84	0.09
Head of Household	-0.073 *	-13.92	-0.043 *	-6.58	0.53
Numbers in Household	0.001	1.53	-0.001	-1.15	4.63
Potential Experience	-0.005 *	-8.15	-0.006 *	-8.52	22.44
Potential Exp.sqrd.	0.00005 *	6.01	0.0001 *	8.51	689.1
Employment Status:					
Self employed	0.182 *	31.04	0.289 *	37.83	0.23
Permanent	-0.132 *	-13.90	-0.271 *	-20.46	0.68
Temporary	0.077 *	9.02	0.136 *	12.23	0.05
Fixed Term	-0.142 *	-9.61	-0.195 *	-10.63	0.03
Piecework	-0.049 *	-4.43	-0.051 *	-3.29	0.06
Seasonal	-0.001	-0.15	-0.037 *	-2.66	0.17
Place of Work:					
Homeworker	0.067 *	11.08	0.100 *	12.94	0.14
Ambulatory	0.015 *	1.98	0.031 *	3.19	0.08
Unionisation& Training:					
Union member	-0.069 *	-6.18	-0.097 *	-7.35	0.07
Trained in last year	-0.064 *	-7.83	-0.077 *	-8.01	0.12
Hours of Work:					
Weekly Hours	-0.007 *	-13.55	-0.010 *	-14.52	48.90
Weekly Hours Sqrd.	0.000 *	11.18	0.000 *	12.04	2580
Establishment Size:					
Size 2-5	0.031 *	5.79	0.042 *	5.99	0.23
Size 6-9	-0.036 *	-4.07	-0.058 *	-5.43	0.06
Size 10-49	-0.126 *	-17.86	-0.166 *	-19.27	0.22
Size 50-199	-0.207 *	-21.94	-0.259 *	-23.48	0.10
Size 200+	-0.220 *	-20.58	-0.302 *	-24.11	0.10

Table 5.3 continued

	Not affiliated		Not Contributing		
Variable	Parameter[a]	t-stat	Parameter[a]	t-stat	Mean
Occupation:					
Manager & Administrator	0.202 *	15.76	0.204 *	13.32	0.05
Professional	0.015	1.15	-0.022	-1.46	0.10
Sales	0.137 *	11.24	0.142 *	9.87	0.06
Personal Service	0.044 *	3.20	0.014 *	0.87	0.04
Agriculture	0.149 *	12.35	0.167 *	11.59	0.09
Skilled manual	0.054 *	4.65	0.053 *	3.97	0.13
Unskilled manual	0.113 *	10.61	0.110 *	9.03	0.34
Transport & Communication	0.085 *	6.75	0.082 *	5.65	0.08
Health Program:					
PublicHealth	-0.326 *	-66.40	-0.426 *	-72.28	0.35
PrivateHealth	0.011	1.79	0.055 *	6.69	0.10
ISAPRE	-0.331 *	-44.45	-0.419 *	-47.63	0.20
Region :					
Region 1	0.000	-0.02	0.042 **	2.34	0.02
Region 2	-0.015	-1.29	0.013	0.93	0.04
Region 3	-0.056 *	-4.54	0.003	0.19	0.03
Region 4	0.026 *	2.95	0.059 *	5.27	0.06
Region 6	-0.045 *	-3.62	0.015	0.99	0.03
Region 7	0.021 *	2.85	0.070 *	7.53	0.11
Region 8	0.014 **	2.03	0.020 **	2.28	0.18
Region 9	0.064 *	5.28	0.071 *	4.57	0.03
Region 10	0.029 *	2.66	0.067 *	5.01	0.04
Region 11	-0.043 *	-2.60	0.026	1.26	0.01
Region 12	-0.008	-0.48	-0.086 *	-4.12	0.01
Metropolitan Region	0.031 *	4.70	0.031 *	3.76	0.25

N= 59,629

LogL = -23,782.7   LogL = -22,440.4
RlogL = -37,228.6   RlogL = -40,132.8
LHS = 0.316   LHS = 0.400
PredLHS= 0.219   PredLHS= 0.330
ZM = 0.625   ZM = 0.671

a. Parameters are the partial derivatives of the probit coefficients evaluated at the mean of the regressors. They can be interpreted as the change in the probability of affiliation, or active contribution, associated with a unit change in the RHS variable.
* means significant at 1 percent.
** means significant at 5 percent.

This is true of the parameters associated with personal characteristics. Compared with the results in Table 5.2, the signs on the parameters are now reversed. Married female workers are more likely not to be affiliated, nor actively contributing, to a pension scheme. And the probabilities of affiliating and contributing are now convex in potential experience.

The parameters within the employment status group indicate that both self-employment and temporary employment increase the probability of non-affiliation and non-contribution. And being in permanent employment, as expected, has the opposite effect. Homeworking and Ambulatory work raise the probability of non-affiliation and non-contribution. Union membership and training are negatively and significantly associated with pension scheme non-participation. Non-participation in pension schemes is concave in weekly hours of work.

Non-participation in pension schemes declines linearly with establishment size. Comparing these results with those reported in Table 5.2 suggest that the decline in participation in the new pension scheme observed for large establishments was due to the availability of alternative pension schemes to workers in large establishments. This is because large establishments were likely to have had high coverage rates in the old pension schemes prior to the reform. The results for non-participation show that workers in large establishments are less likely not to be affiliated or contributing to a pension scheme.

The parameters associated with the Health Program groups show that there is an association between non-participation in pension schemes and non-participation in health insurance programs. Having a private pension insurance plan other than in ISAPRES increases the probability of non-participation in pension schemes.

In sum, non-participation in pension schemes is less likely for married women and the self-employed, and for less skilled workers in small establishments, with less secure or stable employment.

Why do some workers affiliated to an AFP fail to contribute to their retirement accounts?

As noted above around one half of the total numbers of affiliates to the new pension scheme fail to actively contribute to their retirement accounts. The ratio of contributors to affiliates has fallen steadily since the start of the new pension scheme in Chile. There are many reasons why affiliates may stop contributing to their pension plans. The key factors are transitions out of employment into unemployment or inactivity, and transitions within employment across employers or sectors. Changes in personal circumstances, or dissatisfaction with the individual capitalization pension scheme may also be contributory factors. Although longitudinal data would be needed to provide accurate measures of the relative significance of these factors, useful information can be gained from the profile of non-contributing affiliates in CASEN94.[20]

Of those who, in CASEN 94, reported being affiliated but not contributing to an AFP, two thirds were not in employment, and one third were employed. Taking those not in employment first, this group includes both the unemployed and the inactive. Within this group, women outnumber men 2 to 1, reflecting the greater incidence of employment gaps and inactivity among women. Only 10 percent of women reported having looked for employment in the last two months, whereas close to one half of men had done so. From these figures, it is clear that transitions from employment into inactivity were a primary cause of women failing to continue contributing to their retirement accounts, whereas transitions into unemployment were the primary cause for men. This is confirmed with the findings from a study done by the *Asociación Gremial de Administradoras de Fondos de Pensiones*, the organisation representing the AFPs, to the effect that transitions out of employment account for the majority of non-contributing affiliates among dependent workers.

Looking now at the one third of non-contributing affiliates who were in employment, it would be useful to isolate the impact of employment transitions on the failure to make regular contributions. These employment transitions would include workers changing employers, or moving from the formal to the informal or non-covered sector. The residual could provide some indication of the extent to which change in personal circumstances or dissatisfaction with the new pension scheme accounts for non-contribution. Within this group, men outnumber women 3 to 1. When the members of this group are classified according to their employment status it appears that 38 percent of them are own account workers, while a further 17.5 percent are temporary or domestic workers, or unwaged relatives. Over one half of non-contributing affiliates to an AFP can therefore be accounted for by the nature of their employment in the informal or flexible labour force. They may have either moved into this sector from formal sector employment, or simply ceased contributing due to the unprotected nature of their employment.

The remainder, around 45 percent of workers who are affiliated to an AFP, and employed, but are not contributing, work under permanent or fixed term contracts, and have more or less protected employment. It is difficult to determine exactly the reasons for their failure to contribute. Possible reasons include, *inter alia*, low earnings, employment in small establishments, changes in personal circumstances, dissatisfaction with the pension scheme.

In conclusion, two thirds of workers who are affiliated to an AFP, but are not contributing, may be in this situation due to transitions from employment to unemployment or inactivity. The other one third consists of workers who are employed. Their failure to contribute may be accounted for by transitions into unprotected employment in the informal or flexible sector of the labour market. Around one half of the employed group are in this category. The other half of workers who are affiliated and employed but are not contributing are in permanent or fixed term employment. Job or personal transitions may be the cause here, but demand factors cannot be ruled out.

Pension scheme coverage in Latin America

In this section the trends in pension scheme coverage observed in Chile will be compared to those in other Latin American countries. As Mexico, Uruguay, Colombia, and Costa Rica have only recently undergone pension reform, comparison of pension coverage rates is mainly restricted to Argentina and Peru. The coverage of old age and retirement pension schemes and disability and survivor insurance are discussed separately.

Old age and retirement pension scheme coverage

The macroeconomic and labour market conditions in the 1980s and early 1990s did not provide an auspicious start to the new individual retirement pension schemes in Latin America, particularly in terms of pension scheme coverage. Participation in the new individual retirement pension plans rises very fast in the period immediately following their introduction. However, to the extent that this simply reflects workers switching from the pre-existing pension scheme to the newly introduced one, overall pension coverage rates may stay the same, or decline. In fact private pension coverage in developed countries also show a declining trend, a fact that is attributed to labour market changes (Barrientos, 1996b; Barrientos, 1997c; Disney and Stears, 1996; Parsons, 1991). As pension reform has accompanied important changes in labour market conditions, and is in part a response to these changes, it will be difficult to disentangle the pension reform and labour market effects on pension coverage rates.

Table 5.4 provides some indicators of the size of the membership of the new pension schemes in Chile, Argentina and Peru. A common trend can be observed for the new pension schemes to experience rapid growth in the number of participants. This rapid initial growth comes from the widespread switching of a large number of workers from the old pension scheme to the new one, but also from the relatively high number of new entrants into the labour market. The latter reflects the marked growth in the labour force and employment in the 1990s in Latin America.

In Chile, the numbers of active contributors to the private capitalization pension scheme rose from 1 million in December 1982 to 3.1 million in December 1996. Rates of growth of active contributors averaged 13.8 percent in the first five years, but declined to 4.6 percent in the last five. The numbers of affiliates, on the other hand, have continued to grow over the period and are now greater than the numbers in the labour force. In Peru, the number of affiliates to the new private pension scheme grew from 627,156 in December 1993 to 1.7 million by December 1997 (Superintendencia de Administradoras de Fondos de Jubilaciones y Pensiones, 1996). There are no statistics available on the number of active contributors to the Peruvian private pension scheme. In Argentina, the numbers affiliated to the new pension scheme grew from 3.5 million at the start of the reform to 6.2 million in November 1997. Growth in the numbers of active contributors was slower. The numbers contributing to the new private pension scheme rose from 2.1 million in December 1994 to 3.1 million in November 1997. Mexico had just over 10 million affiliates at the start of the new pension scheme in 1997.

Table 5.4
Number of affiliates and contributors to individual capitalization pension schemes in Chile, Peru, Argentina and Mexico

	Affiliates				*Contributors*	
	Chile	Peru	Argentina	Mexico	Chile	Argentina
1982	1,440				1,060	
1985	2,284				1,322	
1990	3,740				1,962	
1993	4,709	627			2,367	
1994	5,014	961	3,502		2,436	2,029
1995	5,321	1,107	4,881		2,490	2,571
1996	5,571	1,550	5,472		2,548	2,762
1997[a]	5,653	1,638	6,222	10,732	2,505	3,175

Source: (Superintendencia de Administradoras de Fondos de Jubilaciones y Pensiones, 1996; Superintendencia de Administradoras de Fondos de Jubilaciones y Pensiones, 1997; Superintendencia de Administradoras de Fondos de Pensiones, several issues)
a. Latest available data.

Although this is usually taken to indicate the early success of pension reform, caution must be exercised for at least two reasons. Firstly, and especially in the context of the new individual retirement pension plans, it is important to distinguish between affiliates and active contributors to pension plans. Affiliates are those individuals who have at any time opened a retirement account with a pension fund manager. Active contributors, on the other hand, are those who make regular contributions to their accounts. The trend is for the number of affiliates to rise rapidly immediately after pension reform, and to continue to rise at significant rates later on. The growth in number of active contributors is also rapid at first, but then it slows down. As a result the ratio of active contributors to affiliates shows a tendency to decline.

Secondly, given the widespread transfer of workers from the pre-existing pay as you go pension schemes to the capitalization schemes, it is important to observe the pension system overall coverage rate. Overall pension coverage rates tell quite a different story. Table 5.5 provides some indicators for the countries concerned. Pension coverage rates for the new pension scheme show a rising trend, but overall pension scheme coverage rates are stagnant, or declining.

The proportion of the labour force actively contributing to the private and public pension schemes in Chile has risen since the early 1980s when pension reform was implemented. In 1995 it was 52 percent, but it is still lower than the levels reached in the early 1970s (just over 70 percent). In Peru, the proportion of the active labour force covered by all pension schemes has remained steady at around 25 percent. In Argentina the rise in coverage of the private pension scheme has not had any effect upon overall pension coverage rates, which remain at around 30 percent. These rates of coverage are very low relative to the rates of pension coverage in the 1970s. In Colombia, overall coverage rates slightly increased after the introduction of individual retirement pension plans. Overall coverage rates were 29.6 percent of PEA in 1992, rising to 32.9 percent in December 1995, with the number of private pension fund participants at 11.5 percent of PEA (Asociación Gremial de AFPs, 1996). The main conclusion is that pension reform has led to a rise in the proportion of the labour force covered by the new individual capitalization pension scheme. This reflects a transfer of workers from the existing pension schemes to the new ones. Overall pension coverage rates, however, have stagnated at the low levels reached in the period prior to pension reform.

Table 5.5
Pension scheme coverage rates for selected Latin American countries

	New pension schemes only				All pension schemes			
	Chile	Peru	Argentina	Colombia	Chile	Peru	Argentina	Colombia
1982	29.0				42.3			
1985	31.2				41.9			
1990	41.5				49.3			
1993	45.3	7.5			51.3	25.2		
1994	46.0	11.2	14.4		51.2	25.9	29.8	
1995	47.2	12.8	17.9	11.5	52.4	25.3	30.7	32.9
1996	45.5		18.9				30.5	
1997	44.8		21.3				30.7	

Source: Pension scheme contributors (Superintendencia de Administradoras de Fondos de Jubilaciones y Pensiones, 1996; Superintendencia de Administradoras de Fondos de Jubilaciones y Pensiones, 1997); PEA data for Chile, Argentina and Peru (Banco Central, several issues; Instituto Nacional de Estadística y Censos, 1995; Instituto Nacional de Estadísticas, 1992; Instituto Nacional de Estadísticas, 1993; Instituto Nacional de Estadísticas, 1995; Instituto Nacional de Estadística y Censos, 1995; Webb and Fernández, 1995). Pension coverage rates is pension scheme contributors as a proportion of the economically active population. New pension scheme coverage refers to active contributors, except for Peru where it refers to affiliates.

Gender and pension coverage. Small gender differentials in pension coverage can also be observed in the countries under examination. For Latin American countries as a whole, the proportion of women workers covered by a pension plan is not very different from that of men. There is significant discrimination in pay and employment against women in Latin America, but their pension coverage holds up well. This is mainly explained by two reasons. Firstly, women in employment are a selected group, likely to have higher skills and qualifications than the average for men. Secondly significant numbers of women work in public administration with higher levels of pension plan coverage.

In Chile as was noted above, rates of coverage for women are slightly higher than rates of coverage for men. In Peru, figures available for March 1995 show that for the universe of private pension plan affiliates, men constituted 69 percent, while women 31 percent. Women's share in private pension plan affiliates is very close to the proportion of women in the labour force (29.7 percent in 1993). Argentina provides a different picture. In Argentina in June 1995, women's share in private and public pension plan affiliates were 25.6 and 33.7 percent respectively. Women appear to have a stronger preference for the public pension scheme. The overall pension coverage rate for women reached 29.2 percent in 1995. This is slightly lower than the overall coverage rate for the labour force as a whole at just over 30 percent.

Employment status and pension coverage. As regards differentials in coverage according to employment status, these are significant. Coverage rates are likely to be higher in formal employment, and much lower in informal employment. Latin American countries experienced a growth in the informal sector of the labour force during the years of recession and later structural adjustment in the 1980s and early 1980s. In Peru, the proportion of the labour force employed in the formal sector in *Lima Metropolitana* decreased from 51.8 percent in 1985 to 47.1 percent in 1994, with informal sector employment growing from 40.5 to 48,4 percent in the same period (Webb and Fernández, 1995). In Argentina, similar trends can be observed.

In contrast to all other Latin American countries, the self-employed in Argentina were covered by the public scheme through a separate social insurance fund (Schulthess and LoVuolo, 1991). While the self-employed share of the labour force was around a quarter in 1994, they accounted for around 26.6 percent of the affiliates to the pension system as a whole. The breakdown of coverage of self-employed workers by pension scheme reveals that they are less attracted to the new capitalization scheme. In December 1995, self-employed workers constituted 34.7 percent of the affiliates to the public scheme, but only 19.9 percent of the affiliates to the private capitalization scheme. As noted above, in Chile only a very small proportion of self-employed workers belongs to the new pension scheme. The new pension scheme has proved to be remarkably unattractive to informal sector workers.

Disability and survivor insurance coverage rates

The coverage of the disability and survivor pension is rather different in that entitlement does not depend on the long term accumulation of contributions and returns, and on reaching a retirement age, but instead on the contribution record prior to the occurrence of the contingency. The contribution period required to secure disability and survivor insurance cover varies across countries and across contingency. In all countries the disability and survivor pension benefit is calculated as a proportion of a reference salary.[21]

As regards disability insurance, most countries provide disability benefits if one half of a worker's productive capacity is lost. Chile and Peru also allow for partial disability where one half and one third of productive capacity is lost. The contribution period required varies from country to country. In Chile entitlement to a disability pension requires that the worker is contributing at the time of the event. For unemployed workers, this is extended for a year after the start of the unemployment spell. Unemployed workers qualify for a reduced benefit. All other countries require a certain density of contributions for qualification. In Mexico this is 150 weeks of contribution. In Uruguay it is two years of contribution and having contributed for six months prior to the event. Colombia requires 26 weeks of contribution in the year prior to disability. Peru requires three consecutive monthly contributions before the disability, or four contributions in the last six months. Argentina has a different approach as entitlement to full benefits requires contributions in 30 out of the last 36 months, or partial benefits if contributions in 18 out of the last 36 months (Barrientos, 1997b; Bertín and Perrotto, 1997).

Most countries deal with survivor insurance in a similar way to total disability and the same requirements apply, but Argentina requires that a worker is contributing at the time of death in order for survivor pension insurance benefits to apply. In the event of death, beneficiaries of survivor pension normally include the (sometimes only female) spouse, dependent children, dependent parents, and in few cases dependant brothers.

The upshot of these rules is that pension scheme coverage for disability and death is severely restricted by contribution gaps (Asociación Internacional de Organismos de Supervisión de Fondos de Pensiones, 1997). These may be the outcome of unemployment spells, quits, lay offs, labour mobility, or employment in the informal sector. The more prolonged the spell the higher the likelihood that the worker will not be covered against death or disability. This is an example of how conditions in the labour market determine pension scheme coverage, and how the latter compounds risks arising from the former.

Pension schemes in which a minimum length of contribution record is required before entitlements are built up, such as the Mexican pension scheme, impose some sort of vesting period on disability and survivor insurance cover. Interestingly, most of the pension schemes do not have a long vesting period and participation in pension schemes is not restricted for those with higher risks. Peru did introduce a six months qualification period for those with terminal illnesses, so that if such illness is diagnosed before the six months elapse, the worker is not covered. [22]

The conclusion of this discussion is that pension coverage rates for long life risks may differ significantly from pension coverage rates for short life or working life risks. Some workers who are currently contributing and are therefore covered for long life may not be covered for short life where they do not fulfil vesting requirements. On the other hand, some workers who are not covered against long life risks because they are not currently contributing, are covered against short life providing they fulfil entitlement requisites.

How to expand pension plan coverage in Latin America?

The pension coverage trends in Latin America following pension reform are not encouraging. Pension coverage rates in Chile, Argentina and Peru, but especially Chile's because of its longer experience with pension reform, have risen for the new private pension scheme, but net overall pension scheme coverage has remained stagnant through the process of pension reform, and after. And compared to the rates of pension scheme coverage achieved in the 1970s, the levels at which pension coverage rates are stagnating are markedly low. Chile's experience with pension reform suggests that it is unlikely that pension coverage rates will significantly rise as a result.

There are, of course, a number of other factors influencing the rates of pension coverage in Latin America. In particular, changes in the labour market and the employment relationship in the 1980s and early 1990s have undoubtedly had a significant impact on pension provision and take up. The dismantling of social insurance programs, and the withdrawal of government support for them, has also led to a decline of pension coverage. It remains difficult to isolate the impact of pension design on pension coverage from these other dominating factors.

What can be postulated on the basis of the available evidence is that the new individual capitalization pension schemes in their current shape are unlikely to provide a strong upward push to pension coverage rates. This is despite the claim that the reformed pension schemes would prove better at accommodating the new conditions in the labour market. Pension coverage rates for the informal and flexible labour force, and for women and other vulnerable workers, are not better than under the old social insurance pension schemes, and in some areas they appear to be worse.

What can be done to improve coverage? The key lies in considering what type of pension scheme would be attractive to workers in the flexible or informal sector of the labour market (Barrientos, 1996b). The illiquid nature of the retirement fund in the new pension scheme strongly militates against participation by self-employed and low income workers. The pension fund can only be drawn upon at retirement, and disability and survivor benefits when the relevant contingencies occur. Self-employed workers may prefer to invest their savings in assets that support their work. Low income workers may be reluctant to tie up a portion of their resources in this long term instrument, especially when their needs may be greater in the short term.

Making the retirement fund more liquid also has its dangers, in that the accumulation of the fund may be undermined by withdrawals. It also has the danger that impatient or myopic workers may inadvisedly drive down their retirement fund. Some compromise may be needed here, but making the retirement fund more liquid will strengthen the incentives for pension scheme participation by self-employed and low income workers. At a more general level, investment in human capital and housing may constitute relatively safe and certainly beneficial uses for the retirement fund.

In all Latin American countries there has been a rise in labour force participation by women. This is projected to continue into the medium term. Changes may be needed to ensure that any gender biased design features in the new pension scheme are eliminated. There are also features in existing pension schemes that ostensibly favour women, such as the lower retirement age, and especial access to survivor insurance. These should be examined carefully. Lower retirement age for women in the context of individual capitalization pension schemes directly result in lower pension benefits, especially if annuity pensions take account of women's longer lives. Gender neutral design, with perhaps a more flexible retirement age, may be preferable, and would provide greater incentives for participation by women.

There is also the issue of the enforcement of the compulsory participation in the new pension schemes. As noted, there may be significant costs for firms associated with collecting and depositing pension contributions which may provide incentives for employers to restrict workers' membership of pension schemes. In addition, the liberalization of labour markets in Latin America has downgraded the role of agencies entrusted with the enforcement of labour market regulations (Marquez, 1995; Marshall, 1996). Where private pension fund managers collect contributions, as in Chile, these have weaker incentives to pursue employers and employees for non-payment of contributions. A central system for collecting contributions may reduce costs for employers, and facilitate the enforcement of compulsory pension contributions. It may also have the effect of raising coverage rates.

Conclusion

What will be the impact of pension reform on labour markets in Latin America? The introduction of individual capitalization pension schemes is expected to have a positive and significant impact on the operation of labour markets, both by removing some of the distortions generated by pay as you go pension schemes, and by contributing to make labour markets more flexible. This chapter has considered whether these expectations are likely to materialize.

The analysis of pension scheme coverage rates can provide a test of the impact of pension reform on labour markets. To the extent that pension reform eliminates or reduces labour market distortions, and that it proves to be better suited to the new conditions in labour markets, pension scheme coverage rates should rise. The broad conclusion from the empirical evidence available is that while pension scheme coverage rates in the new individual capitalization pension schemes have risen rapidly after reform, overall pension scheme coverage rates have stagnated. The newly introduced pension schemes attract large numbers of contributors from the old pension scheme, and a proportion of new entrants. However, taking all pension schemes available into account, pension reform has not been accompanied by a rise in the proportion of the labour force that actively contributes to pension schemes. Pension reform is unlikely to reverse the decline in pension scheme coverage, which has been apparent since the early 1980s.

There is a case for taking this conclusion as provisional. In fact, labour market conditions have been, in the wake of the 1980s crisis in Latin America, particularly adverse, and pension scheme coverage rates have also declined in other countries outside the region. The longer span of evidence on pension scheme coverage rates from Chile, however, seem to indicate that even when labour market conditions improve, pension reform has not been successful in pushing up coverage rates.

The muted impact of pension reform on labour markets has several explanations. The first is that perhaps the distortionary effects of social insurance pension schemes have been exaggerated. This is the main finding emerging from the study by Gruber (1997) to the effect that pension reform in Chilean manufacturing did not have employment effects but only wage effects.

A second explanation is that the changes in pension design may not be significant within the context of labour markets. To put it succinctly, if the demand for pension plans was met by adequate supply before the pension reform, the replacement of social insurance pension schemes with individual capitalization pension plans may have only marginal effects on coverage rates. Employers and employees who, for their own reasons, require a pension plan are going to have one, regardless of its particular design. This accords with the findings of a study in the USA that found it impossible to distinguish the impact of defined benefit from that of defined contribution pension schemes for key labour market variables (Gustman and Steinmeier, 1993).

A third explanation is that some design features of the individual capitalization pension plans in Latin America are not sufficiently accommodating of the new labour market conditions, which emphasize employment flexibility and mobility. The fact that the new pension schemes have not proved to be sufficiently attractive to the self-employed, and other vulnerable groups in Latin America can be used in support of this explanation. This third explanation, if correct, would point to the need to consider design changes to the new pension schemes that remove any barriers to the expansion of coverage. As noted, pension funds would need to be made more liquid, and pension plan participation costs lower, for coverage rates to rise. The need to make pension plan participation more attractive for women workers also constitutes an important challenge.

Coverage requirement for disability and survivor benefits should be of especial concern. At present, active contributor status is in most countries the main qualification for access to these benefits. This is very restrictive in the context of very fluid labour markets, with large, and rising, incidence of non-standard employment. The policy choice between stricter or more relaxed requirements is a difficult one to make. It will be interesting to evaluate the outcomes emerging from whatever diversity exists in the relevant regulations across the Latin American countries studied. As they stand at present, these requirement have the effect of compounding, rather than diversifying, labour market risks.

Notes

1 This finding emerges from simulations of different pension scheme designs.
2 By pure tax it is meant that contributors do not expect to receive any benefits directly from their contributions.
3 Corsetti and Hebbel point to a decline in the share of informal sector employment in Chile from 36 percent in 1980 to 31.1 percent in 1990-2 (Corsetti and Schmidt-Hebbel, 1997).
4 It is only fair to record that both these studies stress that these are very tentative suggestions given the significant impact upon the labour market of other factors, and in particular the impact of labour market liberalization and the sustained growth of the Chilean economy from mid 1980s onwards.
5 Workers switching from the old to the new pension scheme in Chile received a one off increase in pay of around 18 percent to compensate them for the elimination of employee contributions.
6 Gruber's study focuses on manufacturing firms of more than ten employees, and may therefore apply only to the primary sector (Gruber, 1997).
7 In fact, in the Chilean new pension scheme there is a minimum level of pension fund at retirement below which the fund is returned as a lump sum to the worker at normal retirement age, without requiring that a pension benefit is arranged.
8 A more precise measure of pension scheme coverage, in the context of the longevity insurance, is given by the density of contributions throughout a person's working life. This is based on the working assumption that the

greater the fraction of a person's working life that is covered by contributions, the larger will be the accumulated fund at retirement. But this can only be measured at the end of a worker's career.

9 This issue is examined in the next chapter.
10 Members of the armed forces and the police were explicitly excluded from joining the new pension scheme and retained their social insurance pension fund CAPREDENA (*Caja de Previsión de la Defensa Nacional*).
11 Although formal measures to liberalize the labour market in Chile were introduced in early 1980 with the *Plan Laboral*, de facto liberalization came earlier and was a consequence of brutal repression by the military government. See Barrientos and Barrientos (1996).
12 The *Superintendencia de Administradoras de Fondos de Pensiones* argues that while the measure of affiliates as a proportion of the labour force overestimates the actual coverage of the pension scheme, the measure of active contributors as a proportion of the labour force underestimates it. This is because some workers not contributing in a particular months will have, nonetheless, sufficient density of contributions to generate benefits (Superintendencia de Administradoras de Fondos de Jubilaciones y Pensiones, 1996).
13 This is an important issue and will be examined in more detail below.
14 This measure was also used in Figure 5.2 above.
15 See Figure 5.1 above.
16 There is no information available for coverage rates by sex for all social insurance funds prior to the 1981 reform. Data for active contributors to the *Servicio de Seguro Social*, the largest social insurance fund covering mainly blue collar private sector workers, for the period 1975 to 1977 show a significant gender pension coverage gap. When dependent and independent workers are considered, this gap is 13 percentage points in 1975, falling to 5 percentage points in 1977. This gender gap in pension coverage is much larger for dependent workers ranging from 17 percentage points in 1975 and 11 percentage points in 1977. The contraction of the gender pension coverage in this period is due to a rise in female employment and a fall in male employment, most probably resulting from the impact of trade liberalization on manufacturing employment (Barrientos and Barrientos, 1996).
17 The public sector is another sector with a high concentration of female employment and pension covered jobs, but this has declined in Chile.
18 The main purpose of this nationwide survey is to evaluate the impact of social programs.
19 Recall that there were five possible responses to the survey question on pension scheme participation. Participation in the new pension scheme, and non-participation in any pension scheme, were the dominant responses. See Table 5.1.
20 It should be kept in mind that the figures for the ratio of active contributors to affiliates computed from CASEN94 data are at 74 percent much higher than the one obtained from records data (48.5 percent for 1994) reported above. This is due to two reasons. Firstly, in CASEN94 active contribution status is

self-assessed, whereas in the records data it only includes those with contributions in December for earnings in November. Secondly, there may be some response bias. This is likely to arise from underreporting of affiliation, particularly where a long time has elapsed since any contributions were made. Whereas the former has the effect of overstating the number of active contributors, the latter has the effect of understating the number of affiliates.

21 In Argentina the requisites for entitlement to disability and survivor benefits are different across the public and the private schemes.
22 As regards disability, the initial legislation in Peru excluded from the insurance cover those contingencies arising as a result of alcohol, drugs or voluntary acts. Strict application of this rule by the insurance companies created problems. Workers who had been drinking and were involved in, for example, a traffic accident, lost insurance cover as a result. The rule was amended to say that contingencies arising from alcoholism, as opposed to alcohol, were to be excluded from cover. On a different note, a vesting period of one year was imposed before cover for death arising from a voluntary act was covered (Asociación Internacional de Organismos de Supervisión de Fondos de Pensiones, 1997).

6 Retirement income

The assessment of pension reform in Latin America has focused in the previous chapters on the impact it is likely to have on saving and growth, and particularly on the operation of capital and labour markets. This focus arises from the role of pension reform as part of broader structural reforms in the countries concerned, and in part due to the short life span of the new pension schemes. The primary objective of pension schemes is, however, to secure adequate pension benefits for their affiliates. The paramount criteria against which the reformed pension schemes in Latin America ought to be assessed is their capacity to secure adequate standards of living for the retired population, and to insure them against consumption risks. The short life span of the new individual capitalization pension schemes in Latin America makes it difficult to assess the extent to which pension reform will achieve these objectives. At this stage only a highly provisional and tentative evaluation can be performed, but given its importance it should be attempted. This is the issue addressed in this chapter.

The next section examines the scant evidence that is available on the income levels of the old in Latin America, and on the incidence of poverty among them. The main fact that emerges from the study of the evidence is that the incidence of poverty among older groups in Latin America is lower than for the population as a whole. This is most probably a consequence of the success of social insurance programs in extending pension scheme coverage in the 1960s and 1970s, and in reducing old age poverty. The conditions prevailing in the 1980s affected particularly those in the labour force, as their real earnings fell and unemployment rose. Relative to those in work, pensioners derived some protection from − albeit discretionary − increases in benefits in response to inflation, and by a minimum pension benefit floor.

The extent to which the new pension schemes are capable of generating adequate pensions for their affiliates will be dependent on the retirement fund accumulation and on the design of pension benefits. These issues are examined in the two sections that follow. A common feature of the new pension schemes in Latin America is that a choice of pension arrangements is offered to those retiring. This choice includes a phased withdrawal pension, and an annuity pension. The relative advantages of these are studied, as well as the Chilean experience with them. The section also considers minimum pension guarantees.

The accumulation path of the retirement funds, is studied with the aid of simulations. These identify the key factors influencing pension fund accumulation, and the likely adequacy of pension benefits. The section concludes that the labour market experience of participants in the new pension schemes, the rates of return secured by the pension fund managers, and commission levels, are the dominant factors.

A final section provides some conclusions, and speculates on the future incomes of the retired in Latin America.

The elderly, retirement income and poverty

The issue of the incidence and extent of poverty among the elderly in Latin America has not received sufficient attention. There is scant evidence on the economic situation of the elderly, with only a handful of studies aimed specifically at establishing the levels and incidence of poverty among the elderly population in some countries in Latin America.[1] This section brings together existing information on this issue and identifies some trends.

A useful starting point is a World Bank report on *Poverty and Income Distribution in Latin America* which aims to identify and discuss their main trends in the 1980s (Psacharopoulos et al., 1993). The report bases its findings on the analysis of household survey data for Latin American countries. Extracting the figures pertaining to the elderly allows some conclusions to be drawn. Table 6.1 below shows the proportions of the 65 and over age group who can be found in each of the income quintiles generated from the population as a whole. These data are reported for the Latin American countries under examination.

Overall, the figures indicate that the elderly are, for the majority of countries in the Table, over represented in the higher income quintiles. Only in Peru and Costa Rica is the share of the elderly in the lowest quintile higher than that for the population as a whole. And only in Peru and Uruguay were the elderly under represented in the highest quintile. Moreover, this under representation is marginal. These figures indicate that the incidence of poverty among the elderly population is lower than for younger groups, and, given demographic conditions in Latin America, for the population as a whole. In Chile and Colombia, the over representation of the elderly population in the highest quintile groups is significantly larger than for the other countries.

Table 6.1
Income distribution and the elderly in selected Latin American countries

(proportion of population aged 65 and over by income quintile in 1989)

	1st	2nd	3rd	4th	5th	All
Argentina	6.5	10.2	12.7	15.2	11.8	11.3
Chile	4.1	5.3	7.1	7.9	9.0	6.7
Colombia	3.0	3.4	4.4	5.0	5.2	4.2
Costa Rica	6.8	4.1	4.1	4.4	5.0	4.9
Mexico	3.8	4.4	5.3	4.8	5.7	4.8
Peru	4.4	4.9	3.8	3.5	4.0	4.1
Uruguay	6.9	16.6	16.6	14.3	13.5	13.6

Source: Psacharapoulos et al. (1993). Note that the income level for each individual in the entire population is calculated as total household income divided by the number in the household. The income quintiles are for the population as a whole.

Two important caveats should be entered in relation to these data. Firstly, the income variable was constructed by dividing a measure of total household income by the numbers in the household. It was implicitly assumed, therefore, that members of a household share income equally. Secondly, measured income, even if distributed equally within the household, may not be a good indicator of relative well being, in so far as the elderly may require a greater measure of income to achieve the same level of welfare than a young person. As the elderly ages, health and care costs are likely to climb steeply.

The observed under representation of the elderly among the poor is supported by other data. In Chile, the proportion of the population over the age of 60 under the poverty line was 15.7 percent in 1992 and 13.7 percent in 1994, while for the population as a whole the poor represented 32.7 and 28.4 percent respectively (MIDEPLAN, 1996). [2] In Argentina the proportion of the population below the poverty line was in 1992, 13.9 percent for those 60 years old and over, but 17.7 percent for the population as a whole. The overall picture is that the elderly are under represented among the poor.

What factors can account for the fact that poverty is less widespread among the old than among younger groups? One important factor is the relative success of the social insurance programs in Latin America. The spread of pension scheme coverage in the 1960s and 1970s, the accelerated accrual of pension benefits, and the relative generosity of pension benefits improved the standards of living of the old. Arellano (1990) notes that the proportion of the population over retirement age in Chile who were in receipt of a pension benefit jumped from 39 percent in 1961 to 54 percent in 1965 and 63 percent in 1974, after which date the figure stabilised. A 1985 survey of the elderly in Chile finds that pension benefits are an important source of income for this group. For males over the age of 65, receipt of pension income is reported by over 80 percent of respondents, compared to the proportion reporting receipt of income from other family members at only between 10 and 15 percent (Barrientos, 1996b). It is interesting to point out that the accelerated implementation of pension schemes was to an important extent responsible for both the financial deficits of the social insurance schemes, and the improvement in the standards of living of the elderly.

The impact on the elderly of the 1980s conditions in Latin America needs to be examined with some care. Three trends need to be separated out. Firstly, the 1980s economic crisis had a large negative impact upon the standards of living of the elderly, pushing a greater number of them into poverty. Secondly the growth in the elderly as a proportion of the population as a whole is likely to have led to an increase in the proportion of the poor who are elderly. Thirdly, the adverse economic conditions in the 1980s had an even greater impact upon the active population, who suffered from rising unemployment and a decline in the real wage. These contradictory trends make for mixed empirical evidence. Although in absolute terms, the numbers of the elderly poor increased and their standards of living declined, in relative terms, their economic situation deteriorated less than those in work.

This was the case in Argentina, where the poor economic growth performance in the 1980s – GDP fell by 19.4 percent between 1980 and 1989 – had a significant impact on the incomes of the elderly (Lloyd-Sherlock, 1997). Using household survey data Morley is able to report that the incidence of poverty among the elderly in Argentina rose from 3.5 percent in 1980 to 15.1 percent in 1989, a five fold increase. At the same time, poverty was rising fast among the non elderly as well. In fact, the proportion of the poor who are elderly in Argentina rose only from 7 to 9 percent in the same period (Morley, 1995). This change is not large when the demographic growth in the elderly population is taken into account. Colombia, on the other hand, enjoyed healthier macroeconomic conditions in the same period – its GDP grew by 14.1 percent in 1980s – and poverty incidence among the elderly declined. But a growth in the elderly share of the population resulted in a rise of two percentage points in the proportion of the poor accounted for by the elderly.

A significant factor in the decline suffered by the incomes of the elderly was the fall in the purchasing power of pensions as a result of deficient indexation. The rapidly rising inflation of the 1970s and 1980s, together with the deterioration in government finances stretched the capacity of Latin American countries to protect the living standards of the retired population. In Chile, for example, the real value of the average pension fell by more than one third between 1970 and 1977, and the same applied to the minimum pension benefit (Arellano, 1990). Only in 1984 did average pension benefits recover their 1970 level. In Mexico, real average pension benefit levels declined by close to 50 percent between 1980 and 1988, and a recovery later in the decade was not sufficient to restore the real value of pension benefits (Soto-Perez, 1992). Delayed or inadequate indexation of pension benefits was an important factor in the decline in living standards experienced by the retired population.

At the same time, because pension benefits were in most countries indexed to prices rather than to earnings, the decline in living standards of the elderly was relatively less than that for the working population, for whom a decline in real wages compounded the effects of imperfect indexation. While the standards of living of the elderly declined for most countries during the late 1970s and 1980s, pensioners were relatively insulated from the unemployment and fall in real wages that affected the majority of the population.

The fact that the relative incidence of poverty among the elderly is lower than for other groups should not obscure the fact that wide income differentials exist among the elderly, and that a significant proportion of the elderly suffers extreme poverty. To the extent that pension reform replaces a pay as you go pension scheme that included redistributive objectives, with an individual capitalization pension scheme that eschews redistribution, the concern must be that income inequality among the elderly population is likely to increase. And the reformed structure of minimum pension provision in the new pension schemes in Latin America will need to be tried and tested.

There are other sources of income and security apart from pension benefits for the elderly population, but the expectations are that these will be less reliable in the future than they were in the past. For a large majority of the elderly, the possibility of using the labour market as a means of securing adequate living standards is closed. Recent changes in the labour market in Latin America, and particularly the rise in demand for skilled labour (Altimir, 1997), may make it more rather than less difficult for elderly workers to secure employment.

Other sources of support for the elderly groups are state provided health and social security benefits, and the family. The economic conditions in the 1980s have led to a decline in the capacity of these institutions to provide support for the elderly. The state withdrawal from social insurance principles and programs is likely to continue into the near future. The contraction in fiscal expenditure, and therefore in the provision of fiscal programs, throughout Latin America in the 1980s is bound to affect the state's support for the elderly.

The family has traditionally played an important role in supporting the elderly in Latin America, but secular changes which have accelerated in the 1980s have also impacted upon this institution. As a recent report *Health Conditions in the Americas* notes, the family's "capacity to provide support [for the elderly] has been seriously eroded as a result of social, economic, and political changes in recent decades, including, inter alia, the migration of young people to industrial and commercial centres, the weakening of the family structure, the widespread entry of younger women into the labour market, and high inflation"(Pan American Health Organization, 1994, p.96). It is likely, therefore that retirement income will need to play an even larger role in the future in securing the well being of the elderly population.

Pension benefits in the new pension scheme in Chile

Pension reform will bring about important changes to the way in which pension entitlements are acquired and defined. Under the old social insurance pension schemes old age, retirement, and service, pension benefits were acquired through covered employment, and defined in terms of a target replacement rate. In the new pension schemes, entitlement to retirement and old age pension benefits will depend on contributions paid into a workers retirement account, and will be defined primarily by the accumulation of the pension fund. As far as the retirement and old age pensions are concerned, there is no target replacement rate in the new pension scheme.

The level of the pension benefit will depend on a range of factors: the age of the worker and dependants, the size of the accumulated retirement fund, and the conditions in the financial and insurance markets. At retirement individuals will be free to select a pension benefit from a menu that includes the purchase of a pension annuity from insurance companies, a phased program of withdrawals from the retirement fund, and a deferred annuity with a phased withdrawal program at first. This menu of permitted pension arrangements is common to all the countries under examination.

Some pension scheme participants will not reach retirement age, and will therefore make use of their disability and survivor insurance. Entitlement to disability and survivor benefits depends, for most countries, on active contribution at the time of the relevant event. The disability and survivor pension benefits are defined as a fraction of the insured person's salary. In fact, disability and survivor pension benefits are salary related, with a target replacement rate.

In addition, a minimum guaranteed pension is provided in most countries for individuals with significant contributory records but with low retirement funds. Entitlements to a guaranteed minimum pension depend on length of contribution record, and are commonly defined as a fixed amount. In some countries, the minimum pension level is related to some measure of earnings, either the minimum wage as in Mexico, or average contributory earnings as in Argentina. The purpose of this section is to explore the impact of pension benefit design in the new pension schemes on future retirement income. The range of pension benefits in the Chilean new pension scheme will be studied first.

Types of pension benefit available in the Chilean new pension scheme

The different pension benefits available in the individual capitalization pension scheme in Chile are described in Table 6.2 below. In broad terms, there are three main types of pension benefits. Firstly, old age and retirement benefits are financed out of the accumulated pension fund at retirement, these provide the main form of pension provision in the new pension scheme.

Secondly, pension fund managers also provide a disability and survivor insurance for those workers making an additional contribution. Independent workers, and workers above the age of retirement do not pay the additional contribution, and are therefore not covered by the disability and dependant insurance. Only workers who were contributing at the time of the event that causes the insurance entitlement are covered. New regulations introduced in 1990 extended the insurance coverage for unemployed workers for up to 12 months after the last contribution paid, providing the worker contributed for at least six months before the start of the unemployment spell.[3] The pension benefits paid under the disability and dependant insurance are fixed for levels of disability and dependency, are salary related, and are subject to a maximum level.

Finally, for those workers with at least 20 years of contribution, the government guarantees a minimum pension which level is set twice yearly. There are no legal requirements regarding the indexation of the minimum pension, and the government has a large degree of discretion in setting its level. Current levels for the minimum pension are around 80 percent of the minimum wage.[4]

Table 6.2
Pension benefits available in the Chilean individual capitalization pension scheme

type of benefit	financing	requisites	benefit menu	level of benefit
Old age	retirement fund	Men 65, Women 60	-annuity -phased withdrawal -deferred annuity [3]	dependent on retirement fund and annuity values
Early retirement		if potential benefit ≥ 50% of basic earnings[1] and ≥ 110% of the minimum pension	same as above	dependent on retirement fund and annuity values
Lump sum	retirement fund	if potential benefit ≥ 70% of basic earnings and 120% of the min. pension, excess drawn as lump sum		
Disability (Full)	insurance	currently contributing or unemployed for less than 12 months; below retirement age; loss of 2/3 work capacity	same as above	if employed: 70% of basic earnings; if unemployed: 50%
Disability (Partial)[5]	insurance	same as above; below retirement age and loss of 1/2 work capacity	same as above	if employed: 50% of basic earnings; if unemployed: 35%
Survivor[2]: widow	insurance (independent workers or over retirement age not covered; dependants receive balance of fund only)	spouse currently contributing or unemployed for less than 12 months when death occurred	same as above	if children (no child)& spouse employed : 35% (40%) of basic earnings; if children (no child)& spouse unemployed: 25% (30%) of basic earnings

Table 6.2 Continued

Survivor [2]: orphan	insurance (independent workers or those above retirement age not covered; dependants receive balance of fund only)	parent currently contributing or unemployed for less than 12 months when death occurred; child must be dependant, below 18 years of age, or 24 if in full time education	same as above	if parent employed: 10.5% of basic earnings; if parent unemployed: 7.5% of basic earnings
Survivor [2] other: common law wife; illegitimate children; dependant parents	same as above	insured currently contributing or unemployed for less than 12 months when death occurred	same as above	if insured employed: common law wife with children (without) 21% (25%); dependant parents 35% of basic earnings; if insured is unemployed: common law wife 15% (18%); parents 25%
Minimum pension	retirement fund balance and government subsidy	above retirement age and 20 years of contributions (could include up to 3 years of registered unemployment)	phased withdrawal	level set by the government twice yearly (presently around 80% of minimum wage)

1. Basic earnings are the average of last ten years contributory earnings, price indexed. Where the insured has less than 10 years in the labour force, the calculation is done on the number of years worked providing they are more than 2. Before 1987 basic earnings were calculated on the last 12 months of earnings.
2. The sum of pension benefits to all dependants cannot exceed 70% of the participant's basic salary if the insured was employed; or 50% if the insured was unemployed.
3. Deferred annuities were introduced in 1988.
4. The phased withdrawal pension mode was made available for disability and survivor benefits in 1988.
5. Partial Disability was introduced in August 1990

Some considerable time will elapse before the new pension scheme in Chile becomes responsible for the majority of pensions awarded. At present old age and retirement pension levels are in the main determined by entitlements from the old pension scheme. The transitional arrangements provide for a Recognition Bond, which is granted to workers with contributions in the old pension scheme and who switched to the new pension scheme. The Recognition Bond is calculated at the time the workers transferred to the new pension scheme according to a somewhat generous formula.[5] The government guarantees the Bond to increase in value by the rate of inflation plus 4 percent until the worker reaches retirement age, at which point the Bond is redeemed.

These arrangements help the government spread over a longer period of time the payments associated with the pension liabilities from the old pension scheme. As the Bond cannot be redeemed before retirement age, workers who wished to retire early could not make use of it until retirement. In 1988 the Government introduced legislation permitting workers to endorse the Bond to an insurance company in exchange for a pension annuity. This legislative change greatly facilitated early retirement, with a consequent rise in the number of workers taking it. Since 1991 the Recognition Bonds can be traded in a secondary market. The Recognition Bond accounts for the greater part of currently awarded old age and retirement pensions.

Trends in the number and level of pensions awarded under the new pension scheme

Figure 6.1 shows the trends in the number of pensions awarded under the new pension scheme by type, and Figure 6.2 shows the share of the different pension types in the total number of pensions awarded. As would be expected with a new pension scheme, disability and insurance pensions account for the majority of pensions awarded in the earlier stages. Thus, orphans and widows pension account for over 80 percent of pensions in payment in 1982, but their share declines to around 35 percent by 1997.

Disability pensions accounted for around 20 percent of pension benefits in the initial stages of the new pension scheme, but their share declined rapidly after 1989 to around 5 percent in 1997. A key factor here was the tightening up of disability pensions awards in 1988. Until 1987, disability pensions were calculated on the basis of covered earnings of the last 12 months. This rule, together with relatively lax disability certification regulations, encouraged a large number of applications. In 1988 the earnings on which the disability pension benefit calculation was based was extended to 10 years, and the regulations and procedures for disability certification were tightened up and harmonised.

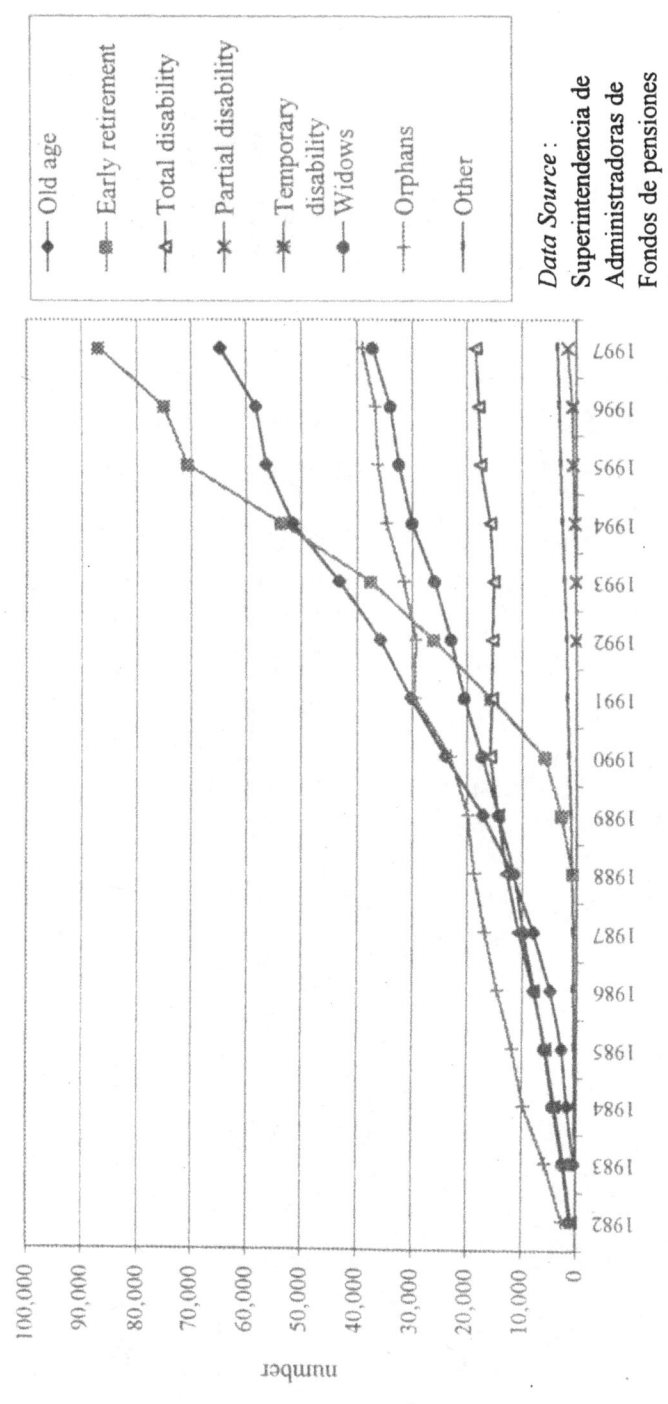

Figure 6.1 Chile: Number of pensions in payment awarded by the new pension scheme, by type

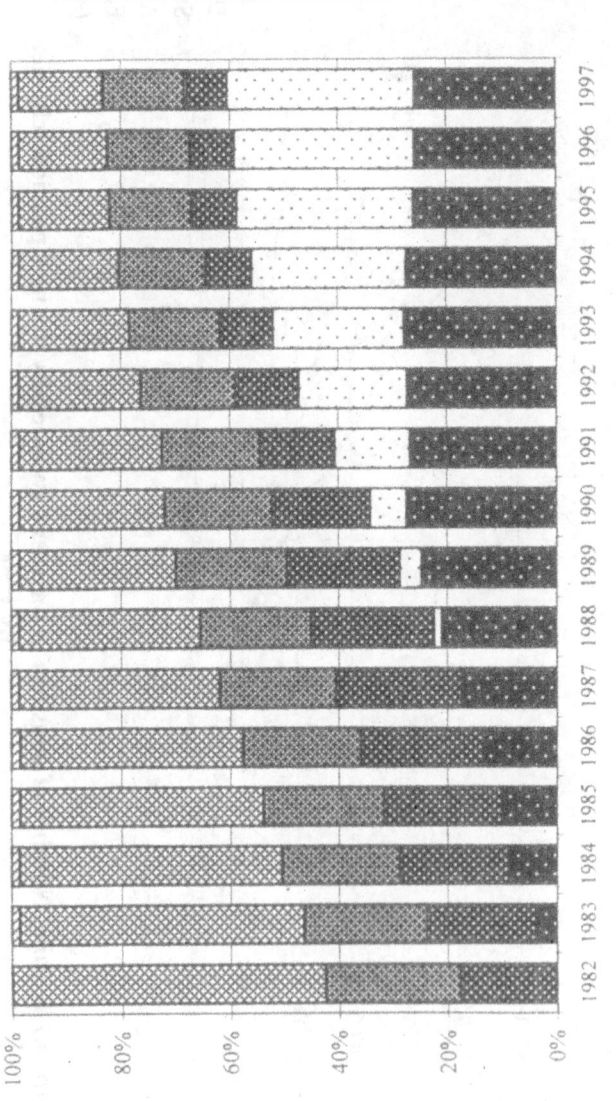

Figure 6.2 Chile: Share of different pension types in the total number of pensions awarded

In 1990, partial disability was introduced to cover workers with between one half and two thirds loss of capacity to work, and a further improvement was made to certification procedures. An important innovation concerned the introduction of temporary disability certification. Workers who are successful in applying for a disability pension are given a temporary disability order for three years after which their disability is reviewed.

In 1988 new regulations facilitated early retirement pensions. Under the original regulations early retirement was possible for workers who could demonstrate their accumulated fund could secure a pension benefit of at least 70 percent of basic earnings, and at least equal to the minimum pension level. The new regulations reduced the required replacement rate to 50 percent, but increased the absolute minimum level to 110 percent of the minimum pension. The extraordinary rates of return secured by the pension funds in the late 1980s and early 1990s, and perhaps the expectation that these will not continue at such high levels into the future, have increased the attractiveness of early retirement. As can be seen from Figure 6.2, the share of early retirement pensions overtook the share of old age pension in 1994 and they have continued to grow at a faster rate.

The provision for early retirement pensions had been complicated in the transitional period by the design of the Recognition Bond. Initially, early retirement was made difficult by the illiquid nature of the Recognition bond, but this was relaxed by legislation in 1987 and 1991. In law, early retirement pensions are not covered by the minimum pension guarantee provided by the government, but in practice it has applied. This may enlarge future government liabilities considerably (Díaz, 1993).

Figure 6.3 shows the share of different types of pensions awarded in the total pension amounts paid under the new pension schemes. It can be seen from the Figure that the share of early retirement pensions easily outstrips the share of old age pensions. By 1997, early retirement pensions account for over one half of the total value of pensions in payment. The decline in the importance of disability pensions can also be clearly observed from this Figure.

Choice of old age and retirement pension arrangements

In the Chilean pension scheme, workers have a choice of pension arrangements including purchasing a pension annuity, organising a phased withdrawal from the retirement fund, or purchasing a deferred annuity with a phased withdrawal first. There are a number of reasons for providing a menu of pension arrangements. These give greater scope for retirees' optimisation of consumption paths, given their individual preferences and information. Individuals have significant diversity in their preferences regarding their consumption path in retirement, bequests, and risk coverage.

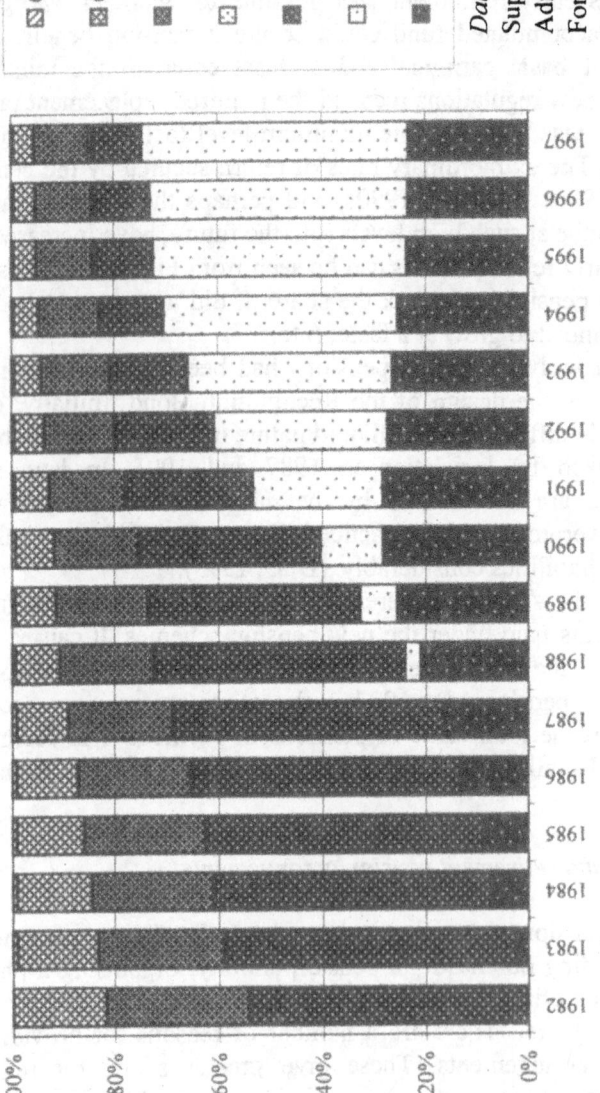

Figure 6.3   Chile: Share of different pension types in total benefit amount

Individuals also have private information on the life expectancy of themselves and their dependants. A menu of pension arrangements would provide a means of accommodating this diversity. The pension reform designers also had other objectives in providing alternative pension arrangements. By restricting insurance companies to providing annuity products, and the AFPs to providing phased withdrawal pensions, pension designers attempted to introduce and enhance competition in the provision of pension benefits. Valdés-Prieto and Edwards (1996) suggest that entrusting the pension fund managers with the provision of phased withdrawal pension was made necessary by the relative underdevelopment of the life insurance sector at the time of pension reform.

The key features of the alternative pension benefit arrangements are summarised in Table 6.3 below. A pension annuity is an irreversible contract by which an individual surrenders the accumulated pension fund in exchange for a monthly benefit for life. The insurance company bears the longevity and investment risks. In Chile, pension annuity contracts are set in real terms, and therefore the insurance company also bears the inflation risk. Variants of the pension annuity contract include fixed term annuities, and joint annuities to include spouses and other dependants. Fixed term annuities pay a pension annuity for a guaranteed length of time. As pension annuities cover longevity risks, they will attract those individuals who are relatively risk-averse, and have expectations of longer lives.

Deferred annuities require that, at retirement, workers both transfer a capital sum to an insurance company, and fix a date for the start of the annuity. Once the contract is agreed, it becomes irreversible although it remains possible to bring forward the start of the annuity by supplementing the insurance premium, or by agreeing to a lower pension benefit. In practice, the deferred annuity variant of pension benefit arrangements is operationally very complex and has proved attractive only to a handful of retirees. Hence the discussion of empirical trends that follows concentrates on pension annuity and phased withdrawal pensions only.

Phased withdrawal pensions, on the other hand, are reversible, in that individuals can take up a pension annuity at a later date. Individuals agree a schedule of withdrawals with an AFP, which is recalculated annually. Under this pension arrangement retirees can withdraw up to the permitted monthly amount. The maximum permitted withdrawals are calculated according to formula set by the pension scheme regulations.[6] The maximum permitted withdrawal is basically the accumulated pension fund divided by a measure of the capital necessary to pay a unitary annuity given the individual's, and his/her dependants', predicted survival. The remaining retirement fund continues to gain returns, or suffer losses, in line with the pension fund, and it can be subject to deductions to cover the commissions and charges of the AFPs.

Table 6.3
Comparison of key features of annuity and phased withdrawal pensions

	pension annuity	phased withdrawal
providers	insurance companies	AFPs
benefit calculation	agreed with insurance company	maximum monthly withdrawals are set annually based on the life expectancy of beneficiary group
charges	two charges: (a) brokers' commission, and (b) insurance company's charges	regulations allow fixed charge and/or percentage of withdrawals; but charges not implemented to date
pension benefit path	constant in real terms	decreasing since after retirement age life expectancy decreases by less than one year per one added year of age; high rates of return on the funds could compensate for this
pension option review and bequests	annuity contract irreversible; bequests possible if fixed term annuity option is taken	transfer to annuity possible at any stage; transfers across AFPs also possible; bequests available
insurance:		
survivor risk	yes	no
longevity risk	yes	no
income risk	yes	no
investment risk	yes	no
inflation risk	yes	no
requisites	accumulated fund at retirement must be sufficient to finance first pension benefit greater than 50% of basic earnings or 110% of minimum pension	until 1992 retirement age; since 1992 early retirement possible with requisites same as for annuity pension
government guarantees and liabilities	annuity fully guaranteed up to minimum pension level, then at 75% up to 45 UF	minimum pension guaranteed if withdrawals fall below it; this guarantee does not apply to early retirement pensions in law, but has applied in practice; pension fund manager rate of return guarantees apply to the residual fund

In fact only one AFP has implemented the permitted commissions and charges to date. Not charging commissions on phased withdrawal pensions gives the AFPs a strong marketing advantage over pension annuity contracts, which do attract significant charges. In the event of the death of the retiree, the remaining funds become part of his/her estate. The retiree assumes the longevity, inflation and investment risks. Clearly, individuals who are less risk averse, and for whom bequests are important, will be especially attracted to this form of pension arrangement. The high rates of return of the pension funds in Chile have enhanced the attractiveness of this form of pension provision.

Whilst the pension annuity provides a constant stream of income in real terms, and therefore supports a constant consumption path, the phased withdrawal pension provides a decreasing stream of income, and therefore a declining consumption path. As noted by some commentators, pension benefits should ideally provide for a rising, or at least constant, stream of income, and therefore consumption (Díaz, 1993; Díaz and Edwards, 1994). This is because old age is associated with rising costs, mainly in terms of health care. The consumption path of a phased withdrawal pension will lead, under most plausible scenarios, to declining living standards for retirees. Phased withdrawal pensions also have poorer insurance properties than pension annuities as they are vulnerable to fluctuations in investment returns and inflation. Phased withdrawal pensions do not cover longevity risk, except to the extent that the minimum pension guarantee is paid for life.

On the other hand, the very high rates of return which pension fund managers have secured in Chile make phased withdrawal pensions attractive, as participants can benefit from the continued accumulation of the pension fund. In addition, pension annuities attract high commissions and charges by insurance companies.

There have been important changes in the regulations concerning old age and retirement pension benefits in the Chilean scheme. As already noted, workers who at retirement cannot finance a pension greater than 50 percent of basic earnings and 110 percent of the minimum pension, are forced to take up a phased withdrawal pension (until 1987 the percentages were 70 and 100 respectively). This requirement is in place to reduce government minimum pension liabilities (phased withdrawal pensions lack dependant survival insurance) and to postpone government subsidies as far into the future as possible by forcing workers to exhaust their funds before the government is required to pay the minimum pension. This has meant workers with low earnings, or poor contribution records, have mainly retired to a phased withdrawal pension.

The evolution of the number and levels of pension annuity and phased withdrawal old age and retirement pensions awarded under the new pension scheme is shown in Figure 6.4 below. As regards the numbers of old age and retirement pensions in payment under each of these two modes, phased withdrawal pensions were more common in the 1980s, but the number of annuity pensions has risen faster in the 1990s. The early dominance of phased withdrawal pensions is in large part explained by the high number of low pension awarded in the initial stages of the new pension scheme. The later dominance of pension annuities has its main explanation in the expansion of early retirement. There a strong correlation between early retirement and annuity pensions, for obvious reasons. And it is likely that the rise in early retirement pension has made annuity pension the dominant pension arrangement.

As can also be seen from the Figure, the average amounts of pension benefits were distinctly higher for annuity pensions in the 1980s. The high rates of return on pension funds in the late 1980s and early 1990s have increased the average value of phased withdrawal pension benefits reversing the earlier situation. The Figure also provides some indication of the level of the minimum pension. As noted, the large number of low pension retirees in the earlier years of the scheme meant that phased withdrawal pension were very close to the minimum pension level.

In making this comparison it should be noted that the distribution of earnings across the population normally has a lognormal distribution. It is therefore likely that pension benefits may also show a lognormal distribution, in which the mean is to the right of the median. The value for the minimum pension is, on the other hand, a constant. The reported average values for the pension annuity and phased withdrawal pensions may significantly overstate the value of pension benefits for the majority of retirees.

Comparison of pension benefit levels in the new and the old pension schemes

A number of factors make a direct comparison of pension benefits under the old and the new pension schemes difficult to interpret. Firstly, pension benefits in the transition period will, initially, be mainly determined entitlements under the old scheme represented by the Recognition Bond. Secondly, the pattern of incentives in place to encourage workers in the old pension scheme to switch to the new pension schemes suggest there was a large measure of self-selection in the resulting groups. Workers who were close to retirement and moved to the new pension scheme did so because their pension benefits would be higher under the new pension scheme. And workers likely to receive higher benefits under the old scheme stayed put.

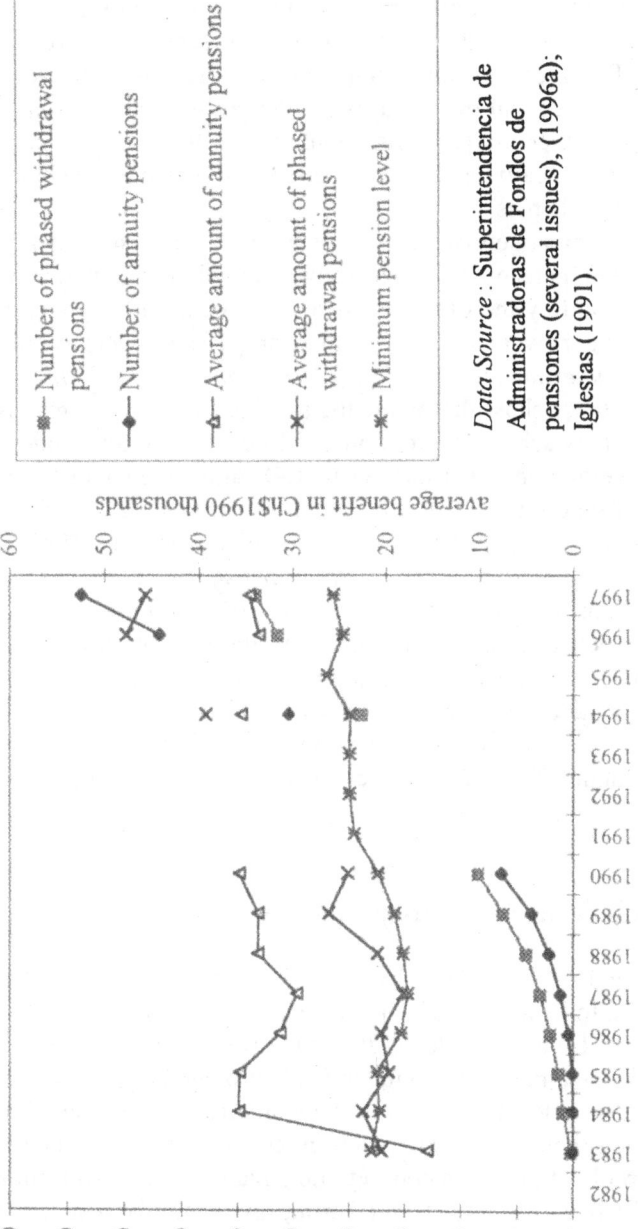

Figure 6.4 Chile: Old age and retirement pensions, number and average amount, and minimum pension level

Thirdly, comparison of pension outcomes in a mature pension scheme with those in an immature one is risky. The new pension scheme has very few pensioners so far. This provides, for example, a large measure of freedom in investment portfolios that will disappear when the pension scheme matures. Rates of return will, other things being equal, fall as the scheme matures. Finally, regulations concerning pension benefit entitlement calculations differ across pension schemes.

Not surprisingly, comparison of pension benefits in payment under both the new and the old pension schemes show that while the majority of pensions are being paid by the old pension scheme, pension benefits levels are higher under the new pension scheme. Comparisons were regularly reported by the *Superintendencia de Administradoras de Fondos de Pensiones*. In 1992 these show that while the number of old age pensions in payment under the new scheme were around 12 percent of those under the old scheme, the average amounts paid were 1.48 times higher in the new pension scheme (Superintendencia de Administradoras de Fondos de Pensiones,). However, comparison of service pension under the old pension scheme with early retirement pension under the pension scheme shows that levels were higher for service pensions than for early retirement pensions. Of course, service pensions are not an option in the new pension scheme. Disability pensions showed a similar disparity in the number of pension in payment, but levels under the new pension scheme were close to two times the level of old scheme pensions. In conclusion a direct comparison of pension benefits under the old and new pension schemes is not very meaningful.

The new pension schemes and retirement income

Will the future benefits generated by the new individual capitalization pension plans prove to be adequate? The evidence discussed in the previous section shows that from the late 1980s, the average pension benefits generated under the new pension scheme in Chile provide benefits well over the minimum pension level. There are few studies of pension benefit adequacy in the new pension scheme using micro data. Baeza and Burger (1995) study a sample of pensions coming into stream in the period January to September 1994 from the AFP *Santa María*, one of the largest AFPs in Chile . They compare pension benefits received with an average of the retirees' last ten years of earnings. Their findings are that, with the exception of disability pensions, average replacement rates for dependant, old age and retirement exceed 70 percent, a standard measure of pension benefit adequacy. Replacement rates were 73 percent for old age and dependant retirees and 83 percent for workers taking early retirement. They conclude that the Chilean new pension scheme is generating good quality pensions.

It is difficult to project this finding into the future for at least two reasons. Firstly, the macroeconomic conditions in Chile in the last decade or so have been extraordinarily good. Conditions in the labour market, and capital market gains, have improved in a sustained fashion since mid 1980s. The rates of the return secured by pension fund managers have averaged an annual 12 percent in real terms. It is unlikely that these, very favourable, conditions will continue into the medium and long term. Secondly, the greater part of the pension benefits paid under the new pension scheme reflects entitlements under the old pension scheme. As the new pension schemes are very recent, simulating the accumulation of the pension funds under a range of assumptions can provide some indication of likely future benefits. This section discusses the findings of simulation exercises concerning the future levels of pension benefits by the new pension scheme.

Simulating pension benefits in the new pension scheme

Under the new pension schemes, benefits will come to depend, aside from the demographic characteristics of the beneficiary, on the accumulated pension fund at retirement, and on the conditions affecting the convertibility of this pension fund into a stream of pension benefits. The accumulation of the pension fund depends in turn on the amount and timing of contributions to the individual retirement accounts, the returns secured on these contributions by the pension fund managers, and the costs charged. The accumulated pension fund at retirement can be translated into a pension benefit in two ways: phased withdrawals and annuitisation. These have differential costs and returns also affecting pension benefits received.

In order to find out what will be the impact of pension reform on the retirement income of the elderly it is important to predict pension benefit levels under the new pension scheme. As the new pension schemes will take a long time to mature, simulation of the accumulation of pension entitlements can help to develop an understanding of future evolution of retirement income (Barrientos and Firinguetti, 1995a; Margozzini, 1988). The simulation of future pension benefits will also provide some information on the factors likely to determine the size of pension benefits at retirement. There are a number of factors that enter into the simulation. These are discussed below.

Contribution history and labour market conditions

The pattern of contributions paid in by workers will depend on the path of their earnings and their employment record. Three main factors account for the evolution of earnings over time: changes in productivity, tenure related rise in earnings, and worker mobility.

Economy or sector-wide improvements in productivity lead to rising earnings for workers. In the longer run, these improvements in productivity can be represented as a steady rise in earnings. As a general rule, long term improvements in productivity and hence real wages of around 1 to 2 percent a year can represent a safe assumption for the Latin American economies under study. In the short or medium term, however, productivity and earnings may stagnate or decline. Altimir (1997) reports that between 1950 and 1980 Latin American economies experienced an average rate of growth of GDP per capita of 2.5 percent a year, but that the average growth of productivity of all the factors was only 1.2 percent a year.[7] In the 1980s, on the other hand, both economic growth and productivity declined, or at best stagnated.

A second source of rise in earnings for an individual may be tenure related. An often repeated finding from estimation of Mincer-type wage equations is that earnings are concave in tenure or age (Mincer, 1974). Earnings appear to rise after entry to the labour market, peak and then decline later in an individual's working life. An explanation for this evolution of lifetime earnings is provided by the human capital approach. Education and training are normally concentrated earlier on an individual's working life. The evolution of earnings thus appears to reflect rising individual productivity arising from human capital investment, and their depreciation in later life. In addition to human capital, deferred compensation explanations point to rising pay as a result of the productivity enhancing properties in employment contracts (Lazear, 1981). By agreeing to upward sloping pay schedules, firms can improve recruitment and retention, and can provide productivity incentives for their workers.

Finally, workers mobility also influences earnings. Voluntary quits are normally associated with improved wage offers and higher productivity resulting from better matching to jobs. Involuntary layoffs, on the other hand, are normally associated with financial penalties as they may signal a workers' productivity deficit. Quits and layoffs will therefore have an impact upon the evolution of earnings for particular workers.

The employment record of individual workers is a another important determinant of the accumulation of a pension fund. This is especially true of individual retirement accounts where the incidence and timing of employment, and hence contribution gaps, will have important effects upon pension fund accumulation. There are a number of factors affecting the employment profile of individual workers. Unemployment and involuntary layoffs are likely to enforce contribution gaps, especially since all new pension schemes in Latin America preclude contributions by the unemployed. Employment in the non-covered sector adds to contribution gaps. Gaps in employment related to household responsibilities are more prominent among women employees. Illness and temporary disability are also a source of contribution gaps.

Two points are important here. Firstly, contribution gaps tend not to be randomly distributed. Unemployment and informal sector induced contribution gaps are more likely to concentrate on low paid and low skilled workers. Contribution gaps induced by household or family commitments are focused on women. Secondly, the timing of these contribution gaps may be important in the accumulation of the pension fund. Given the nature of the new pension schemes in Latin America, earlier contribution gaps will have more significant effects upon pension benefits than later ones, due to the compounding of pension fund returns.

Accumulation of the pension fund

The contributions minus charges and commissions are deposited into the individual's retirement account. These are collected into a pension fund, which is in turn invested in a range of assets yielding returns. The rate of return that applies to the pension fund for a given period of time is then applied to the individual retirement accounts. Rates of return of the pension fund, and charges and commissions, are therefore key to the rate of accumulation of an individual's pension fund. Where there are many pension fund managers, rates of return may differ across fund managers.

Under most plausible conditions, the accumulation of returns has a much larger impact upon the size of the pension fund at retirement than the contributions themselves. For a worker with an uninterrupted employment record of 40 years, a constant wage rate growth of 2 percent per year, and constant rate of return applying to the pension fund of 5 percent, the contributions paid account for only one third of the total pension fund at retirement. Given this, contributions made earlier in an individual's career have a much greater weight upon the pension fund at retirement than later ones. This is in contrast to final salary pension schemes, in which earnings later in an individual's employment have a much greater weight on the pension benefit.

The services provided by the pension fund managers are charged to the contributors through a mixture of commissions and charges. As noted above, these are closely regulated as regards their incidence, but free as regards their level. The commissions and charges vary in their level and complexity across countries. For the purposes of the simulation, the commission charges will be assumed to be a fraction of contributions, although in some cases these are collected as a fraction of the individual pension fund value, or as a combination of these.

Translating the pension fund at retirement into a pension benefit

There are basically two main pension benefit arrangements available under the new pension schemes. On the one hand, workers at retirement can purchase a life annuity from insurance companies. As noted above, there is considerable diversity in the development of the insurance market across the countries being studied here. As a rule, insurance companies will assess the expected life expectancy of demographic groups, and offer annuities based on the age of the beneficiary as well as the number and age of dependants.

Insurance companies will also deduct charges and commissions from the pension fund before calculating annuity values. These charges and commissions are not immediately obvious as they can be charged directly as a deduction from an individual's capital sum, or indirectly through the interest rates assumed in the calculations of the annuity value. As the means of raising charges and commissions vary across insurance companies, annuity costs comparisons across providers are difficult to compare. In the simulations that follow charges and commissions will be modelled as a fraction of the pension fund.

An alternative pension arrangement is to take up a phased withdrawal program with a pension fund manager. The phased withdrawal program specifies maximum amounts than can be withdrawn monthly from the beneficiary's pension fund. The remaining pension fund continues to accumulate returns.

Simulation of pension benefits

The pension fund at retirement PF(R) is modelled as

$$PF(R) = \Sigma^R_t \, [\, c(1-m) \, W_t \, (1+g) \,] \, (1+r)^{(R-t)} \tag{6.1}$$

where c is the contribution rate; m is the pension fund manager's commission rate; W_t is total earnings in year t; g is the economy/sector-wide annual rate of growth of earnings; r is the rate of return of the individual pension fund; and R is the normal retirement age.

The conversion of the pension fund at retirement into a pension annuity is defined as

$$pa = [PF(R) \, (1-n)] \, / \, A \tag{6.2}$$

where pa is the pension annuity, n is the commission rate charged by the insurance company and A is the annuity rate determined by the expected life expectancy of the beneficiary and the number and age of his/her dependants.

It would be useful to focus on the pension benefit replacement rate as a measure of adequacy (Barrientos and Firinguetti, 1995a). The pension benefit replacement rate is pa / W(R) and is a standard way of evaluating the extent to which the pension benefit yielded allows a beneficiary to sustain a level of consumption in retirement similar to the level of consumption while in work.

Table 6.4 below shows the results from a simulation of the replacement rate generated by an individual capitalization pension plan. Panel A reports on the replacement rates secured by a male worker with an uninterrupted work history, who joins the labour market at 20 and retires at 65. The simulation assumes constant wage growth and rates of return rates as stated. Panel B introduces contribution gaps of varying length to capture the impact of likely labour market conditions. The replacement rates under different assumptions regarding wage growth and rate of return for a married worker are reported.

The results from the simulation exercise suggest a number of important points:

- in broad terms, for workers with continuous employment a one percentage point rise in the rate of return increases the replacement rate by around a quarter, and therefore the impact of rates of return on pension annuities is paramount;
- if a measure of pension benefit adequacy is set at 0.70 replacement rate, rates of return must exceed rates of wage growth by at least two percentage points for pension benefits to satisfy this adequacy level; if the measure of adequacy is lower at 0.50 replacement rate, rates of return must exceed rates of wage growth by at least one percent for pension annuities to be adequate for full career workers;
- contribution gaps have a large impact upon replacement rates; simulations that assume workers with full contribution records are likely to produce over-optimistic replacement rates (Gillion and Bonilla, 1992; Margozzini, 1988);
- with rates of return at 5 percent, the replacement rate for a married worker with a full (45 year) contribution record is 0.71, but it declines to 0.51 with an early 10 year gap, 0.40 if the gap is 15 years long, and 0.37 if the gap is 20 years long;
- the timing of the contribution gaps is also important, with earlier gaps being more damaging as a result of the compounding effect of rates of return on individual's pension funds; the fall in the replacement rate with an earlier contribution gap is roughly three times larger than if the contribution gap happens late in someone's career;
- using the higher adequacy level of 0.70 replacement rate, a ten year contribution gap is sufficient to push pension annuities below this point;

- with a lower adequacy level of 0.50, pension annuities can still be adequate providing that higher rates of return apply to the funds, or the contribution gaps happen later;
- a twenty year contribution gap pushes the married workers well below the lower adequacy level.

Table 6.4
Simulations of pension replacement rates under different assumptions

Panel A.
Assumes worker joins labour force at age 20, retires at age 65, and works continuously. Pension benefit replacement ratio is pension benefit to final salary net of pension contributions.

		rate of return (r)			
		2%	3%	4%	5%
wage growth rate (g) = 2%	single male	0.46	0.58	0.73	0.94
	married male/ single female	0.38	0.48	0.61	0.78

Panel B.
As in Panel A, but now worker is assumed to have varying contribution gaps

		10 year gap starts at age 20	10 year gap starts at age 30	10 year gap starts at age 40	10 year gap starts at age 50
g = 2 % ; r = 3%	married	0.42	0.44	0.45	0.46
g = 2 % ; r = 5%	married	0.51	0.58	0.63	0.67

		15 year gap starts at age 20	15 year gap starts at age 35	15 year gap starts at age 50	20 year gap starts at age 25
g = 2 % ; r = 3%	married	.30	.32	.34	.25
g = 2 % ; r = 5%	married	.40	.54	.62	.37

The simulation assumes the pension contribution rate is 13 percent of earnings and the pension fund manager commission is 3 percent of earnings. Annuity rates are assumed at 10 percent for single male and 12 percent for married male with spouse five years younger. Annuity rates for married males are roughly in line with those for a single female. Annuity provider's commission is 10 percent of pension fund at retirement.

The overall conclusion yielded by the simulation exercise is that favourable conditions will be required in both the labour and capital markets to secure adequate pension benefits for future pensioners.

Pension benefits under a phased withdrawal program are likely to be similar to those reported in the table above for pension annuities at retirement, but will decline over time because of the formula used in calculating them. Figure 6.5 below shows the phased withdrawal and annuity pension benefit replacement rates for a worker using the same assumptions as in Panel A of Table 6.4. The simulation of phased withdrawal pension benefits is based on the relevant mortality tables for Chile, for males and females, and assumes a rate of interest of 5 percent. As can be observed for the Figure, phased withdrawal pension benefit replacement rates are higher than pension annuities initially, as the former does not include any charges and commissions. However, phased withdrawal replacement rates decline with the age of the beneficiary, and fall below the pension annuity replacement rate soon after retirement.

The results of these simulations need to be considered carefully for at least two reasons. Firstly, the simulations rely on steady market conditions that are considerably at odds with the past record of the Latin American economies. Negative interest rates in the 1970s and helter-skelter conditions in financial markets in the 1980s are in clear conflict with the simulation assumptions of steady positive and high real rates of return. The labour market has shown no less change and upheaval, with negative rates of real wage growth and stagnant productivity in the 1980s.

Secondly, the representative worker used in the simulation has a much steadier employment experience than the large majority of workers in Latin America. When evaluating public policy it is more desirable to focus on the more vulnerable workers (Barrientos and Firinguetti, 1995b).

When these two points are taken into consideration the results of the simulation above may be presumed to overestimate likely future outcomes of pension reform in Latin America. The value of the simulations is that these show the conditions that are needed for the individual capitalization pension schemes to generate adequate pension benefits. These are high rates of return on the pension funds coupled with low rates of wage growth. And a labour market environment that fosters continuous employment and high earnings. These are very demanding conditions in the context of recent trends in Latin America.

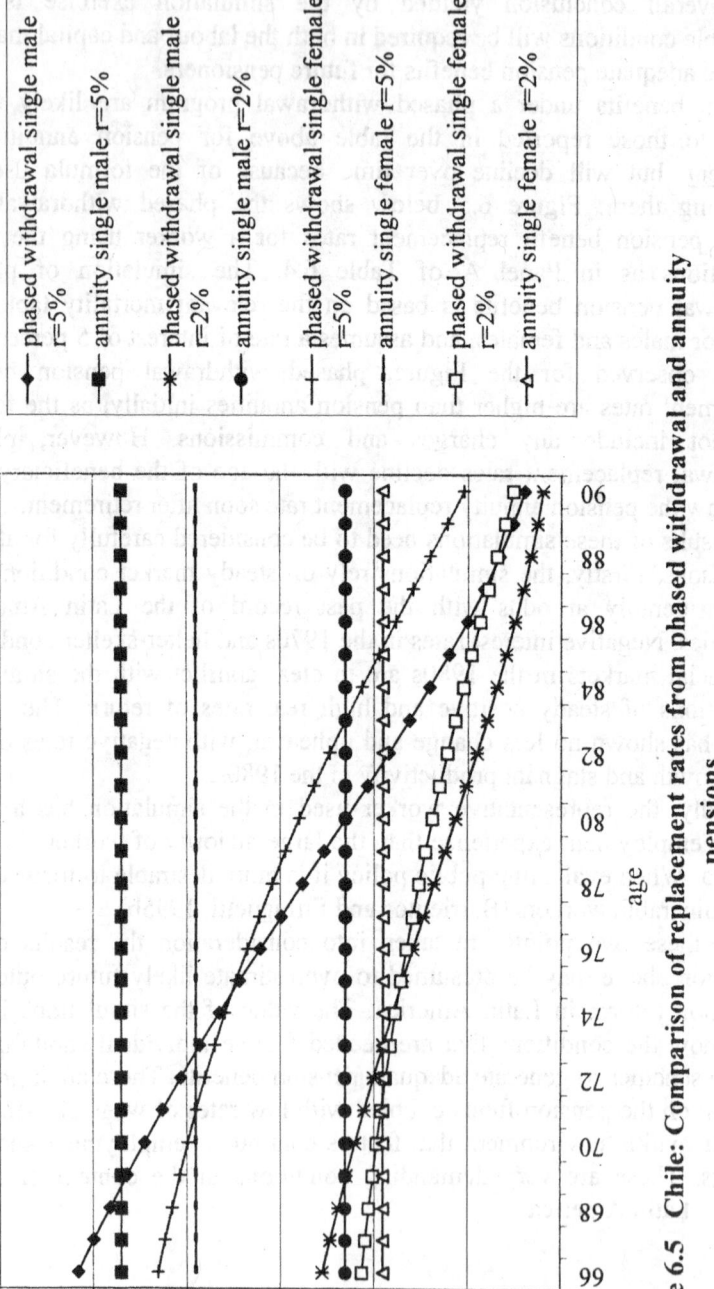

Figure 6.5 Chile: Comparison of replacement rates from phased withdrawal and annuity pensions

Comparison of pension benefit adequacy across reformed pension systems

The simulations of future pension benefits have focused so far on the Chilean new pension scheme. Although sharing a common structure, the conditions regarding contributions and entitlements vary across the Latin American countries studied. A simulation of the likely pension benefits generated by these reformed pension schemes, and the comparison of likely outcomes, would be helpful in evaluating the impact of differences in pension design on future retirement incomes. As the reformed pension schemes in Latin America are in their initial stages, the comparison rests on highly stylized assumptions, and its results need to be considered with great care.

The basis for the simulation of pension entitlement accumulation in the countries concerned is provided by age earnings profiles constructed from wage regressions reported in Psacharopoulos and Tzannatos (1992a). These are shown in Figure 6.6 for females, and Figure 6.7 for males. The data used in the estimation of the wage regressions comes from household survey data from the period 1985-1987. It is important to keep in mind that the cross-sectional nature of the data implies that these age earnings profiles correspond to a snapshot of earnings of workers at different ages, rather than from longitudinal observations of the same cohort at different points in time. Thus, it is implicitly assumed that current younger cohorts will have a future labour market experience that is essentially similar to the labour market experience of current cohorts.

From these constructed age earning profiles, the pattern of contributions required by the pension scheme regulations is identified. These contributions are accumulated at constant rates of return. Translating the pension fund at retirement into a pension benefit is done using assumptions similar to those used in the previous section to simulate pension benefits in the Chilean pension scheme. Where necessary, the simulation incorporated differences in pension scheme rules regarding normal retirement age and pension benefit modalities existing across countries. The results of the simulation are reported in Table 6.5 below.

The simulations show the impact on replacement rates of pension design, the level of contribution rates, and the slope of the age earnings profiles. The simulations assume a representative worker with full, 45 year, contribution record, and a constant rate of return on the pension funds of 3 percent.

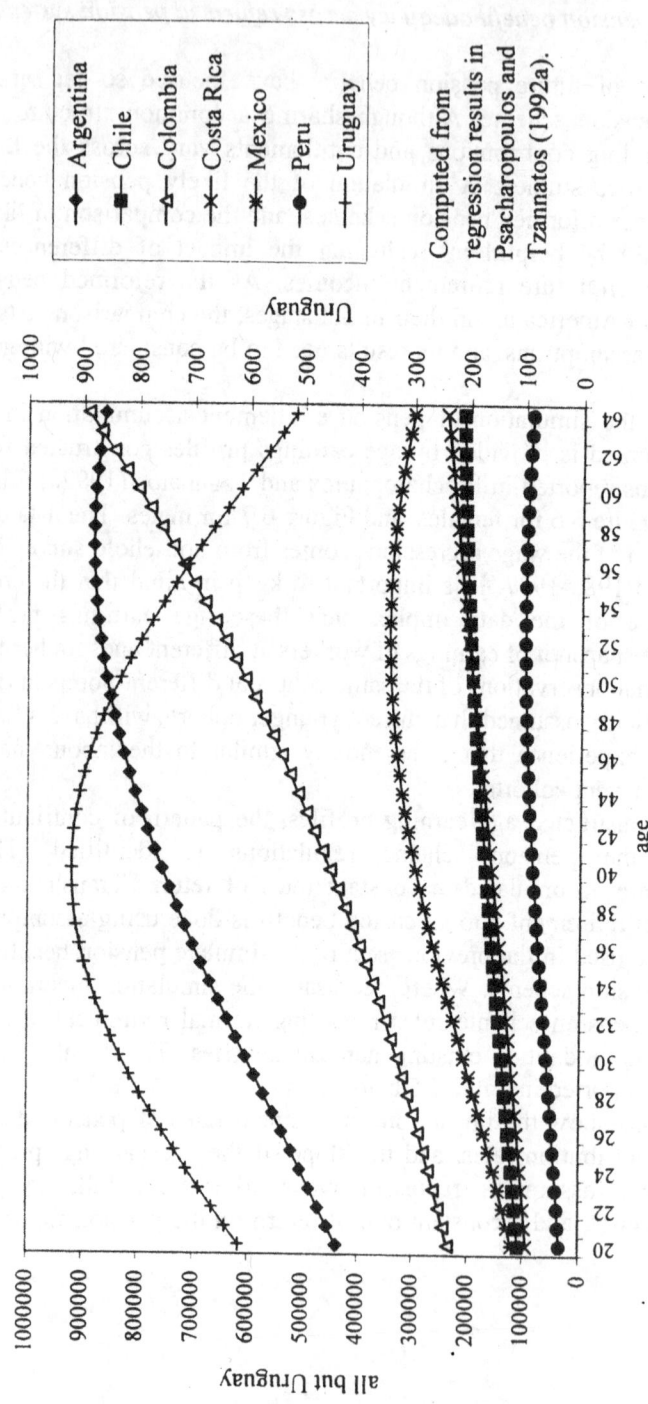

Figure 6.6 Annual age earnings profiles for female workers in selected Latin American countries (domestic currency)

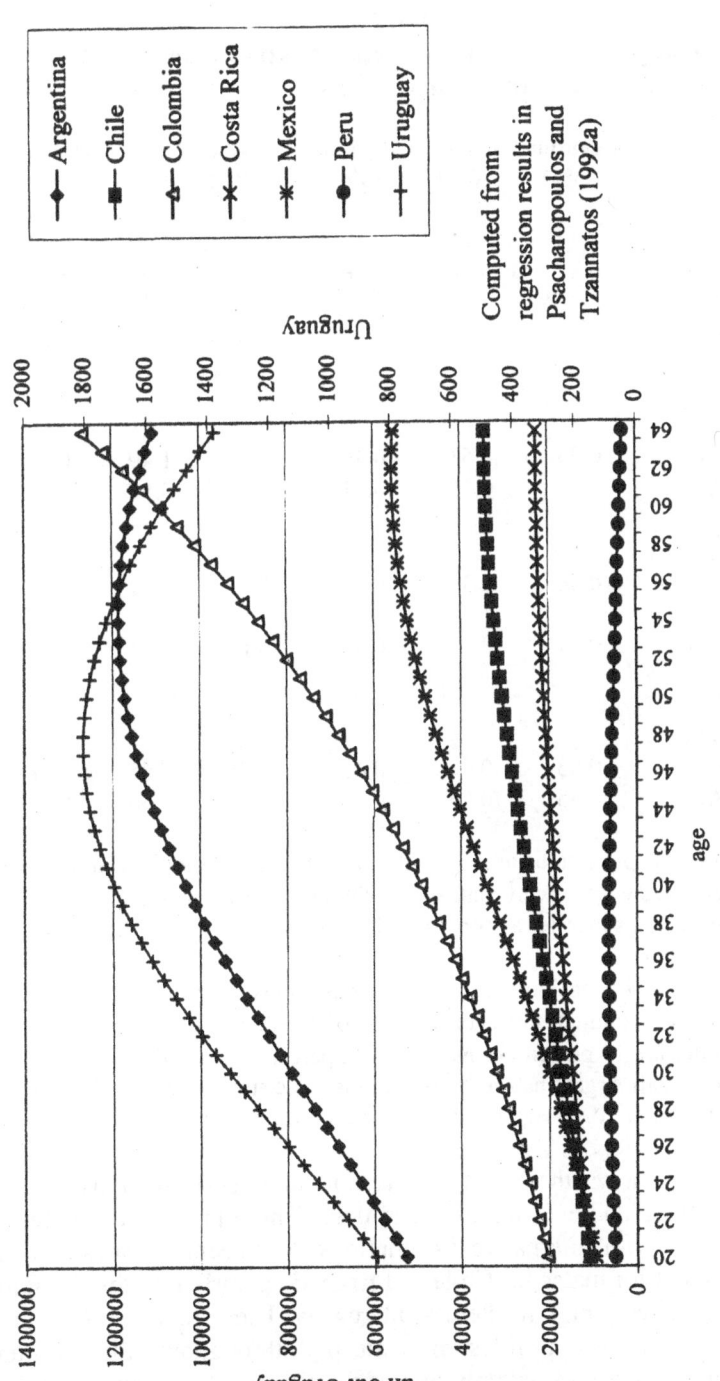

Figure 6.7 Annual age earnings profiles for male workers in selected Latin American countries (domestic currency)

233

Table 6.5
Simulation of pension benefit replacement rates for selected Latin American countries

Country (contribution rate)	Argentina (7.5%)	Chile (10%)	Colombia (10%)	Mexico (6.5%)	Peru (10%)	Uruguay (15%)
Males						
capitalization scheme only	0.57	0.58	0.36	0.32	1.74	1.44
if Chile's pension reform	0.75	0.58	0.36	0.50	1.74	0.96
if Argentina's pension reform:						
PBU+AFAP	0.75	0.63	0.46	0.56	1.49	0.91
PBU+PAP	0.59	0.56	0.51	0.57	0.67	0.62
Females						
capitalization scheme only	0.46	0.57	0.38	0.41	0.61	1.75
if Chile's pension reform	0.61	0.57	0.38	0.63	0.61	1.17
if Argentina's pension reform:						
PBU+AFAP	0.65	0.62	0.47	0.66	0.65	1.06
PBU+PAP	0.58	0.56	0.53	0.60	0.60	0.65

Replacement rate is pension benefit to final salary. The simulations assume:
- a representative worker who contributes without interruption for 45 years, with age earnings profiles as constructed;
- no wage growth;
- contributions as in pension scheme regulations minus commission;
- pension fund accumulates at a constant rate of 3 percent;
- annuity rates are 10 percent for males and 12 percent for females.

For simulations with Argentina's features, PBU is basic state pension, AFAP is capitalization pension, PAP is pay as you go social insurance pension.

The first row shows the results of a simulation performed using each country's earnings and contribution conditions. These provide a benchmark for comparison with alternative assumptions. Replacement rates are just above 50 percent for males for Chile and Argentina, fairly low for Colombia and Mexico, and very high for Peru and Uruguay. They are low in Colombia because age earnings profiles rise steeply throughout the worker's employment. In Mexico it is a mixture of the slope of the earnings profiles and a relatively low contribution rate. In Peru and Uruguay the replacement rates are very high. In Peru this is because of the steep decline of earnings at later ages of the representative worker. In Uruguay, it is a mixture of this factor and the relatively high contribution rates. The pattern of replacement rates for females is very similar.

The second row shows the results of imposing Chile's contribution rates on the other countries. This has no effect on Colombia's and Peru's since they have the same contribution rate, but it lowers the replacement rates in Uruguay and raises them in Argentina. This simulation shows more clearly the impact of altering replacement rates.

The next two rows report on a simulation using Argentina's pension reform features on all other countries. This is interesting because of Argentina's mixture of a basic state pension, and alternative capitalization and final salary second pillar pensions. Taking first the results emerging from imposing Argentina's pension system structure with the capitalization scheme as the second pillar shows that replacement rates rise for all countries except Mexico and Uruguay. This is because of the combination of a lower contribution rate, and a sharp decline in the slope of the earnings profile at later ages. The impact of a decline in earnings in later years is greater if workers select the state pay as you pension scheme as their second pillar pension, because in a lower the final salary has a strong impact upon the pension benefit. In Colombia and Mexico, where the rise in the age earnings profile is steep, the pay as you pension scheme delivers higher replacement rates. The impact of differences in pension design is less important for females due to their flatter age earnings profiles.

The simulations assumed away the impact of variations in rates of return, and the impact of employment or contributory gaps. They highlight the fact that labour market conditions in the future will have a crucial effect upon replacement rates. To an important extent, pension design would be less important in itself if the labour market could provide stable and favourable conditions. The impact of pension design will be accentuated by adverse labour market conditions. Workers with earnings that rise with age or experience would benefit from final salary pension schemes. On the other hand, workers with flatter age earning profiles will be better served by capitalization pension schemes, at least where these can secure positive returns.

Two other important points arise from the simulation. The first one is that with the exceptions of Peru and Uruguay, the presence of a first pillar pension scheme appears to generate higher pensions than alternatives. This is perhaps not surprising since the basic state pension is financed out of general tax revenues. The second point is that the variance in replacement rates is markedly lower across the different countries with a two pillar pension scheme, and with a final salary scheme second pillar, as in Argentina. This would be even more apparent if comparisons could be made between workers at different points in the earnings distribution, simply because the distribution would be truncated at low earnings. The capitalization pension schemes, by avoiding intentional redistribution, have the effect of increasing the variance in replacement rates.

Conclusion

This chapter began by discussing the economic position of the elderly in the recent past in Latin America. Its main findings were that the elderly were under represented in the lower income groups and over represented in the medium and upper income groups in the region. A number of factors suggest that this situation may not continue into the future. The relative well being of the elderly was a result of the expansion in social insurance pension schemes in the 1950s and 1960s, and indicates a measure of success by these programs in reducing old age poverty. Demographic trends, the dismantling of government programs, and changes in the family, will leave the elderly more exposed in future. The relative prosperity of pensioners in the 1980s rested on very specific conditions. Pensioners were affected by the 1980s recession, but to a lesser extent than those in work. This is because their benefits were loosely adjusted with inflation, while the wage of those in work declined in real terms. It would not be surprising if the economic situation faced by the elderly in Latin America were to deteriorate in the first two or three decades of the next century.

The capacity of the reformed pension schemes to provide adequate pension benefits in the future will be essential in accommodating these trends. The design properties of the pension benefits introduced by the capitalization pension schemes will be an important factor. The two main types of pension benefit introduced by pension reform, life annuities and phased withdrawals, were studied. It was found that phased withdrawal pensions have fewer insurance properties than life annuities. Moreover, phased withdrawal pensions provide, under most plausible scenarios, a declining consumption path. On the other hand, life annuity pensions are subject to significant charges and commissions, in part due to the underdevelopment of the insurance markets in Latin America. The success of pension reform will require the rapid development and modernization of insurance markets in Latin America.

The short life span of the reformed pension systems in Latin America means that the adequacy of future pension benefits can only be studied in the context of very stylised simulations. While highly speculative and tentative, these simulation exercises point to some of the requirements needed for the reformed pension systems to provide adequate pension benefits in the future. A simulation done on the basis of the Chilean capitalization pension scheme shows that a key requirement will be that the rates of return secured by the funds exceed rates of wage growth by a significant margin. Contributory gaps, especially if they occur early in an individual's career, could have large adverse effects on pension benefits.

A simulation of pension benefits generated by the different reformed pension systems in the Latin American countries under examination provided some useful, although again speculative, pointers. Firstly, it showed that labour market conditions are key to the success of the new pension schemes. Secondly, it suggested that a two pillar pension system, as in Argentina, has the effect of reducing the variance in replacement rates. Thirdly, it showed that workers with age earnings profiles that rise more steeply, are better off in capitalization pension schemes. In the simulation, the differences in pension design have less significant effects upon women workers, as their age earnings profiles are flatter. Two important factors are not captured in this simulation. These are the impact of employment gaps, and the impact of varying rates of return on the pension fund.

The overall conclusion is that favourable conditions in the labour market, and the economy in general, will be needed to ensure the reformed pension schemes in Latin America are successful in providing adequate pension benefits in the future.

Notes

1   In the 1980s and early 1990s the Pan American Health Organisation commissioned a number of studies on the needs of the elderly in Latin America and the Caribbean countries (Pan American Health Organisation, 1989; Pérez, Restrepo and Colsner, 1993). These are an important source of information.

2   The poverty line was defined in this study as the money value of a basic food basket adjusted by a factor of 2 for the urban population, and 1.75 for the rural population.

3   By 1990 the proportion of the unemployed in Santiago who were unemployed for more than a year was just under 20 percent, down from 26 percent in 1982 and from 35 percent at the peak of the 1980s unemployment (Paredes and Riveros, 1994).

4   Assistential pensions are also available for elderly persons without alternative sources of income. These are paid out of government general revenues, are administered by local authorities, and have a value of less than a quarter of the minimum wage. Many other Latin American countries offer non-contributory pensions for the very elderly, over 70 years of age, without other sources of income.

5   The formula used in the calculation of the Recognition Bond (RB) is as follows:

$$RB = (0.8 \bullet \Sigma nW/n) \bullet 12 \bullet T/35 \bullet z \bullet A \qquad (A6.1)$$

Where W are monthly earnings on which contributions were paid before June 1979 price adjusted to this date; n are months with n=1,2,...,12; T are years in which contributions were made up to a maximum of 35; z is an gender adjustment factor with a value of 10.35 if male and 11.35 if female; and A is an age adjustment factor with a value of 1 if male at or below 60, and 1.1 if aged 65 or more; and 1 if female aged 41 or less, and 1.31 if aged 60 or above.

To qualify for a Recognition Bond, workers needed to have contributed to the old pension scheme for at least 12 months in the five years before June 1979. The Recognition Bond set at June 1979 prices is then price adjusted to the time the worker joins the new pension scheme. After that, the Bond is guaranteed by the government to accumulate at 4 percent a year in real terms.

6   The formula used to calculate the maximum pension withdrawal takes account of the life expectancy of the beneficiary and dependants, and of the continued accumulation of the pension fund. The AFPs are required to use mortality tables produced by the National Institute of Statistics, and the formulas set out by the Superintendencia de Administradoras de Fondos de Pensiones. For example, the formula used to calculate a monthly maximum withdrawal PW for a single male is given by :

$$PW = (PF - PVFB) \bullet (1/12) \bullet 1/(Nx/Dx - 11/24) \qquad (A6.2)$$

where PF is the accumulated pension fund at retirement, $PVFB$ is the present value of the funeral benefit (15 UF). Dx is the product of Lx and Vx, where x indexes ages in years, Lx is the number of a 100,000 cohort still alive at the beginning of x, and Vx is a discount factor $(1/1+i)$. Nx adds Dx over the future. Assuming a unitary annuity (say £1) Nx is the sum of all discounted payments to a cohort.

The rate of interest i used in the discounting of future payments, is in effect the rate of return at which the remaining retirement fund is expected to accumulate. Since 1988, the formula required by regulation for the computation of i is

$$i_h = (0.2 \bullet R_h) + (0.8 \bullet IPA_{t-1}) \qquad (A6.3)$$

where h indexes AFPs. R is the average of the rates of return attained by AFP h in the last five years. And IPA is the average of the implicit rates of interest of pension annuities in the previous year. Note that to the extent that rates of return differ across AFPs these will have different rates of discount, and hence will offer different maximum withdrawals for a given retirement fund.

7   This is a simple average of trends for Argentina, Chile, Colombia, Mexico and Venezuela. It includes four of the seven countries under study.

Conclusion

An assessment of pension reform in Latin America

The examination of pension reform in Latin America presented in the preceding chapters suggests a number of conclusions. The new individual capitalization pension schemes introduced by pension reform have successfully established themselves, and pension reform has set in place the foundations on which these will develop into the future. There is, of course, a considerable time to go before the new pension schemes mature, and their capacity to ensure adequate pension benefits for their members can be fully tested. Judging by their very short life spans, the reformed pension systems, and the new pension plans within them, will be subject to constant and searching modifications in line with experience.

The early experience of pension reform in Chile has created high expectations as to the rapid growth and development of the new pension schemes. Compared to Chile, the development of the new pension schemes in Argentina, Peru, and Colombia, has been slower. This applies especially to Peru, where the individual capitalization pension scheme stagnated after an initial period, and had to be relaunched in 1995. There a number of explanations for Chile's faster development of pension reform. In Chile, the new individual capitalization pension scheme did not have to find an accommodation with the old social insurance pension schemes. Pension reform benefited from adequate preparation, and from very auspicious economic conditions from mid 1980s onwards. The pension scheme affiliation options offered to Chilean workers in the early 1980s were stacked in favour of switching to the new pension plans. In Peru it could be argued that the situation was the other way around. In terms of labour force coverage, and pension fund size, it does not look as if the new pension schemes in other Latin American countries will reach the same rates of growth that Chile's had in its initial stages.

Perhaps the most important factor in explaining the rapid establishment of the Chilean individual capitalization pension scheme lies with the high rates of return achieved by the pension fund managers. Since its inception in 1981, the average real rate of return of pension funds in Chile has been just over 12 percent. This reflects the high rates of investment returns available in Chilean economy in the last decade or so, rather than any outstanding achievement by the pension fund managers. The high rates of return secured by pension funds are unlikely to be sustained in the future, as the factors that have contributed to these high rates of return cannot be safely projected into the future. These include the privatization of utilities, the emerging markets premium, the sustained growth of the Chilean economy, and the growth in financial asset demand from the pension funds themselves.

The evaluation of pension schemes must necessarily focus on their longer term prospects. Pension funds rates of return have been exceptionally high in the last decade. The point is how much lower rates of return will be in the medium to the long term. The longest term assets in Chile, around 15 years' maturity, can currently secure rates of return of between 5 and 6 percent. If the expectations implicit in these rates of return materialize, the new pension schemes will be moderately successful. Providing workers contribute on a regular basis, and throughout their working lives, these rates of return will ensure adequate pension benefits. The investment risk attached to pension fund portfolios will be a factor of the variation of rates of return over time, rather than of their long term average level.

The second most important factor in the success of the Chilean new pension scheme derives from the willingness of the government, and the regulators, to provide effective supervision and regulation. Some suggest that the extent of regulation, as well the particular form it takes, may adversely affect the performance of the new pension plans (Shah, 1997). It is difficult to fully agree with this claim. Chile's banking liberalization in the 1970s, and the introduction of personal pensions in the UK in late 1980s, provide ample evidence of fact that the absence, or inadequacy, of regulation can seriously undermine financial reform. This was a lesson the Chilean government had learned before embarking on pension reform. This is not to say that all regulation has been helpful in the Chilean case, but that the willingness to regulate demonstrated by the government has been a crucial ingredient in the rapid establishment and development of the capitalization pension plans in Chile. It will also be a determining factor in the development of pension reform in other countries.

In addition to regulation and supervision, the government provides a number of guarantees. Their role is more difficult to evaluate. The provision of government guarantees applying to pension funds' performance and solvency, and to pension benefits, was crucial in securing public confidence in the new pension scheme. In most Latin American countries, these guarantees enjoyed a high profile in the legislative scrutiny of pension reform proposals, or were the result of amendments to the legislation. These guarantees may have played a significant a role in the initial phase of pension reform. At the same time, it is noteworthy that these guarantees either have a large discretionary element or can be easily changed in line with fiscal constraints. In Chile, for example, the minimum pension guarantee is not indexed to prices or earnings. In Argentina, the basic pension guarantees were quickly scaled down after the 'tequila' crisis. The short life span of the new pension schemes means these guarantees, and especially the pension benefit guarantees, are as yet untested. There is also a question mark over the impact of financial guarantees on the risk propensities of pension fund managers.

The implementation of pension reform in Latin America has underlined some important weaknesses in the reformed pension systems, and in the new individual capitalization pension plans. The articulation of pay as you go and individual capitalization pension schemes within the reformed pension systems does not appear to be sufficiently stable or solid. In Peru the legislators initially placed the individual capitalization plans at a disadvantage relative to the pay as you go pension scheme regarding contribution rates. This was later amended and the two schemes were put on a level playing field. In Argentina, on the other hand, the legislators initially encouraged the switch of workers to the new individual capitalization pension plans, but later amendments have relaxed, albeit for a limited period, the constraints on workers' freedom to return to the pay as you go pension scheme. As can be seen from the experience of the Latin American countries studied here, subtle changes in regulations could transform the pay as you go pension schemes from being a residual scheme to being a competitor for the individual capitalization scheme, and vice versa.

The problem is that pay as you go pension schemes require, to be viable, a balanced demographic distribution of its members. In practice, the design properties of pay as you go and capitalization pension schemes dictate that the former will be more attractive to older workers, while the latter will be especially attractive to younger workers. In the UK, where workers can move between a capitalization pension scheme and a public salary related pension scheme, it has been shown that the optimal strategy is for workers to start in the former, and to switch to the latter in mid working life (Disney and Whitehouse, 1992). One of the implications of this is that government future pension liabilities are uncertain, and may be very large. Accommodating a pay as you go public pension scheme with a capitalization pension scheme within a single pension pillar will provide an important challenge to the reformed pension systems in Latin America.

A different set of problems beset countries like Argentina and Uruguay where first pillar public pension schemes must be accommodated with second pillar capitalization pension schemes. Here a key problem is how to finance the first pillar. With the partial exception of Uruguay, all other countries intend to finance their minimum or basic pension out of general tax revenues. This is in line with the recommendations of the World Bank (World Bank, 1994). It is, of course, appropriate for the government to assume these liabilities. These also provide a strong justification for close supervision and regulation of the new pension schemes by the government. The government future liabilities in this respect will be dependent upon the success of the new pension schemes as regards their coverage rates and pension fund accumulation. There are very few studies projecting government future expenditure arising from these liabilities. Studies focusing on Chile provide a rough estimate of this expenditure when the new pension scheme matures at between 3 and 5 percent of GDP (Corsetti and Schmidt-Hebbel, 1997; Marcel and Arenas, 1992; Ortúzar and Peña, 1986).

The implementation of pension reform has also thrown into relief some important weaknesses of the new pension schemes. The most important of these is to do with the high costs of the new pension schemes in Latin America, reflected in high levels of charges and commissions. These amount to between 2.4 and 3 percent of contributory earnings, or between a quarter and a third of pension contributions. International comparisons of pension plan costs show the cost levels of the new pension plans in Chile to be at the upper end of the scale, and certainly much higher than public pay as go pension schemes. When the cost trends in the new pension schemes in Latin America are analysed in more detail, two points emerge. Firstly, marketing and sales personnel costs are the main contributors to the costs of the new pension schemes. Moreover, in Chile these have tended to rise over time. It is difficult not to come to the conclusion that a large proportion of marketing and sales personnel costs provide little added value, and that they will significantly reduce future pension benefit levels. Secondly, the pattern of incentives present in the pension fund market is such that pension providers have little pressure to reduce costs, or to pass lower costs on to affiliates in the form of lower charges.

In large part this is due to a another main weakness of the new pension schemes, the limited role of competitive forces in securing efficiency in pension provision. Affiliates to the individual capitalization pension plans are relatively insensitive to the longer term parameters affecting the accumulation of their pension funds (Diamond, 1996b). The quantity and quality of sales personnel and marketing appear to have a stronger effect upon market share than pension fund performance indicators. Allied to this are the lack of direct correlation between the operational costs of the new pension schemes, and the structure of commissions and charges. This means that pension fund managers have scope for distributing charges in line with marketing objectives, and that charges and commissions are to a large extent insulated from competitive forces.

There are well known reasons why financial, and pension, markets may not operate as in the textbook version of competitive markets. The long term nature of the product, and the complexities of financial products, may seriously limit competitive behaviour in these markets. Pension designers in Latin America have taken some of these issues on board. The complexities of pension products have been reduced to a minimum by the standardisation built into the individual capitalization pension plans in Latin America. Extensive regulation is in place to buttress the pension fund management market. These measures are not always successful. The balance of regulation and competition is a difficult one, and the specifics of regulating a private pension fund management market are very complex. Some commentators have suggested the limitations of competition in the new pension schemes are simply the flip side of extensive regulation (Shah, 1997; Valdés-Prieto, 1995). All things considered, the overall assessment of the new pension schemes in Latin America must be that competition has worked only to a very limited extent.

After Chile's pension reform, other countries have sought ways of reducing the costs of their new pension schemes. These have included centralising some of the pension scheme functions that could benefit from economies of scale, such as the collection of contributions and record keeping (as in Argentina), or the provision of disability and survivor insurance (as in Mexico). Restrictions imposed on the ability of affiliates to transfer from one pension fund manager to another have also been included in most countries. It is interesting to note that these will have the effect of further reducing the scope for competition in securing the efficiency of pension provision.

Another important weakness in the new pension schemes has to do with the decline or stagnation in pension system coverage rates for the countries involved in pension reform. Although the coverage rates for the new pension schemes show a rising trend, this is largely explained by workers transferring from the old pension schemes, and by the rise in employment. Pension reform has not succeeded in raising overall pension coverage rates. This is particularly apparent in the case of independent workers, who have very low pension coverage rates .

The decline or stagnation in overall pension coverage rates may be explained by the recent changes in labour market conditions in Latin America. Labour market liberalization, the stagnation of real wages, and the informalisation of employment relationships, all contribute to lower pension coverage. These trends have been reversed in Chile in the 1990s, but pension coverage rates have changed only marginally. The experiences of Chile, Argentina, and Peru, do not support the claim that the new individual capitalization pension plans will be better at accommodating the new labour market conditions in Latin America.

This leads to the issue of the impact of pension reform on vulnerable groups of workers. An important feature of the new individual capitalization pension plans is that they provide more limited insurance for social and economic risks than the old social insurance pension schemes. The new pension scheme provides full longevity insurance only if a life annuity is chosen at retirement, or if the worker is entitled to a minimum pension. Entitlement to disability and survivor insurance is in most cases limited to workers who are currently contributing to a pension plan. The basic features of the new pension schemes compound labour market risks. On the other hand, it is possible to add products to the individual capitalization pension plans that provide access to financial diversification. Chile's severance saving accounts, and more broadly voluntary saving accounts, do precisely that.

Overall, the new individual capitalization pension plans do not improve the situation of vulnerable workers with regards to retirement income risks. It is admittedly difficult to design individual pension plans for workers who experience irregular employment and pay, or whose poverty dictate high intertemporal discount rates. These workers will continue to rely on basic income government programs, or on informal family support. As unemployment, pay, and poverty deteriorated in the 1980s, and social insurance programs have been downsized or dismantled, poverty in old age is likely to rise in Latin America.

Lessons for other countries

The model of pension reform provided by Chile and the other Latin American countries has figured prominently in discussions of pension reform in other countries. The spread of pension reform in Latin America shows that the essentials of pension reform can be adapted, and applied, to other countries. In this context it may be useful to outline the lessons other countries can be learn from pension reform in Latin America.

The transition

As with any public policy reform, care should be taken to phase in the reforms gradually, and ameliorate the losses of those adversely affected by the reform. The pension reform in Latin America has been gradual to the extent that membership of the new pension schemes was made compulsory only for workers entering the labour force. The pre-existing entitlements of workers were protected by retaining the social insurance pension schemes, and by giving these workers the choice to switch to the new capitalization pension plans. The way in which entitlements under the old pension scheme are transferred varies across countries. In Chile, the recognition bond served to make explicit existing pension debt, and to spread pension payments over a longer period. As a consequence, government expenditure related to the old scheme pension liabilities is expected to rise over the first two decades of the next century, and decline thereafter. In Argentina, the pension liabilities under the old social insurance pension scheme will also be spread over a longer period, but will take the form of pension benefits, that are dependent upon demographic and mortality factors.

In Latin America, pension reform has been introduced as part of wider structural reforms. On the one hand, this has reduced the range of options regarding pension design. On the other, accompanying economic reforms have facilitated and supported the development of the new individual capitalization pension plans. This raises the issue of sequencing pension reform in the context of wider structural reforms (Vittas, 1995). In Chile, for example, the privatization program and the reform of financial market regulation, were crucial to the success of pension reform. Pension reform will be greatly facilitated if pre-existing pension provision is streamlined, and if government social security deficits are under control. Capital market reforms must be in place to ensure the absorption of large pension saving flows. The reform of the insurance sector will needed to follow the introduction of individual capitalization pension plans. In Chile, pension reform has been greatly facilitated by very favourable economic conditions.

The government input

Pension reform in Latin America has considerably extended the scope for private pension provision. The role of government remains, however, central to the effective operation of the reformed pension systems. This is not just because in most countries, except Chile and Mexico, a reformed pay as you go public pension scheme remains. The government has a central role to play in authorising, regulating, supervising, and guaranteeing the new individual capitalization pension schemes. These will be successful only on the basis of continued government support and supervision. Moreover, the indications are that governments in Latin America will have to assume a large role in pension provision, to the extent that efforts to reduce costs lead to centralised contribution collection and record keeping. The lesson here is that successful pension reform requires that governments are willing to maintain a high profile in pension provision.

Pension design

Pension reform in Latin America has resulted in diversity in pension system design. The basic features of the individual capitalization pension plans are very similar across countries, but the way in which these are articulated with the overall pension system vary. Two points are important here. The first is that it is inevitable that pension schemes built around two pension pillars will prevail. In some of the countries examined here, notably Chile, Mexico, and Colombia, there is no explicit first pillar. In their place there is a minimum pension, with entitlements varying in requisites and generosity. In addition, many countries pay a discretionary pension benefit to the very old who lack alternative sources of income. Given economic conditions in Latin America, and pension coverage rates, it is likely that these will become a basic pension pillar, and it would be better to design them accordingly. There are, as noted, important incentive effects arising from the financing and provision of a basic pension pillar. It would be helpful to design the first pillar pensions to minimize the adverse incentive effects.

The second point is that individual pension plans have significant drawbacks which can be minimized by offering group pension plans as an alternative. The advantages of individual pension plans are that they place choice and responsibility for pension arrangements on individual workers themselves, that they permit a closer correspondence between contributions and benefits, and that they do not obstruct worker mobility. At the same time they suffer from corresponding drawbacks, in that they are costly to administer, they provide no scope for employers to use them to support productivity enhancing objectives, and they have fewer redistributive and insurance properties. Allowing for group capitalization pension plans, in which the entitlements of individual members could be identified, may provide a fruitful alternative to existing plans.

Enhancing pension coverage

An important lesson emerging from pension reform in Latin America is that the introduction of individual capitalization pension plans does not in itself increase pension coverage. The new pension schemes in Latin America have not been particularly attractive to independent workers, nor to workers in less formal employment. The Chilean pension reform has, however, resulted in the elimination of the gender gap in pension coverage.

One possible explanation for the stagnation of pension coverage rates is to do with the lack of liquidity of the pension fund. Pension savings can be drawn upon only when the beneficiary retires, becomes disabled, or dies. This feature of the new pension schemes precludes savers using their retirement saving for investment in human or physical capital, or in housing.

There is a justification for restricting the use of pension funds, based on the perception that failure to do so may result in individuals failing to save enough for retirement, or misusing the pension funds. In addition, it may be administratively costly to monitor other uses of the pension fund. There is a case, however, for studying ways of allowing workers to use their pension funds for alternative capital investments.

Pension reform does not raise saving

An important claim made on behalf of pension reform is that the introduction of individual pension plans would result in increased household saving. The experience of Latin American countries is that the saving effects of pension reform are marginal.

Minimizing pension scheme costs

The high costs of individual capitalization pension plans are of some concern. The need to minimize these costs will need to be a primary objective of pension designers aiming to emulate pension reform in Latin America. Cost minimization features fall within two main headings. The first includes those features that economize on the use of markets. Markets provide an effective means of organizing pension provision, but they can also be very costly. In the new individual capitalization pension schemes there are a number of services which can be provided more cheaply by a central agency. These include those services enjoying significant economies of scale, such as the collection of contributions, record keeping, and benefit payment. Enforcing the payment of contributions, and their collection and processing by employers, could be done more effectively and cheaply by a central agency with access to existing government records. In addition, there are other services that involve significant economies of scope, and could be bundled together. These include, for example, the provision of voluntary saving accounts together with retirement accounts.

A different set of cost minimization features has to do with restricting the pursuit of market power and rent seeking by pension providers. These features should be concerned with restricting the rising marketing and sales costs of pension fund managers. Some countries have introduced regulations restricting transfers across fund managers, for example. It is difficult to identify features that would not, at the same time, have the effect of reducing competition. It has been suggested in Chile that offering group pension plans may provide affiliates with a means of countervailing the power of pension providers. In Argentina the existence of a government sponsored pension fund manager may ensure best practice.

The most effective way to restrict pension providers' market power is to bring as far as possible their commissions and charges into line with their costs. An important issue here is to aim as far as possible to unbundle services with different cost structures. In existing individual capitalization pension plans, both regulations and practice result in services with different cost structures being bundled together. For example, fund investment services costs are, if anything, related to the size of the fund, but account management and record keeping are most likely to be related to the number of affiliates. Where these are bundled together it is likely that commissions will be out of line with costs. The lessons here are, firstly, to economize on the use of markets where appropriate, and, secondly, to align commissions as closely as possible to costs.

Insurance provision

The importance of the insurance properties of pension funds cannot be overstated. Pension reform in Latin America will alter the insurance provided by pension schemes in at least two ways. Firstly, the range of insurance provided by the new individual capitalization pension plans is narrower than under the old social insurance pension schemes. Secondly, the reform has the effect of compounding labour market risks. This is because longevity risks will depend on the density of contributions over an individual's working life, and disability and survivor insurance cover is dependent upon active contributor status. The combination of pension reform and recent labour market trends will enhance economic insecurity. Moreover this will take place against a background of government withdrawal from social insurance, and significant changes in the family. Other countries embarking upon pension reform will need to consider this carefully. Getting the right conditions in the labour market will be crucial to the future evolution of pension reform.

Solidarity and redistribution

The new individual capitalization pension schemes in Latin America explicitly avoid redistributive properties. Redistribution is still present in the reformed pension systems, through the provision of minimum pensions, and the distribution of costs among pension scheme affiliates. There is, however, no attempt at redistributing from the rich to the poor, or from the successful to the unsuccessful. Other things being equal, there will be greater inequality in retirement income as a consequence of pension reform.

Some countries, Colombia and Peru for example, have incorporated solidarity objectives in their reformed pension systems by levying contributions explicitly aimed at protecting the disadvantaged. In all countries, the minimum pension guarantee will provide some safety net retirement income, but the entitlement requisites will restrict these to a fraction of the elderly. Other countries wishing to emulate pension reform in Latin America will need to play close attention to how the solidarity and redistributive objectives could be integrated within the new pension schemes.

Future trends and research agenda

It is likely that pension reform will continue to spread in Latin America, and elsewhere. The future course of pension reform in the countries studied in this book will depend on the development of the pension fund management market, and of the insurance and capital markets. Crucially, the future conditions in the labour market will determine whether the high expectations of pension reform are fulfilled.

It will be interesting to see how the articulation of pay as you go and capitalization pension schemes evolves over time. Current trends suggest that the reformed social insurance pension schemes will become a residual scheme and gradually decline. It will also be interesting to see how the mix of regulation and competition evolves in the future. As the new pension schemes develop, it is likely that regulation may become less significant, whilst continuing to buttress the reformed pension systems.

A longer run of the reformed pension systems in Latin America will permit a more conclusive analysis of whether pension reform has contributed to the economic growth and development of the economies in the region.

The evolution of the new individual capitalization pension plans in Latin America will focus attention of other areas of research (Arrau and Schmidt-Hebbel, 1994). The development, regulation, and supervision of the life insurance sector has not been adequately explored, in part because there are few pensioners in the new pension schemes. The performance of the life insurance sector will be an essential factor in the evolution of the new pension schemes. The examination of the life insurance market in developed countries, and especially the USA raises important issues of regulation and supervision (Friedman and Warshawsky, 1990). Allied to this is the issue of the appropriateness of current pension benefit options (Díaz and Edwards, 1994; Valdés-Prieto and Edwards, 1996).

Two other areas of research have been largely ignored in the literature. Firstly, the similarity in the individual capitalization pension plans in Latin America, and their portability, should facilitate worker mobility across Latin American countries, contributing to economic integration (Asociación Internacional de Organismos de Supervisión de Fondos de Pensiones, 1997). Secondly, pension reform should facilitate flows of pension fund investment and know how across the developed and developing world (Davanzo and Kautz, 1992; Fischer and Reisen, 1994; Reisen and Williamson, 1997).

The introduction of individual capitalization pension plans in Latin America constitutes a radical attempt at pension reform. Chile provided the initial model of pension reform in 1980s. Peru, Argentina, Colombia, Uruguay, Mexico and Costa Rica have followed suit in the 1990s. This book has aimed to provide an extensive analysis and evaluation of pension reform in Latin America. Due to the short life span of the reforms, many of its findings and conclusions must be taken to be provisional. This book would be successful in its aims if it encourages, and contributes to, an ongoing debate on how to best secure adequate retirement income and economic security for the elderly of the future.

Bibliography

Abuhadba, M. (1994), 'Aspectos Organizacionales y Competencia en el Sistema Previsional', mimeo, March, Santiago.

Agosín, M. (1994), 'Saving and Investment in Latin America', Documento de Trabajo 126, August, Universidad de Chile, Departamento de Economía: Santiago.

Agosin, M.R.; G. Crespi and L. Letelier (1996), 'Explicaciones del Aumento del Ahorro en Chile', mimeo, August, Banco Interamericano de Desarrollo: Washington DC.

Altimir, O. (1997), 'Desigualdad, Empleo y Pobreza en América Latina: Efectos del Ajuste y Cambio en el estilo de Desarrollo', *Desarrollo Económico*, Vol. 37, No.145, pp.3-29.

Arellano, J.P. (1990), 'El Desafío de la Seguridad Social: El Caso Chileno', Documento de Trabajo 340, February, PREALC: Santiago.

Arrau, P. (1994), 'Fondo de Pensiones y Desarrollo del Mercado de Capitales en Chile: 1980-1993', Serie Financiamiento para el Desarrollo 19, May, CEPAL/PNUD: Santiago.

Arrau, P. and K. Schmidt-Hebbel (1994), 'Pension systems and reforms: Country experiences and research issues', *Revista de Análisis Económico*, Vol. 9, No.1, pp.3-20.

Arriagada, I. (1994), 'Changes in the urban female labour market', *Cepal Review*, No.53, pp.91-110.

Asociación Gremial de AFPs (1996), *II Congreso Iberoamericano Sistemas de Fondos de Pensiones*, AGAFPS: Santiago.

Asociación Internacional de Organismos de Supervisión de Fondos de Pensiones (1997), *Primer Seminario Internacional sobre Fondos de Pensiones*, AIOSFP: Buenos Aires.

Atkinson, A.B. (1989), 'Social Insurance and Income Maintenance', in A.B. Atkinson (ed.), *Poverty and Social Security*, Harvester Wheatsheaf: Brighton.

Ayala, U. (1992), 'Un Sistema de Capitalizacion Individual para Colombia', in A.Uthoff and R.Szalachman (eds.), *Sistema de Pensiones de America Latina*, CEPAL/PNUD: Santiago.

Baeza, S. and R. Burger (1995), 'Calidad de las Pensiones del Sistema Privado Chileno', in S. Baeza and F. Margozzini (eds.), *Quince años después. Una mirada al sistema privado de pensiones*, Centro de Estudios Públicos: Santiago.

Baeza, S. and F. Margozzini (eds.)(1995), *Quince años después. Una mirada al sistema privado de pensiones*, Centro de Estudios Públicos, Santiago.

Banco Central de Chile (1989), *Indicadores Económicos y Sociales*, Banco Central de Chile: Santiago.

Banco Central (several issues), 'Boletín Mensual', Banco Central de Chile: Santiago.

Barrientos, A. (1993), 'Pension Reform and Economic Development in Chile', *Development Policy Review*, Vol. 11, No.1, pp.91-107.

Barrientos, A. (1996a), 'Ageing and Personal Pensions in Chile', in P. Lloyd-Sherlock and P. Johnson (eds.), *Ageing and Social Policy: Global Comparisons*, Suntory-Toyota Center for Economics and Related Disciplines: London.

Barrientos, A. (1996b), 'Pension Reform and Pension Coverage in Chile: Lessons for Other Countries', *Bulletin of Latin American Research*, Vol. 15, No.3, pp.309-322.

Barrientos, A. (1997a), 'The Changing Face of Pensions in Latin America: Design and Prospects of Individual Capitalisation Pension Plans', *Social Policy and Administration*, Vol. 31, No.4, pp.336-353.

Barrientos, A. (1997b), 'Pension Reform and the Individual Capitalisation Pension Scheme Stampede in Latin America', Working Paper UHBS 1997:8, University of Hertfordshire Business School: Hertford.

Barrientos, A. (1997c), 'Supplementary Pension Coverage in Britain', Working Paper UHBS 1997:14, University of Hertfordshire Business School: Hertford.

Barrientos, A. (1998), 'Pension reform, personal pensions and gender differences in pension coverage', *World Development*, Vol. 26, No.1, pp.125-137.

Barrientos, A. and S. Barrientos (1996), 'Labour Market and Trade Liberalisation and Women's Employment in Chile', Working Paper UHBS 1996:17, University of Hertfordshire Business School: Hertford.

Barrientos, A. and L. Firinguetti (1995a), 'Individual capitalisation pension plans and old-age pension benefits for low-paid workers in Chile', *International Contributions to Labour Studies*, Vol. 5, pp.27-43.

Barrientos, A. and L. Firinguetti (1995b), 'Planes de Pensión de Capitalización Individual y Beneficios Previsionales para Trabajadoras de Bajos Ingresos', *Estudios de Economía*, Vol. 22, No.1, pp.17-44.
Barrientos, A. and L. Firinguetti (1996), 'Pension Reform and Low Paid Workers', *Contribuciones Científicas y Tecnológicas*, Vol. 25, No.113, pp.234-47.
Barúa, R. (1995), 'El Caso de Peru', in CIEDESS (ed.), *El Ahorro Previsional: Impacto sobre los mercados de capitales y de la vivienda*, Corporación de Investigación, Estudios y Desarrollo de la Seguridad Social: Santiago.
Bateman, H.; J. Pigott and S. Valdés (1995), 'Australia y Chile: Pensión Privada con Normas Diferentes. Comparación de Regulaciones y Comisiones de Administración', Discussion Paper 176, February, Instituto de Economía, Pontificia Universidad Católica de Chile: Santiago.
Berger, A.N.; W.C. Hunter and S.G. Timme (1993), 'The Efficiency of Financial Institutions', *Journal of Banking and Finance*, Vol. 17, pp.221-249.
Bertín, H. (1997), 'Desempeño de las AFJP 1994-1996', in Superintendencia de Administradoras de Fondos de Jubilaciones y Pensiones (ed.), *Estudios sobre el Régimen de Capitalización Argentino 1996*, SAFJP: Buenos Aires.
Bertín, H. and A. Perrotto (1997), 'Los nuevos regímenes de capitalización an America Latina: Argentina, Chile, Colombia, Costa Rica, México, Perú y Uruguay', Serie Estudios Especiales 9, May, Superintendencia de Administradoras de Fondos de Jubilaciones y Pensiones: Buenos Aires.
Bodie, Z. (1990), 'Pension as Retirement Income Insurance', *Journal of Economic Literature*, Vol. 28, pp.28-49.
Bodie, Z.; A.J. Marcus and R.C. Merton (1988), 'Defined Benefit vs. Defined Contribution Pension Plans: what are the trade-offs?', in Zvi Bodie; J. Shoven and D. Wise (eds.), *Pensions in the US Economy*, University of Chicago Press: Chicago.
Brugiavini, A.; R. Disney and E. Whitehouse (1993), 'Choice of pension arrangements under uncertainty in the UK', Working Paper, April, Institute for Fiscal Studies: London.
Cáceres, J. (1996), 'El Sistema Privado de Pensiones Peruano', in Asociación Gremial de AFPs (ed.), *II Congreso Iberoamericano Sistemas de Fondos de Pensiones*, AGAFPS: Santiago.
Cassoni, A.; G.J. Labadie and S. Allen (1995), 'Uruguay', in G. Marquez (ed.), *Reforming the Labour Market in a Liberalized Economy*, Inter-American Development Bank: Washington DC.
CEPAL/PNUD (1995), 'Reformas a los Sistemas de Pension en América Latina y el Caribe', Serie Financiamiento para el Desarrollo 26, February, CEPAL: Santiago.

Cheyre, H. (1991), *La Previsión en Chile Ayer y Hoy*, Centro de Estudios Públicos: Santiago.
Chile Finanzas (1997), Mercado Asegurador Latinoamericano - 1996, in Chile Finanzas, December 1997: http://ww.finanzas.cl/vys/seglat96.htm.
CIEDESS (1994), *Modernización de la Seguridad Social en Chile. Resultados y Tendencias*, Corporación de Investigación, Estudios y Desarrollo de la Seguridad Social: Santiago.
CIEDESS (1995), *El Ahorro Previsional: Impacto sobre los mercados de capitales y de la vivienda*, Corporación de Investigación, Estudios y Desarrollo de la Seguridad Social: Santiago.
Corsetti, G. and K. Schmidt-Hebbel (1997), 'Pension Reform and Growth', in S. Valdés-Prieto (ed.), *The Economics of Pensions. Principles, Policies and International Experience*, Cambridge University Press: Cambridge.
Creedy, J.; R. Disney and E. Whitehouse (1992), 'The Earnings-related State Pension, Indexation and Lifetime Redistribution in the UK', Working Paper W92/1, January, Institute for Fiscal Studies: London.
Davanzo, L.E. and L.B. Kautz (1992), 'Toward a Global Pension Market', *Journal of Portfolio Management*, pp.75-85.
Diamond, P. (1993), 'Privatization of Social Security: Lessons from Chile', Working Paper 4510, October, National Bureau of Economic Research: Cambridge, Mass.
Diamond, P. (1996a), 'Government Provision and Regulation of Economic Support in Old Age', in M Bruno and B. Pleskovic (eds.), *Annual World Bank Conference on Development Economics 1995*, The World Bank: Washington DC.
Diamond, P. (1996b), 'Proposals to Restructure Social Security', *Journal of Economic Perspectives*, Vol. 10, No.3, pp.67-88.
Diamond, P. (1997), 'Insulation of pensions from political risk', in S. Valdés-Prieto (ed.), *The Economics of Pensions. Principles, Policies, and International Experience*, Cambridge University Press: Cambridge.
Diamond, P. and S. Valdés-Prieto (1994), 'Social Security Reforms', in B. Bosworth, Dornbusch,R. and Laban,R. (ed.), *The Chilean Economy: Policy Lessons and Challenges*, The Brookings Institute: Washington DC.
Díaz, C.A. (1993), 'Análisis crítico de las modalidades de pensión y propuestas alternativas', Documento de Trabajo 156, June, Instituto de Economía, Pontificia Universidad Católica de Chile: Santiago.
Díaz, C.A. and G. Edwards (1994), 'Anualidades vitalicias variables: una nueva modalidad de pensión', Documento de Trabajo 166, May, Instituto de Economía, Pontificia Universidad Católica de Chile: Santiago.
Disney, R. (1995), 'Occupational Pension Schemes: Prospects and Reform in the UK', *Fiscal Studies*, Vol. 16, No.3, pp.19-39.
Disney, R. (1996a), *Can we afford to grow old?*, MIT Press: London.

Disney, R. (1996b), 'Pensions as Insurance', *The Geneva Papers on Risk and Insurance*, Vol. 21, No.79, pp.258-270.

Disney, R. and G. Stears (1996), 'Why is there a decline in defined benefit plan membership?', Working Paper W94/4, March, Institute for Fiscal Studies: London.

Disney, R. and E. Whitehouse (1992), *The Personal Pension Stampede*, Institute for Fiscal Studies: London.

Disney, R. and E. Whitehouse (1993), 'Will Younger Cohorts Obtain a Worse Deal from the UK State Pension Scheme?', Working Paper 93/7, May, University of Kent: Canterbury.

Durán, V. (1993), 'La Evasión en el Sistema de Seguridad Social Argentino', Serie Política Fiscal 50, December, CEPAL: Santiago.

Edwards, S. (1995), *Crisis and Reform in Latin America, from despair to hope*, Oxford University Press: New York.

Engen, E.; W. Gale and J. Scholz (1996), 'The Illusory Effects of Saving Incentives on Saving', *Journal of Economic Perspectives*, Vol. 10, No.1, pp.113-138.

Errázuriz, E. (1987), 'Capitalización de la Deuda Externa y Desnacionalización de la Economía Chilena', Working Paper 57, August, Programa de Economía del Trabajo: Santiago.

Even, W.E. and D.A. Macpherson (1990), 'The Gender Gap in Pensions and Wages', *Review of Economics and Statistics*, Vol. 72, No.2, pp.259-265.

Even, W.E. and D.A. Macpherson (1994), 'Gender Differences in Pensions', *Journal of Human Resources*, Vol. 29, No.2, pp.555-587.

Ferguson, P.R. and G.J. Ferguson (1994), *Industrial Economics*, Macmillan Press: London.

Fischer, B. and H. Reisen (1994), 'Pension Fund Investment from Ageing to Emerging Markets', Policy Brief 9, OECD Development Centre: Paris.

Friedman, B.M. and M.J. Warshawsky (1990), 'The Cost of Annuities: Implications for Saving Behaviour and Bequests', *Quarterly Journal of Economics*, No.420, pp.135-154.

Gillion, C. and A. Bonilla (1992), 'Analysis of a national private pension scheme: The case of Chile', *International Labour Review*, Vol. 131, No.2, pp.171-195.

Ginn, J. and S. Arber (1993), 'Pension Penalties: the Gendered Division of Occupational Welfare', *Work, Employment and Society*, Vol. 7, No.1, pp.47-70.

Glinding, T.H. and A. Berry (1994), 'Costa Rica', in S. Horton; R. Kanbur and D. Mazumdar (eds.), *Labor Markets in a Era of Adjustment*, Vol. 2 The World Bank: Washington DC.

Godoy, O. and S. Valdés-Prieto (1997), 'Democracy and Pensions in Chile: Experience with two systems', in S. Valdés-Prieto (ed.), *The Economics of*

Pensions. Principles, Policies, and International Experience, Cambridge University Press: Cambridge.

Goldin, C. (1994), 'The U-shaped Labour Force function in economic development and economic history', Working Paper 4707, April, National Bureau of Economic Research: Cambridge, Mass.

Gravelle, J. (1991), 'Do Individual Retirement Accounts increase Savings?', *Journal of Economic Perspectives*, Vol. 5, No.2, pp.133-148.

Gruber, J. (1997), 'The Incidence of Payroll Taxation: Evidence from Chile', *Journal of Labor Economics*, Vol. 15, No.3, pp.S72-S101.

Grushka, C. and M. de Biase (1997), 'La Movilidad de los Afiliados a las AFJP. Hipótesis y Evidencias', in Superintendencia de Administradoras de Fondos de Jubilaciones y Pensiones (ed.), *Estudios sobre el Régimen de Capitalización Argentino 1996*, SAFJP: Buenos Aires.

Gustman, A.; O. Mitchell and T. Steinmeier (1994), 'The Role of Pensions in the Labor Market: A Survey of the Literature', *Industrial and Labor Relations Review*, Vol. 47, No.3, pp.417-438.

Gustman, A.L. and T.L. Steinmeier (1993), 'Pension Portability and Labor Market Mobility: Evidence from the Survey of Income and Program Participation', *Journal of Public Economics*, Vol. 50, pp.299-323.

Holzmann, R. (1996), 'Pension Reform, Financial Market Development, and Economic Growth: Preliminary Evidence from Chile', IMF Working Paper wp/96/94, August, International Monetary Fund: Washington DC.

Holzmann, R. (1997), 'Pension Reform, Financial Market Development, and Economic Growth: Preliminary Evidence from Chile', *IMF Staff Papers*, Vol. 44, No.2, pp.149-178.

Horton, S.; R. Kanbur and D. Mazumdar (1994b), *Labor Markets in a Era of Adjustment*, Vol. 1, The World Bank: Washington DC.

Horton, S.; R. Kanbur and D. Mazumdar (1994a), *Labor Markets in a Era of Adjustment*, Vol. 2, The World Bank: Washington DC.

Huber, E. (1996), 'Options for Social Policy in Latin America: Neoliberal versus Social Democratic Models', in G. Esping-Andersen (ed.), *Welfare States in Transition. National Adaptations in Global Economies*, Sage: London.

Hurd, M.D. and J.B. Shoven (1985), 'The distributional impact of social security', in David Wise (ed.), *Pensions, Labor and Individual Choice*, University of Chicago Press: Chicago.

IFC (1990), *Emerging Market Factbook 1990*, International Finance Corporation: Washington DC.

IFC (1995), *Emerging Market Factbook 1995*, International Finance Corporation: Washington DC.

IFC (1997), *Emerging Market Factbook 1997*, International Finance Corporation: Washington DC.

Iglesias, A. and R. Acuña (1991), *Chile: Experiencia con un Régimen de Capitalización 1981-1991*, CEPAL/PNUD: Santiago.
Iglesias, A.; R. Acuña and C. Chamorro (1991), *Diez Años de Historia del Sistema de AFP*, AFP HABITAT: Santiago.
ILO (1995), *World Labour Report 1995*, International Labour Office: Geneva.
Instituto Nacional de Estadística y Censos (1995), 'Proyección de la Población Urbana y Rural y de la Población Economicamente Activa', Serie Análisis Demográfico 1, INDEC: Buenos Aires.
Instituto Nacional de Estadísticas (1981), *Chile Series Estadísticas 1981*, INE: Santiago.
Instituto Nacional de Estadísticas (1992), *Empleo. Encuesta Nacional 1986-1991*, INE: Santiago.
Instituto Nacional de Estadísticas (1993), *Encuesta Nacional del Empleo 1992*, INE: Santiago.
Instituto Nacional de Estadísticas (1995), 'Cifras Preliminares 1993-4', INE: Santiago.
Instituto Nacional de Estadísticas y Censos (1995), *Situación y Evolución Social. Síntesis 3*, INDEC: Buenos Aires.
Ippolito, R.A. (1991), 'Encouraging long term tenure: wage tilt or pensions?', *Industrial and Labor Relations Review*, Vol. 44, No.3, pp.520-535.
James, E. (1996), 'Comment on "Government Provision and Regulation of Economic Support in Old Age," by Peter Diamond', in M. Bruno and B. Pleskovic (eds.), *Annual World Bank Conference on Development Economics 1995*, The World Bank: Washington DC.
James, E. (1997a), 'New Systems for Old Age Security', Working Paper 1766, May, The World Bank: Washington DC.
James, E. (1997b), 'Pension Reform. Is there a trade-off between efficiency and equity?', Working Paper 1767, May, The World Bank: Washington DC.
Larrain, F. (1995), 'Instrumentos Financieros', in CIEDESS (ed.), *El Ahorro Previsional: Impacto en los mercados de capitales y de la vivienda*, Corporación de Investigación, Estudio y Desarrollo de la Seguridad Social: Santiago.
Larroulet, C. (1996), 'Impact of Privatisation on Welfare. The Chilean case 1985-1989', in W. Glade (ed.), *Bigger Economies, Smaller Government, The Role of Privatization in Latin America*, Westview: Oxford.
Lazear, E. (1981), 'Agency, Earnings Profiles, Productivity and Hours Restrictions', *American Economic Review*, Vol. 71, No.4, pp.606-620.
Lazear, E.P. (1985), 'Incentive Effects of Pensions', in D. Wise (ed.), *Pensions, Labor and Individual Choice*, University of Chicago Press: Chicago.

Lewis, M.K. and K.T. Davis (1987), *Domestic and International Banking*, Philip Allan: London.

Lloyd-Sherlock, P. (1997), *Old Age and Poverty in the Developing World. The Shanty Towns of Buenos Aires*, Macmillan: London.

Lo Vuolo, R. (1996), 'Reformas Previsionales en América Latina: una visión crítica en base al caso Argentino', *Economia e Sociedade*, Vol. 6, June, pp.153-181.

Lo Vuolo, R. and A. Barbeito (1993), 'La reforma del sistema previsional argentino: el mercado de trabajo y la distribución del ingreso', *Estudios del Trabajo*, Vol. 6, No.2, pp.23-52.

MacKie-Mason, J.K. (1990), 'Do Firms Care Who Provides their Financing?', in G.R. Hubbard (ed.), *Asymmetric Information, Corporate Finance, and Investment*, University of Chicago Press: London.

Marcel, M. and A. Arenas (1992), 'Social Security Reform in Chile', Ocassional Paper 5, Inter-American Development Bank: Washington DC.

March, J. (1995), 'Desarrollo de la Bolsa de Valores', in CIEDESS (ed.), *El Ahorro Previsional: Impacto en los mercados de capitales y de la vivienda*, Corporación de Investigación, Estudio y Desarrollo de la Seguridad Social: Santiago.

Marfán, M. and B.P. Bosworth (1996), 'Saving, Investment and Economic Growth', in B.P. Bosworth; R. Dornbusch and R. Labán (eds.), *The Chilean Economy. Policy Lesons and Challenges*, The Brookings Institution: Washington DC.

Margozzini, F. (1988), 'Estimaciones de las Pensiones de Vejez que otorgará el Actual Sistema de Pensiones', in S. Baeza and R. Manubens (eds.), *Sistema Privado de Pensiones en Chile*, Centro de Estudios Públicos: Santiago.

Marquez, G. (1995), 'Reforming the Labour Market in a Liberalized Economy', in G. Marquez (ed.), *Reforming the Labour Market in a Liberalized Economy*, Inter-American Development Bank: Washington DC.

Marshall, A. (1996), 'Weakening employment protection in Latin America: incentive to employment creation or to increasing stability?', *International Contributions to Labour Studies*, Vol. 6, pp.29-48.

Martínez, G. (1996), 'El Mercado Asegurador y su Relación con el Sistema de Pensiones', in Asociación Gremial de AFPs (ed.), *II Congreso Iberoamericano Sistemas de Fondos de Pensiones*, AGAFPS: Santiago.

Mayer, C. (1990), 'Financial Systems, Corporate Finance, and Economic Development', in G.R. Hubbard (ed.), *Asymmetric Information, Corporate Finance, and Investment*, University of Chicago Press: London.

McGreevey, W. (1990), 'Social Security in Latin America: Issues and Options for the World Bank', Discussion Paper 110, The World Bank: Washington DC.

Mesa-Lago, C. (1989), *Ascent to Bankruptcy: Financing Social Security in Latin America*, University of Pittsburgh Press: Pittsburgh.
Mesa-Lago, C. (1991), 'Social Security in Latin America and the Caribbean: A Comparative Assessment', in E. Ahmad; J. Dreze; J. Hills and A. Sen (eds.), *Social Security in Developing Countries*, Clarendon Press: Oxford.
Mesa-Lago, C. (1994), *Changing Social Security in Latin America: toward alleviating the social costs of economic reform*, Lynne Rienner Publishers Inc.: Boulder.
Mesa-Lago, C. (1996), 'Pension Reform in Latin America: Importance and Evaluation of Privatization Approaches', in W. Glade (ed.), *Bigger Economies Smaller Governments, The Role of Privatization in Latin America*, Westview Press: Oxford.
Mesa-Lago, C. (1997), 'Social Welfare Reform in the Context of Economic-Political Liberalization: Latin American Cases', *World Development*, Vol. 25, No.4, pp.497-517.
MIDEPLAN (1996), 'Realidad Económico-Social de los Hogares en Chile', Documento, Ministerio de Planificación y Cooperación: Santiago.
Mincer, J. (1974), *Schooling, Experience, and Earnings*, Columbia University Press: New York.
Miranda, E. (1994), 'Evidencia de Economías de Escala en las Administradoras de Fondos de Pensiones', *Estudios de Administración*, Vol. 1, No.1, pp.45-79.
Mitchell, O.S. (1996), 'Administrative Costs in Public and Private Retirement Systems', Working Paper 5734, August, National Bureau of Economic Research: Cambridge, MA.
Morandé, F. (1996), 'Savings in Chile: What went right?', Working Paper I-92, April, ILADES: Santiago.
Morley, S. (1995), *Poverty and Inequality in Latin America. The Impact of Adjustment and Recovery in the 1980s*, John Hopkins University Press: London.
Mosley, P.; J. Harrigan and J. Toye (1991), *Aid and Power. The World Bank & Policy-based Lending*, Routledge: London.
Mullin, J. (1993), 'Emerging Markets in the Global Economy', *Federal Reserve Bank of New York Quarterly Review*, pp.54-83.
Munnell, A. (1982), *The Economics of Private Pensions*, The Brookings Institution: Washington DC.
Myers, R.J. (1992), 'Chile's Social Security Reform, After ten years', *Benefits Quarterly*, Third Quarter, pp.41-55.
Notisar (1997), Noticias del Sistema de Ahorro para el Retiro, in Notisar, December 1997: http://www.notisar.com/notisar.
Ortúzar, P. and J. Peña (1986), 'El Nuevo Sistema Previsional y la Situación de los Trabajadores más Pobres', mimeo, September, ODEPLAN: Santiago.

Pablo, R. (1991), 'Efectos de la Participación de la Banca en la Administración y Gestión de la Previsión', mimeo.

Pan American Health Organisation (1989), 'El Reto del Envejecimiento en America Latina. Resultados de las encuestas de necesidades de los ancianos en cinco países', May, PAHO Program on the Health of the Elderly: Washington DC.

Pan American Health Organization (1994), 'Health Conditions in the Americas 1994 ed.', Scientific Publication 549, PAHO: Washington DC.

Paredes, R. and L.A. Riveros (1994), 'Chile', in R. Paredes and L.A. Riveros (eds.), *Human Resources and the Adjustment Process*, Inter-American Development Bank: Washington DC.

Parsons, D.O. (1991), 'The Decline of Pension Coverage in the US', *Economics Letters*, Vol. 36, pp.419-423.

Paul, L.H. (1995), 'Vínculos entre los Sistemas de Pensiones y el Mercado de Capitales', in CIEDESS (ed.), *El Ahorro Previsional: Impacto en los mercados de capitales y de la vivienda*, Corporación de Investigación, Estudio y Desarrollo de la Seguridad Social: Santiago.

Pérez, A.; W. Restrepo and H. Colsner (1993), 'Análisis comparativo del envejecimiento en Brazil, Colombia, El Salvador, Jamaica y Venezuela', Technical Paper 38, Pan American Health Organisation: Washington DC.

Piñera, J. (1991), *El Cascabel al Gato: La Batalla por la Reforma Previsional*, Zig-Zag: Santiago.

Psacharopoulos, G.; S. Morley; A. Fiszbein; H. Lee and B. Wood (1993), 'Poverty and Income Distribution in Latin America', Regional Studies Program Report 27, December, The World Bank: Washington DC.

Psacharopoulos, G. and Z. Tzannatos (1992a), *Case Studies on Women's Employment and Pay in Latin America*, The World Bank: Washington DC.

Psacharopoulos, G. and Z. Tzannatos (1992b), *Women's Employment and Pay in Latin America*, The World Bank: Washington DC.

Queisser, M. (1995), 'Chile and Beyond: The Second Generation Pension Reform in Latin America', *International Social Security Review*, Vol. 48, No.3, pp.23-39.

Reisen, H. and J. Williamson (1997), 'Pension funds, capital controls, and macroeconomic stability', in S. Valdés-Prieto (ed.), *The Economics of Pensions. Principles, Policies and International Experience*, Cambridge University Press: Cambridge.

Riveros, L.A. (1994), 'Argentina', in S. Horton; R. Kanbur and D. Mazumdar (eds.), *Labor Markets in a Era of Adjustment*, Vol. 2, The World Bank: Washington DC.

Rofman, R. (1997), 'Evolución, Componentes y Efectos de las Comisiones del Régimen de Capitalización', in Superintendencia de Administradoras de Fondos de Jubilaciones y Pensiones (ed.), *Estudios sobre el Régimen de Capitalización Argentino 1996*, SAFJP: Buenos Aires.

Rofman, R. and G. Stirparo (1997), 'Proyección del tamaño de los fondos de jubilaciones y pensiones', in Superintendencia de Administradoras de Fondos de Jubilaciones y Pensiones (ed.), *Estudios sobre el Régimen de Capitalización Argentino 1996*, SAFJP: Buenos Aires.

Rosen, S. (1984), 'Some Arithmetic of Social Security', in R.D. Campbell (ed.), *Controlling the Cost of Social Security*, Lexington Books: Lexington.

Sales, C.; F. Solís and A. Villagómez (1996), 'Pension System Reform: The Mexican Case', Working Paper 5780, September, National Bureau of Economic Research: Cambridge MA.

Schmidt-Hebbel, K.; L. Serven and A. Solimano (1994), 'Saving, Investment and Growth in Developing Countries. A Review', Working Paper 1382, November, The World Bank: Washington DC.

Schulthess, W. and G. Demarco (1993), *Argentina: Evolución del Sistema Nacional de Previsión Social y propuesta de reforma*, CEPAL/PNUD: Santiago.

Schulthess, W. and R. LoVuolo (1991), 'Transformación del Sistema Previsional de Autónomos: Paso Inicial para una Reforma en la Seguridad Social', *Desarrollo Económico*, Vol. 30, No.120, pp.551-571.

Schwarz, A. (1993), 'The Trade-off between Redistribution and Savings in alternative Pension Systems', mimeo, October, National Foreign Affairs Training Center: Arlington.

Shah, H. (1997), 'Towards better regulation of private pension funds', Working Paper 1791, June, The World Bank: Washington DC.

Soto-Perez, C.J. (1992), 'El Sistema Mexicano de Pensiones', in A. Uthoff and R. Szalachman (eds.), *Sistema de Pensiones de América Latina*, CEPAL/PNUD: Santiago.

Stiglitz, J.E. (1989), 'Financial Markets and Development', *Oxford Review of Economic Policy*, Vol. 5, No.4, pp.55-68.

Superintendencia de Administradoras de Fondos de Jubilaciones y Pensiones (1996), *Reformas a los Sistemas de Pensiones. Argentina, Chile, Peru*, SAFJP: Buenos Aires.

Superintendencia de Administradoras de Fondos de Jubilaciones y Pensiones (1997), *Memoria Trimestral 11*, SAFJP: Buenos Aires.

Superintendencia de Administradoras de Fondos de Pensiones (1992a), *Boletín Estadístico*, SAFP: Santiago.

Superintendencia de Administradoras de Fondos de Pensiones (1992b), 'Fondo de Pensiones y Ahorro Previsional: 1981-1991', *Boletín Estadístico*, No. 110, No.April, pp.16-18.

Superintendencia de Administradoras de Fondos de Pensiones (1996a), *El Sistema Chileno de Pensiones*, SAFP: Santiago.

Superintendencia de Administradoras de Fondos de Pensiones (1996b), *Evolución del Sistema Chileno de Pensiones*, SAFP: Santiago.

Superintendencia de Administradoras de Fondos de Pensiones (1996c), 'Límites de Inversión para los fondos de pensiones', *Boletín Estadístico*, No.126, pp.25-34.

Superintendencia de Administradoras de Fondos de Pensiones (several issues), *Boletín Estadístico*, SAFP: Santiago.

UNCTAD (1994), *Statistical Survey of Insurance and Reinsurance Operations in Developing Countries 1983-1990*, United Nations: New York.

Uthoff, A. (1993), 'Pension System Reforms and Savings in Latin American and Caribbean Countries with Special reference to Chile', in Y.Akyuz and G. Held (eds.), *Finance and the Real Economy: Issues and Case Studies in Developing Countries*, CEPAL/PNUD: Santiago.

Valck, E. (1995), 'Caso Práctico de Administración de Portafolios', in CIEDESS (ed.), *El Ahorro Previsional: Impacto en los mercados de capitales y de la vivienda*, Corporación de Investigación, Estudio y Desarrollo de la Seguridad Social: Santiago.

Valck, E. and E. Walker (1995), 'La Inversión de los Fondos de Pensiones. Historia, Normativa y Resultados', in S. Baeza and F. Margozzini (eds.), *Quince años después. Una mirada al sistema privado de pensiones*, Centro de Estudios Públicos: Santiago.

Valdés-Prieto, S. (1992), 'Selección de AFP y Regulación de la Información', Working Paper 140, January, Instituto de Economía, Pontificia Universidad Católica de Chile: Santiago.

Valdés-Prieto, S. (1994), 'Administrative Charges in Pension in Chile, Malaysia, Zambia and the United States', Working Paper 1372, October, The World Bank: Washington DC.

Valdés-Prieto, S. (1995), 'Vendedores de AFP: Producto del Mercado o de Regulaciones Ineficientes?', Documento de Trabajo 178, March, Instituto de Economía, Pontificia Universidad Católica de Chile: Santiago.

Valdés-Prieto, S. and G. Edwards (1996), 'Jubilación en los sistemas pensionales privados', Documento de Trabajo 182, December, Instituto de Economía, Pontificia Universidad Católica de Chile: Santiago.

Vittas, D. (1994), 'Argentina: Rebuilding Capital Markets' Institutional Investors', mimeo, February, World Bank: Washinton DC.

Vittas, D. (1995), 'Sequencing Social Security, Pension, and Insurance Reform', Policy Research Working Paper 1551, December, The World Bank: Washington DC.

Vittas, D. (1997), 'Private Pension Funds in Argentina's New Integrated Pension System', Working Paper 1820, August, The World Bank: Washington DC.

Vittas, D. and A. Iglesias (1992), 'The Rationale and Performance of Personal Pension Plans in Chile', Working Paper WPS 867, June, The World Bank: Washington DC.

Walker, E. (1993a), 'Desempeño Financiero de las Carteras Accionarias de los Fondos de Pensiones en Chile: Ha tenido desventajas ser grandes?', *Cuadernos de Economía*, Vol. 30, No.89, pp.35-75.

Walker, E. (1993b), 'Desempeño Financiero de las Carteras de "Renta Fija" de los Fondos de Pensiones en Chile. Ha tenido desventajas ser grandes?', *Cuadernos de Economía*, Vol. 30, No.89, pp.1-33.

Webb, R. and G. Fernández (1995), *Anuario Estadístico. Peru en Numeros 1995*, Cuánto S.A.: Lima.

World Bank (1994), *Averting the Old Age Crisis*, Oxford University Press: London.

World Bank (1995), 'Labor and Economic Reform in Latin America and the Caribbean', Regional Perspectives on World Development Report 1995, August, The World Bank: Washington DC.